FORGOTTEN
SOLDIERS
OF THE FIRST WORLD WAR

About the Author

David R. Woodward is Professor of Modern European History at Marshall University in the United States, and the author of Lloyd George and the Generals. He is currently writing a major anthology of 'voices' of soldiers who fought in the First World War, also for Tempus. He lives in West Virginia.

FORGOTTEN SOLDIERS

OF THE FIRST WORLD WAR

DAVID R. WOODWARD

TEMPUS

This edition first published 2007

Tempus Publishing Limited
The Mill, Brimscombe Port,
Stroud, Gloucestershire, GL5 2QG
www.tempus-publishing.com

© David R. Woodward, 2006, 2007

The right of David R. Woodward to be identified as the Author
of this work has been asserted in accordance with the
Copyrights, Designs and Patents Act 1988.

This edition has been published by arrangement with the
University Press of Kentucky.

British Library Cataloguing in Publication Data.
A catalogue record for this book is available from the British Library.

ISBN 978 0 7524 4307 2

Typesetting and origination by Tempus Publishing Limited
Printed in Great Britain

Contents

Abbreviations

ADC	Aide De Camp
Adjutant	Served as chief of staff in a battalion; normally a captain
ALH	Australian Light Horse
ANZAC	Australian and New Zealand Army Corps
Army Corps	Formation made up of several divisions
ASC	Army Service Corps
Bde	Brigade
BEF	British Expeditionary Force
BGC	Brigadier General Commanding
Bn	Battalion
CGS	Chief of the General Staff
CID	Committee of Imperial Defence
CIGS	Chief of the Imperial General Staff
C in C	Commander in Chief
CO	Commanding Officer
COY	Company
CRA	Commander Royal Artillery
CTC	Camel Transport Corps
Div	Division
DMO	Director of Military Operations
DMS	Director of Medical Services
ECTC	Egyptian Camel Transport Corps

EEF	Egyptian Expeditionary Force
ELC	Egyptian Labour Corps
GHQ	General Headquarters
GOC	General Officer Commanding (Division, Corps, or Army)
GCMG	Knight Grand Cross of the Order of St Michael and St George
HE	High Explosive
HOW	Howitzer
HQ	Headquarters
ICC	Imperial Camel Corps
MG	Machine Gun
MGC	Machine Gun Corps
NCO	Noncommissioned Officer
OC	Officer Commander (usually a company or platoon)
OP	Observation Post
OTC	Officer Training Corps
RAF	Royal Air Force
RAMC	Royal Army Medical Corps
RE	Royal Engineers
RFA	Royal Field Artillery
RGA	Royal Garrison Artillery
RHA	Royal Horse Artillery
RS	Royal Scots regiment
RWF	Royal Welch Fusiliers
TBD	Torpedo Boat Destroyer
TF	Territorial Force
VC	Victoria Cross

Preface

The British soldiers in Egypt and Palestine whose own words constitute a large part of this book fought in a theatre very different from France and Flanders. The Egyptian Expeditionary Force, advancing some 500 miles from the Suez Canal to Aleppo, marched in the footprints of ancient armies and experienced extraordinary changes in soil, climate and scenery: the Sinai Desert, the green fields of Palestine, the rugged and treacherous Judean hills, and the suffocating humidity of the Jordan Valley. They baked on marches across the arid desert and froze in the chilly winter rains in the hills above Jerusalem. The remains of those who died are found in places such as El Arish and Kantara, where row upon row of markers rise from sandy wastes under a blazing sun.

These British soldiers and their allies were involved in a campaign that has not received the attention that it deserves. Although considered a 'sideshow' when compared with the western front, the Palestinian front developed into Britain's second most important theatre of operations. After playing a key role in destroying the Ottoman Empire, London then took the lead in redrawing the map of the Arab Islamic heartlands, with ominous implications for the future.

Not only has the campaign in Egypt and Palestine been neglected in the historiography of the war, the ordinary British soldier has not been given his due. T.E. Lawrence and the stout-hearted Australians have captured the imagination of the public and are the subjects of the two best-known films on this theatre of war, *Lawrence of Arabia* and *The Light Horsemen*. One can easily get the impression that if Lawrence with his individual heroics did not defeat the Turks, the Australians did with their famous hell-for-leather charge against the Turkish defenders of Beersheba. 'We used to wonder sometimes', wrote Antony Bluett, a British soldier who served with the Egyptian Camel Transport Corps, 'whether the people at home knew there was an army at all in Egypt and Palestine; an army, moreover, longing, wistfully for the merest crumb from the table of appreciation just to show that our "bit" was known and recognised.'[1]

Among the participants, the Territorials have been especially overlooked. The Yeomanry, the cavalry of the Territorial Force,[2] and the Territorial divisions were called on to do most of the fighting in the battles for Gaza and the conquest of Jerusalem, with Territorials suffering over ninety per cent of the casualties during this phase of the campaign. Casualty figures underscore the role of the Territorials in this theatre. Excluding sick, the Territorials suffered 32,274 casualties for officers and other ranks in Egypt and Palestine. The casualties for the Regular Army (12,683), Indian and native troops (9,980), Australians (4,725) and New Zealanders (1,684) pale in comparison.[3]

No formation represented the amateur tradition in the armed forces better than the Territorial Force, which had been organized shortly before the First World War to defend Britain against raids in the event of war. Not surprisingly, the professionals were sceptical of the effectiveness of these citizen-soldiers, who were led primarily by middle-class officers. 'Peace time soldiering in the Territorial Army was largely a matter of evening and occasional weekend "drills" with an Annual Camp in the park surrounding some stately home', recalled J.W. Wintringham, a subaltern in the Lincolnshire Yeomanry.[4] How could these 'weekend warriors', many in the War Office reasoned, be successful against the powerful German Army on the western front?

Members of the EEF resented the view that Turks were lesser opponents than Germans and that conditions in their theatre were 'cushy' when compared with the western front. 'In France, with its incessant shelling, pouring rain, and waterlogged trenches', Major

C.S. Jarvis noted in his memoirs, 'the soldier envied and in fact felt intensely hostile to his opposite number in Egypt, who in his opinion, was having a "cushy" time basking in the warm sunshine and being fanned to sleep by lovely houris.'[5] Major Lord Hampton, a squadron commander in the Worcestershire Yeomanry, sarcastically wrote, 'I have been told that it was at one time the vogue in England to consider the soldiers, whom fate and the War Office had condemned to serve in Egypt, only one degree better than a conscientious objector.'[6] Nothing could be further from the truth, as this account of Britain's forgotten soldiers will demonstrate.

A detailed account of the war in Egypt and Palestine can be found in the official histories, but one must look elsewhere for the personal and individual side of this campaign. This is my focus, with the participants speaking for themselves through their own accounts, most of which have the rigour and directness that comes from being written at the time, by men coping as best they could with the harsh conditions of what proved to be one of the most strenuous and demanding campaigns of the First World War.

The spelling, capitalization, and punctuation of the many quotations have been quoted exactly with the following exceptions: The initial letters may have been changed to a capital or a lowercase letter to make a quotation conform to the syntax of the text. Also, in a few instances, spelling or punctuation has been silently changed to make a quotation comprehensible.

Acknowledgements

Writing history has always been a collective effort for me, and I owe a great debt to Marshall University and its faculty and staff members, who have afforded me support. The university provided assistance in many ways: a summer research grant, a reduced teaching load for several semesters, and a sabbatical during the spring semester of 2002. The staff of the Drinko Library secured many books that were essential to my research through interlibrary loan. Some of my colleagues in the history department were generous with their time. Professor Daniel Holbrook was always available when I had a word-processing query; Professors Alan B. Gould and Robert Sawrey read my manuscript and offered suggestions. Teresa Dennis, the departmental secretary, helped me in more ways than I can list. Professor James Leonard, Department of Geography, produced the four maps used in the text.

I am also grateful for the support of many outside the university. Eugene Pofahl served as another reader of the manuscript. The staff members of the British archives in which I conducted research could not have been more helpful, especially Dr Simon Robbins, Department of Documents, Imperial War Museum, and Katie Mooney, Liddell Hart Centre for Military Archives. I wish to give special recognition to two individuals who sustained and assisted me in the completion and publication of this work: R.W.A Suddaby, the brilliant keeper of the Department of Documents, Imperial War

Museum, and Malcolm Brown, the prolific military historian, who serves as a model for those who would write about ordinary soldiers in the Great War.

I have made every effort to contact copyright holders of the material reproduced in this volume and I apologize for any possible oversight in this regard. For permission to quote from written documents and sound recordings and reproduce photographs to which they hold copyright, I thank the following: the British Library; Public Record Office (now part of the National Archives); Department of Documents, Sound Archive, and Photograph Archive, Imperial War Museum; Master and Fellows of Churchill College, Cambridge; National Army Museum; The Beaverbrook Foundation; House of Lords Record Office; and the Trustees of the Liddell Hart Centre for Military Archives. I also express my great appreciation to individual copyright holders who have given me permission to use quotations in publication: Her Majesty Queen Elizabeth II, C. Everard, Rupert Dawnay, Peter Hodgson, Winifred Bryant, Alisdair Murray, Kathryn E.W. Blunt, Sylvia Clark, Peggy Howe, Richard Blaksley, Lady Sinclair, Patricia K. Bettany, Margaret Cant, Joyce Overall, James Collier, and Janet Betterworth. I also thank the copyright holders of the papers of A.M. McGrigor, B. George, and W. Knott, who do not wish their names to be made public.

To all who helped in this volume, my sincere thanks.

1

Eastward Bound

In September 1915, Private A.S. Benbow experienced perhaps the most exciting day of his young life. He had worked for London Assurance in Pall Mall before his Yeomanry unit had been mobilized. Marching through the streets of Liverpool, he was on his way to a foreign land. His memory of that moment was that 'a lot of people had gathered on either side of the road and many were in tears as we marched (or rather staggered) along; one old woman, I remember, called out "God bless you all and bring you back soon." Gaining the dockside at last we were awed at the mighty size of the good ship we were to travel on, and almost leaping with excitement up the long gangway we found ourselves (for the first time for many of us) on board an ocean going liner.' As his liner, the White Star *Olympic* left the dock and moved towards the open sea, 'all liners in dock and the river, the ferry boats passing up and down and in fact every ship with enough steam up let go with their sirens in farewell to the men going abroad, many of whom, we knew, would never come back'.[1]

Benbow and the other members of 'D' Squadron of the West Kent Yeomanry were uncertain of their destination, but they discovered soon enough that they were destined to fight Turks. Not surprisingly, many of these young soldiers who had never been on foreign soil before had an *Arabian Nights* image of Turks. Captain T.H. Chamberlain, 1/1st Berkshire Yeomanry, who fought at Gallipoli before serving in Palestine, discovered that his men 'had heard of the Turks but few had ever seen one – some had vague memories of a picture in a school book showing a large dark man, bare chested, large muscles and an enormous sword'.[2]

Just before Britain's entry into the war, Turkey had concluded a secret treaty with Berlin. Within days of this agreement, two German warships, the *Goeben* and the *Breslau*, anchored at Constantinople in clear violation of international law. Despite the presence of these enemy warships, London tried to keep Turkey neutral. The Turks, however, edged toward war. Turkish leaders, egged on by the Germany Military Mission (which had arrived in Turkey the previous year), prepared plans to attack both the Russians and British. On October 29, the *Goeben* and *Breslau*, now a part of the Turkish navy and renamed, respectively, *Sultan Selim Yanuz* and *Midilli,* attacked Russian installations. Russia declared war against Turkey on November 2; Britain followed suit three days later. Turkey responded by invoking a jihad, or holy war against the infidels.

The emergence of this Turko-German threat to the British Empire came at a time when the war was going disastrously for the British Regular Army. Dispatched to the Continent, the British Expeditionary Force found itself in the path of a massive German flanking movement through Belgium and into northern France, the so-called Schlieffen Plan. British losses in the retreat from Mons and in the ensuing battles were horrendous and beyond anything that the War Office had anticipated. The question that demanded an immediate answer was how could the War Office field the necessary forces to maintain its position in France and also defend the Empire against the global threat posed by the Turko-German alignment?[3]

Prewar reforms of the military had created two British forces: a professional army (the Regulars) and a home force (the Territorials). In 1914, the Territorial Force consisted of fourteen formed infantry divisions and fifty-three voluntary mounted regiments called the Yeomanry. Lord Kitchener, the Secretary of State for War, was leery of these summer and weekend soldiers, who represented the amateur tradition in British warfare. His study of the US Civil War led him to conclude that the hastily raised American armies had represented little more than armed mobs, with little cohesiveness and scant knowledge of the art of war. Dismissing the Territorials as 'a town clerk's army', he feared that they promised to be no better. Indeed, the Territorials, in the words of A.J. Smithers, 'always seemed something like a social club with sporting and military overtones',[4] especially in the Yeomanry and in the London units, which were largely composed of white-collar workers.

Not surprisingly, a gulf existed between many career officers and newly minted Territorial officers. When the Territorials were mobilized in 1914 and their units brought up to strength, many of their junior officers were products of the Officer Training Corps, which had recently been established at the universities and at large public schools such as Eton and Harrow. But their amateur status did not disqualify them from becoming excellent soldiers and leaders when given seasoning. In many ways, they represented the best that civil society had to offer in what was going to be Britain's greatest and most costly war. In Smithers's apt characterization, 'The Territorials were from top to bottom the civilian English with a sense of duty.'[5]

Although Kitchener underestimated the value of the Territorial Force, he could not wage war without them, given the heavy losses suffered by the Regulars in the opening battles of the war. His solution was to send Territorials to the far corners of the Empire, initially to release Regulars for duty on the western front and later to fight in the Turkish theatres. Even then he was forced to send some Territorials to France, not as divisions at first, but by units such as the London Scottish in their gray kilts, and the Herfordshires. The Territorials fought with true grit in France and elsewhere, earning seventy Victoria Crosses in the war.

Massive casualties to the original units and Kitchener's decision to create a mass army by raising a new fighting force – the New Army – tended to obscure the role of the Territorials in France, in contrast to the role that they played in the Turkish theatres, especially in Egypt and Palestine. The War Office chose to fight Turkey with Territorials and imperial troops, primarily from Australia, New Zealand and India. This was partly because these Territorials were readily available as the war with Turkey expanded to theatres in Gallipoli, Mesopotamia and Egypt. But it also reflected the insulting view that these amateur soldiers might not be able to hold their own with the German Army.

The War Office initially was inclined to discount the effectiveness of the Turkish army that had been overwhelmed by the Greeks, Serbs, Bulgarians and Montenegrins in 1912. The director of military operations, Colonel Henry Wilson, after touring the Balkans, concluded that 'the Turkish Army is not a serious modern Army... [it shows] no sign of adaption to western thought and methods. The Army is ill commanded, ill officered and in rags.'[6] There was truth to what Wilson wrote: the Ottoman army had recently undergone a revolution and some disastrous campaigns. But the British soldier, as reflected in his letters, diaries and memoirs, developed considerable respect for the fighting ability of the enemy, especially the Anatolian Turk. The Turkish peasant proved tenacious in defence and courageous in attack. Although often poorly supplied, his powers of endurance proved extraordinary, as did his ability to cover ground on foot. What W.T. Marchant, who served as a signaller with the 160th Brigade, 53rd Division, before being posted in September 1918 to the Divisional Ammunition Column, Royal Artillery, wrote in his diary was similar to what most British soldiers concluded:

> The Turks as fighters are among the best, being without fear, and rather courting death as a means of reaching heaven. They have their characteristics, surrendering when beaten, rather than being taken, if there's any difference. It's a fine point. Their free desertion at times is probably due to their being provided with such scanty and poor food and clothing. They fight fiercely and fire rapidly and carefully with their powerful mauser rifles... On the whole we have little fault to find with the Turk as a fighter.[7]

The failed Gallipoli campaign in 1915 demonstrated that the British military and political leadership had badly underestimated the Ottoman forces. As the British commander in chief, General Sir Ian Hamilton, lamented: 'I did not know, to tell you the truth, that they [the Turks] were nearly as good as they turned out to be.'[8] It is true that the British faced Turkey's best combat divisions at Gallipoli, but later British defeats at Kut and Gaza, as well as the daring Turkish crossing of the Sinai Desert to attack the Suez Canal, underscore the assessment that ordinary British soldiers made of their enemy in the Middle East.

Before British soldiers engaged the Turks in Egypt and elsewhere, their troopships had to navigate the submarine-infested Mediterranean. The War Office routed some soldiers overland by rail to Mediterranean ports such as Taranto in Italy and Marseilles in France for their voyage to Egypt; others such as Benbow were sent on the direct sea route through the Straits of Gibraltar. When A.S. Benbow departed in the autumn of 1915, the threat from German torpedoes was quite real. To enforce their war zone in British waters, the Germans increased their submarine fleet with telling effect. Before February 1915, only ten British merchant ships had been lost to torpedoes; in August 1915, however, a shocking forty-two British ships were sunk. The navy responded by aggressively patrolling the sea routes. This had a limited effect and served to direct U-boat commanders to their targets. Although Benbow's ship was packed with some 9,000 men, the *Olympic*, the sister ship of the *Titanic,* had no naval escort. In other instances, troopships on the outward voyage were escorted only to the Straits of Gibraltar. 'The essential point, that the way to counter submarines was not by going in search of them', noted Trevor Wilson, 'but by standing between them and their quarry, escaped Britain's naval strategists throughout 1915 – and for a good while after that.'[9]

After the sinking of two British passenger liners, the *Lusitania* and the *Arabic,* American pressure forced the Germans in October 1915 to suspend their attacks on the west coast of England and in the Channel. In the Mediterranean, where American citizens were much less likely to become victims, the U-boat campaign continued unabated.

British soldiers began their voyage to Egypt with drills to deal with the U-boat threat. Matters did not always go smoothly. Yeoman George Stanley, who served with the Imperial Camel Corps (later renamed the Imperial Camel Corps Brigade), offers a less than flattering account of his training: 'There was a life-belt and life-boat parade in the morning. At the sound of a whistle from the Captain we all rushed below and put on life belts, and then came up and paraded under selected officers at our respective boats. The life-belts are kept below. There are enough for every man but I doubt if every man could get one in time in case of accident as they are in a very awkward place.'[10] Frederick Thomas Mills, who served in the Royal Engineers, provided an even more alarming glimpse of the training he received on this voyage from Taranto to Alexandria: 'We had a practise call to quarters – hopeless confusion. We, who were quartered in the stern had to go up to the bow; those in the bow had to come to the stern. God help us if anything does happen.'[11]

A serious omission in most of these drills was that men were not trained to lower lifeboats. When the HMT *Transylvania* was torpedoed on May 4 1917, R.G. Frost, a driver for No. 905 Company in the Motor Transport, recalled that

> ...the life boats were in shocking order, some of them turning upside-down and hurling the occupants into the sea. None of the men knew how to lower them as there had been no lifeboat drill and one end of a boat would go down while the other stuck. One boat was lowered on top of another and, it is thought, killed many of the underneath boats companions. In several cases the wrong ropes were cut, and the boats fell into the sea or hung suspended by one end.

Frost also observed that 'most of those which were lowered safely, either had the caulks out or were in an unseaworthy state'.[12]

Some boats were rotten and were quickly reduced to matchwood. 'Submarine spotters', frequently armed with loaded rifles, were stationed every ten paces around the deck. These spotters, recalled D.H. Hiorns, a member of 'C' Squadron, County of London Yeomanry, who departed for Egypt in April 1915, 'were bawled out for reporting submarines which turned out to be either porpoises, dolphins or whales, yet strangely enough we went through the Mediterranean with lights on and nightly concerts in the well deck'.[13]

These concerts might not have been advisable under the circumstance. Still, they boosted morale on troopships in which men were packed like sardines. As Mills observes, 'in peacetime there are about 1,000 people on board. All told there are now 3,000 so one can understand what it is like.'[14] Norman Francis Rothon, who had been conscripted on his thirty-seventh birthday and served as a mule driver in the Royal Garrison Artillery, minced no words in describing the overcrowding on his ship from Marseilles to Alexandria: 'Life in a troopship is a fearful pickle, everything upside down. Our quarters are like the black hole of Calcutta. There are over 300 men cooped up in there, it will be wretched when the boat starts rolling.'[15] Rothon chose to sleep on deck, where sleeping comrades occupied almost every available inch of deck space.

Insufficient and poor rations were another complaint. Converted from peacetime use and crowded from stern to bow, it is no surprise that organization suffered aboard the troopships. The food was 'cooked and served under conditions so revolting as to turn the stomach at the bare sight of it', lamented Antony Bluett, who served with the Egyptian Camel Transport Corps. 'It was an unspeakably horrible voyage, but most of the troops traveling East experienced the same conditions.'[16]

H.J. Earney, a teacher before the war who served as a signaller with the Royal Garrison Artillery, bitterly resented the privileged position of the officers and what he saw as their indifference to the conditions of their men during his voyage from Taranto to Egypt in September 1917. On the upper decks he observed 'a luxurious smoking lounge, comfort in every corner' and a dining saloon with 'white linen, shining cutlery and glass – dining chairs around the table in real hotel style'. The officers' sleeping accommodations with baths included reminded him of what 'I once enjoyed'. When he descended to his quarters:

> ...the first thing that strikes one is the smell of mules assailing the nostrils, combined with the unholy smell which rises from imperfectly ventilated spaces from between decks. Side by side with the mules and in the remaining stalls many men have their quarters, taking their food there and many of them sleeping there. Lower again on the mess deck are the remainder of the men. At mealtimes there is almost a fight for food especially if there is any shortage.[17]

Despite the primitive conditions for the rank and file on many troopships, the adventure of foreign travel offered solace to many. When Captain O.P. Boord had rejoined the Territorials in early 1915, he had 'had visions of gloomy weather and exciting times in the muddy trenches of Flanders'. But to his surprise and delight, he was posted to Egypt as a member of the 1st Garrison Battalion, Devonshire Regiment. 'The dream of my life had been to visit Egypt', he later recalled, 'but in my wildest moments I had never conceived the possibility of being ordered to proceed there.'[18]

There was thus the aspect of soldier as tourist as these young men sailed toward unknown and foreign lands. Hiorns marvelled at the natural beauty of the sea and got his first glimpse of a whale. When he sailed along the North African coast, he was 'aware of the glare of the Libyan Desert, and the strange smells from the land'. The evening before they reached Alexandria, the sea was 'an oily calm and the water was streaked with solid bands of blue, red and green, each band yards wide and on both sides of the ship as far as the eye could see. The wake was a glorious mixture of them all. I have never seen anything like it again.' As he later recalled, 'I was thrilled to be seeing strange places – all free.'[19]

Despite the prospect of visiting the land of the Pharaohs, many soldiers could not avoid thinking when or if they would ever see home again. Decades after the war, the eyes of George Horridge, a lieutenant with the 1/5th Battalion, Lancashire Fusiliers, filled with tears as he recalled a song that he and his comrades often sang in their singalongs on the deck of the *Neominee* as they sailed for Egypt in 1915:

Homeland, homeland, when shall I see you again?
Land of my birth, dearest land on earth.
Homeland, homeland, when shall I see you again?
It may be for years, when shall I see you again?
It may be for years or it may be forever,
Dear Homeland.[20]

The U-boat presented an immediate threat to the passengers of these troopships. On the night of July 26 1916, R.W. Macey, a private in his late thirties in the 2/4 Battalion, Hampshire Regiment, was approaching Egypt on the transport *Geramie*. He was awakened by the:

...sound of guns booming. The ship began to put on speed and so we knew something was the matter. Utter darkness down below, and soon pandemonium reigned. Men cussing, praying, crying, and all crowding in the dark towards where we knew the stairs were leading to the upper deck. I could not find my boots, so thought it best to get back into my hammock for my toes' sake. After what seemed an interminable time word came down to us that all was well. We had been chased by a submarine, whose two torpedoes had missed us.[21]

Other ships were not so lucky. The admiralty faced a crisis in protecting seaborne traffic as 1916 came to an end. Over forty ships of all nationalities were sent to the bottom of the sea from October to December.[22]

The new year got off to an ominous start. On January 1 1917, the troopship *Ivernia*, weighing 14,278 tons, encountered off Matapan a U-47 with its torpedo tubes loaded and ready. 'A bit on edge', Private Doug H. Calcutt had sailed on the *Ivernia* from Marseilles with some 3,000 passengers. Calcutt, brought up by a widowed mother, had been educated at the London Orphan Asylum. When the war began, he was employed as a civil servant in the Home Office. His superiors, bowing to the growing pressure for ever more recruits, had agreed to release him for service. According to Calcutt, both he and his superiors expected him to fail the physical examination for medical reasons. They were wrong, and he was accepted in the Queen's Westminster Rifles. 'This was a horrifying result for me', Calcutt remembers. 'To be strictly honest with myself even at this late date I should have rejected the idea. But I was "all right up to now" and had a secret fear that I was a coward as compared with all these other apparently brave fellows.'[23] He was classified B1 (fit for service abroad but not for general service) and attached to a garrison battalion before serving with the 2/16th London Regiment, 179th Brigade, 60th Division.

On the morning of January 1, Calcutt was taken off cookhouse fatigue and sent above to watch for submarines. Once on deck, he followed orders to wear a lifebelt and remove his socks and shoes. At 10.55a.m., he felt a 'dull thud' and was covered with water. 'At first

I thought I must be under the water', he records in his diary, 'but it was the huge column of water sent up by the explosion running from poop deck to "A" and from "A" to "B" decks. I grabbed on my glasses and conscious of the weight of water pouring on my head rushed down the gangway to "B" deck.' When he arrived at his designated lifeboat, he found it filled with water from the torpedo explosion. When lowered, it 'fell into pieces like matchwood'. When someone suggested that they find another lifeboat, he responded: '"No, ours is gone, we will stand by, we have no place in the others."'[24]

Unlike Calcutt, A.W. Fletcher, who had left England as part of a draft for the Lincolnshire Yeomanry, 22nd Mounted Brigade, was not a stickler for orders when circumstances differed from the drills. When the torpedo struck 'sudden as death' and 'the great liner staggered like a beast reeling from the blow of the axe', Fletcher tried to find his assigned lifeboat. 'I found the hope of my reaching it entirely impossible', he later recalled:

> ...owing to the push from below completely filling the gangway. The only course open was to proceed up the one close at hand which was against orders. Without hesitating I was on the upper deck just in time to see a boat being lowered over the liner's side. This was my chance now or never so I dropped into the boat in spite of those on either side crashing to pieces and falling useless into the sea. Fortunately my boat was amongst the four that succeeded in getting away from the wreckage. The position of those less fortunate was disastrous – to describe such a scene is far from my mind.[25]

Despite the danger that the *Ivernia* might sink at any moment – the *Lusitania* had gone to the bottom in eighteen minutes – many soldiers remained remarkably calm. According to Calcutt, 'there was no panic or wind up discernible at this juncture but not much organization either. Inertia if anything was the order of the day.' Calcutt was acutely 'conscious of the frightful quietness of the vessel as she seemed to wallow on an even keel, after 4 days of the steady thud thud thud of the engines as she ploughed on her way'. Without central direction, confusion reigned.

The ship's Officers did their best as opportunity offered. Troops sat in the top boat of stacks of these waiting to float off when she sank! or as if angels could lower the boats... One ship's Officer with a lovely Eton and Harrow Oxford and Cambridge accent shouted through a megaphone 'Get going you chaps, the Archangel will not be coming to lift you off.' The Navy at its best. The ropes of the lifeboats proved to have been painted into the davit blocks and things worked very stiffly indeed. No one seemed to know how to lower a boat from the davits. Troops were standing on the edge of the 'Ivernia' with the boat behind them that was trying to be lowered, and they with their backs to the boat. The wireless was going and trawlers and destroyers were at hand.

With escape by lifeboats unlikely, Calcutt's chances of survival seemed slim. But help abruptly arrived. A destroyer dashed alongside in a style reminiscent of 'a lady going through the hoops at a circus', he continued in his diary:

> It cuts down the dangling boats and churns up some already afloat...
> I looked over the side and saw bodies and men in the water between
> the destroyer and the 'Ivernia.' Some were alive, some life belted bodies
> floated with a red stain where the head should have been, they having
> been churned up by the propellers. Troops swarmed down on to the
> destroyer by ropes and ladders but Daymond and I do not attempt it.
> Some slide down on pulleys and things with nothing on the other
> end. The destroyer cannot stay long in one place on account of the
> submarine being still present presumably and cuts away on an instant
> and leaves the air full of dangling figures. Some climb back and some
> fall in. Rumsey was one of the dangling ones who climbed back very
> excited and gives us an account of it.

When a trawler, the *Stratheden,* suddenly came alongside, Calcutt shouted to his friend Daymond, 'lets get on this trawler', and they 'got on to ladder swinging round and round. At one time over the trawler, and then over the sea. Men are in the sea below us. Now we are flat against the "Ivernia". Land on the trawler, pulled on by hands, turn round to help others. Parsons after me on the ladder treading on my hands. Get him in and help Daymond in.' Another comrade, Medium, 'gets mixed up in the ladder astride of a rung as if to paint the side of the ship. We tip him upside down. He lets go and we pull him in.' Chaos reigned on all sides, with men about to be crushed between the two ships. 'The trawler and "Ivernia" swing together and then away again', Calcutt recalled. 'One falls in and the others pull him out. All this time a raft having got between the trawler and the "Ivernia" is being crushed to matchwood, the space on which "they" are getting gradually smaller and smaller, and they [are] in imminent danger of getting crushed. I see all this while helping to pull in men.' As the trawler pulled away from the *Ivernia*, Calcutt almost lost his life:

> We find that about four or five of us are in the centre of a coiled rope that is somehow connected with both the 'Ivernia' and the 'Stratheden.' The rope tightens round us tying us up like a bundle of asparagus and spinning us round and round as she pays out tightening into our flesh from feet to hips. There are shrieks of 'cut the rope cut the rope,' but we had only clasp knives against a great ship rope. The rope cut into my companions thigh about 3 inches deep, lifted us off our feet and commenced to drag us off the trawler, towards the 'Ivernia'. The rope got into an angle of machinery and paid out without carrying any of us out. The man with the badly cut thigh was bound up with a field dressing, me being merely badly bruised and very tender.

Safely aboard the *Stratheden*, Calcutt witnessed scenes of horror on every side as a storm developed and the wind picked up:

> The trawler cruises about picking up survivors: boat load after boat load. The Chaplain General arrives. Daymond is being sick behind me. The trawler is rolling in the rising wind. The spray is coming in over us now. We are huddled together on the deck of this trawler, shivering, no clothes, wish we had our cardigans discarded on account of that projected cook house fatigue. We continue to cruise around picking up men from the side of upturned boats, and others submerged. Those in command crying 'Take your time' 'Take your time' more and still

more boats. Our boat, only a trawler is getting very full now. About 300 on board. Those in command cry 'Sit down' to lower the centre of gravity. Then get over to the right, and sit down. Then get over to the left and sit down. There are the cries of the drowning, wreckage and bodies floating by as we pass. There is difficulty in saving in the now heavy seas. Some are drowned before our eyes. The destroyer is still dashing about unable to remain for long stationery owing to danger from the submarine. Our boat is getting fuller and fuller. The 'Ivernia' gets lower and lower in the Water. The trawler stands by. At 3.50p.m. after nearly five hours after being struck the 'Ivernia' heels over and sinks. Her huge bulk which somehow must have been a comfort while she was still afloat disappears and the sea suddenly seems horribly empty. The trawlers are still around picking up men.

One of these men happened to be Fletcher, who had perhaps saved his life by disobeying orders.

After the *Ivernia* disappeared beneath the waves, the *Stratheden* found itself in a perilous situation when its propeller became fouled. Calcutt described the frantic efforts of a destroyer to attach a tow line:

Daylight goes in frantic efforts to get taken in tow. There are many tries in the heavy seas. We are all urged forward to make room on the deck for operations. Forward still more to make room to move. Then it proves impossible to get out the tow rope. Then we are all urged all aft, all aft. At this point I am sick. I lay down on the deck running with water, clutching a deck ring with one hand, an iron pillar with other and am '*ill*.' I have no interest in anything for the moment except I suppose to see I do not allow myself to be washed overboard.

This was a real possibility for, as Calcutt observed, 'the boat is so overloaded we are nearly under the water, with no means of getting at right angles to the waves. The sea is pouring in over the gunwales.'

When the destroyer abandoned its rescue effort, the auxiliary patrol trawler *Princess Mary* took its place and successfully attached a tow line. But Calcutt and his mates were still not out of danger.

I stand up in half fear of getting tipped over or capsizing. The sides of trawlers are not very high. We are drenched time after time as waves as high as the ship sweep across us… Injured men lying on the deck all awash. I work my way towards the cabin door. I dry by hot fumes from below by putting my head in a doorway. Some men are crouching under an awning. Ship taking the most dangerous looking rolls. I take about four hours to get down into the cabin. I perch on the stairs and cling for some time. The contrast from outside is great. Now we are all nearly suffocated. People smoking cigarettes! Get a drink of water in a tin lid. It is horrible in the cabin for hours on end. There are half naked men, injured men. One is attempting to smoke. There is acetylene gas for illumination. The din is terrible. Every time the ship rolls the propeller swings from one side to the other and back again. Things roll about over deck and make an exaggerated sound down below. The water on deck makes a fearful row washing on and off, and all the time fear of capsizing down below with all this lot and the possibility of the submarine having another go. Men (including me) spewing again now, urinating on the floor, and in a fireplace, everyone groaning and lying in a comatose condition for hours and hours and hours and hours. I lay on the floor under a table. Then I fear the table will collapse on me so I get up. Men all lying on one another to make more room. There is one little wild eyed boy. After what seems ages the boat gets a bit quieter and steadier and eventually we (sail if that is the word) into Suda Bay in Crete.[26]

Coated with salt where the sea water had washed over him, dried, and then washed over him again, Doug Calcutt was reunited with many of his comrades. Some 2,000 men had been rescued.

When their time came, many men and women rose to the occasion in the frightening and chaotic environment of a torpedoed troopship. The courageous acts that Calcutt had witnessed by naval personnel and fellow soldiers were not unusual. As the HMT *Transylvania* began to disappear beneath the waves, Frost observed brave and selfless acts: Red Cross nurses singing and laughing although their lifeboat was almost full of water, a 'cool as a cucumber' sergeant major cracking jokes to keep his men calm, and a member of the Royal Army Medical Corps resuscitating a half-drowned soldier rather than save himself. A veteran cavalryman assisted men who were jumping aboard a destroyer that had moved alongside. 'He managed to keep order', Frost wrote, 'and helped each man up on to the ship's rail and gave him a push to help him clear the jump. He could quite easily have saved himself, but he stuck to his self-allotted duty, and when the T.B.D. [Torpedo Boat Destroyer] moved away, he waved to the men on sea and wished them good luck.'[27]

The loss of the *Ivernia* created consternation in the Egyptian high command. Major General A.L. Lynden-Bell, the EEF's chief of staff, wrote to the War Office: 'The sinking of the *Ivernia* was a bad business... These naval people *must* take up the question of the protection of important ships. There is far too much haphazard about their methods.'[28] After Germany launched unrestricted U-boat warfare in February 1917, the admiralty was forced to change its approach. Troopships arriving in Egypt now sailed in convoys protected by destroyers and watched over by planes from Cairo that met the ships as they approached Alexandria.

Zigzagging was now compulsory night and day. Because all lights, including navigation lights, were extinguished, there was the danger of a collision between the troopships and their escort vessels. Sublieutenant Jack D. Walters recalled a near miss when his ship, the HMS *Lobelia,* almost collided with a merchant ship at night as it suddenly altered course. Another time his convoy narrowly avoided colliding with another convoy at night.[29]

Anxiety over lurking U-boats and accidents at sea was replaced by curiosity aboard the troopships as the shining white buildings of Alexandria came into view. 'Even the least imaginative traveller would experience a certain wondering curiosity upon arriving at an Eastern port', observes Bernard Blaser, who served with the 2/14 London Regiment ('London Scottish'), 179th Brigade, 60th (London) Division, 'confronted as he is by new scenes and strange people rendered the most attractive by reason of tales and traditions of world-wide renown. As I was about to set foot on the land of this historic people I was all speculation as to what the modern Egyptian would be like.'[30]

The only Egyptians whom Blaser had previously seen were Egyptian students dressed in European clothes. Instead of the educated and well-dressed student that Blaser had known in London, he was greeted by dockworkers who he characterized as 'a dirty howling mob'.[31] Blaser's reaction was typical. J.R. Tozer wrote in his diary when he arrived in Egypt in December 1915: 'We have a very amusing time watching the Egyptians in the docks, a low, dirty degraded lot of beings, eat anything that we throw at them, bullie, biscuits, etc. They scrambled and were ready to fight for.' Tozer, who served in a machine gun section with the Devon Yeomanry, Second Mounted Brigade, was appalled by the ragged clothing of the natives. 'Dressed in just a few loose rags which they pick up. Old clothes which our fellows throw out the port holes into the water they pulled out', he noted.[32] The loud gibbering of strange tongues also shocked many soldiers. Reacting to the chanting and shouting of the dockworkers, H.S. Scott, a gunner with the 75th Division, scribbled in his diary: 'One of the first impressions of the country we got was I think of the extraordinary nosiness of the Arabs.'[33]

Although some soldiers were able to look beyond the noise, disorder, hunger and clothing of the dockworkers and admire their work ethic, most were not. Compared with Blighty, this foreign culture was not only different, it seemed to them decidedly inferior. The short march from the ships to the railway station in Alexandria seemed to confirm this view. Egypt looked and smelled different. 'We were quickly disillusioned', recalled A.R. Surry, a signaller with the 1/7th Battalion, 161st Brigade, 54th Division, 'for dirty dilapidated shops and dwellings greeted us as we left the docks. The smells and other obnoxious odours were a decided revelation and the natives seemed to be in keeping with the general surroundings.'[34]

Merchants frequently exploited these unworldly soldiers. Blaser observed men before they boarded their train buying for the lordly sum of twenty-five piastres what appeared to be champagne 'in dark coloured bottles bearing a well-known label, the corks of which were bound in the usual way'. As the train pulled away, mugs were produced and the expensive liquid poured. 'The *cherished* hopes of those thirsty warriors', Blaser recalled, 'were immediately dashed to the ground (and beyond) upon tasting the contents of that dearly purchased bottle, which turned out to be nothing stronger than WATER – and none of the purest at that.'[35] This was the first of many unwelcome surprises for British soldiers in this foreign land.

2

Land of the Pharaohs

The massive flow of troops and equipment to Egypt eventually made that country the greatest British military base outside of Britain and France. Before 1916, however, the actual defence of the Empire's lifeline, the Suez Canal, depended almost entirely on Indian troops. The original garrison of British Regulars had been recalled to Europe shortly after Britain's declaration of war against Germany in August 1914, and the New Zealand and Australian troops in the country were kept back from the canal zone for training and organization.

Berlin, of course, posed little threat to the Empire's lifeline until Turkey became an ally in November 1914. A Turkish force, numbering between 12,000 and 15,000 men and existing on 'desert rations' of biscuits, olives and dates, performed an amazing feat in January 1915 when it crossed the Sinai, an almost waterless desert some 150 miles wide, with artillery, rafts and pontoons. Not a single Turkish soldier lost his life. The Turkish commander, Djemal Pasha, hoped to capture Ismailia and spark a general revolt of Egypt's Muslims.

British defences in 1915 were primitive compared with what they would become during the following year: the Suez Canal, which was over 200 feet wide, was part of the defensive system, with most of the forces positioned on the western bank. Nonetheless, the Turkish assault at the beginning of February failed. Although three boatloads of soldiers got across the Suez, the attack was easily repulsed and the Turks put to flight, with perhaps as many as 2,000 casualties. Losses to the defenders were minimal. The British suffered four killed and eighteen wounded; the Indians had twenty-five killed and 110 wounded.[1] Until autumn, the Turkish threat to the canal was reduced to harassing tactics to disrupt shipping. Turkey had to concentrate its forces in Gallipoli to meet the British threat there. The Sinai, although still controlled by the Turks, remained relatively quiet.

Battle in the Turkish theatres took an alarming turn as 1915 came to an end. London abandoned its Gallipoli campaign. Meanwhile, in Mesopotamia, an Anglo-Indian force of some 20,000 men advancing on Baghdad was forced back and encircled at Kut. With Baghdad secure and triumphant in Gallipoli, Turkey could apply increased pressure on Egypt. This Turkish menace was more serious because of the prospect of assistance from Berlin in 1916. With the conquest of Serbia and the addition of Bulgaria as an ally, Germany now had direct access to the Turkish theatres.

An additional British concern was the emerging threat on Egypt's western frontier posed by the Senussi, a puritanical sect of Islam. German and Turkish agents, bolstered by U-boat activity along the coast, were busily encouraging these tribesmen to launch a holy war against the British. If the Senussi recruited the Bedouins (nomadic rather than settled Arabs) to their cause, the Nile Valley would be endangered.[2]

In Sollum, Egypt's westernmost outpost, Chief Petty Officer G.V. Sharkey, who served with a Royal Naval Armoured Car Squadron that was attached to the 29th Division, witnessed the opening stages of the Senussi revolt:

That night [November] 20th–21st we laid in our overcoats on the hillside by our guns listening to the chanting of the priests away in the distance & it reminded us of Gallipoli. The moon was very bright & we felt that if anything should happen our position could be easily located… A rifle shot rang out just as I was falling asleep & then another… The native sentries fell back to redoubts connecting the guns & all our men stood to. Then all was quiet… A wireless message was received from *Barrani* [a town forty-eight miles east of Sollum] stating that they were being heavily attacked & two armoured cars were even at the gate firing into the Arabs.[3]

The small Anglo-Egyptian garrison at Sollum that included Sharkey boarded the coast guard cruiser *Rasheed* on the morning of November 23. They were outnumbered and now in a state of war with the Senussi. 'During the evacuation', Sharkey's dramatic account continued, 'no shots were fired directly at us as far as we could make out but as the last man got aboard the gunboat thousands of Arabs swarmed down the hills, firing, shouting & brandishing swords in the air. They prevented a few refugees from reaching the boat. The governor's house was soon ransacked, our tents pulled down & fighting commenced amongst the natives. The horsemen galloped round & round, whipping natives & striking with their rifles a few Egyptian soldiers who cut off now endeavoured to reach us.' Sharkey's last glimpse of this revolt was one he would never forget. As his boat steamed away, he saw 'at least 6,000 Senussi Arabs on the hill sides & shores still firing, shouting, galloping round in circles & what appeared to us fighting amongst themselves. I never saw such a mob or sight in my life as those hills at Sollum covered with their thousands of white figures.'[4]

This campaign in the western desert, in which the British deployed cavalry and armoured cars to pursue an elusive enemy, was essentially won on February 26 1916 at Agagiya, in an action that included a cavalry charge by the 1/1st Dorsetshire (Queen's Own) Yeomanry, Western Frontier Force, over open country against infantry supported by machine guns, the first of several British mounted assaults with the sword in this eastern theatre.

The British, advancing to reoccupy Sollum, on that day encountered the enemy entrenched. After infantry dislodged the Senussi from their defences, the Dorsets, commanded by Lieutenant-Colonel Hugh Maurice Wellesley Souter, who had fought in India, Gallipoli and France, harassed the retreating foe. By 3:30p.m. infantry had lost contact with the Senussi, and three of the four pursuing armoured cars had become stuck in sand. The Dorsets had not watered their horses since 4a.m., and the men themselves were almost spent. Souter, who feared that the Senussi would escape if he did not take decisive action, had the led horses whistled up and gave the order to mount and form ranks. Lieutenant J.H. Blaksley, 'B' Squadron, recalled that he was surprised by this order.

> Imagine a perfectly flat plain of firm sand without a vestige of cover and 1200 yards in front of us a slight ridge; behind this and facing us were the four machine guns and at least 500 men with rifles. You might well think it madness to send 180 yeomen riding at this. The Senussi, too, are full of pluck and handy with their machine guns and rifles… We were spread out in two ranks, eight yards roughly between each man of the front rank and four yards in the second. This was how we galloped for well over half-a-mile straight into their fire.

Fortunately for Blaksley and his fellow troopers, the Turks proved poor marksmen. At first, bullets fell short. As the Dorsets closed with drawn swords – the regimental cooks who rode swordless brandished their cleavers – the panicked enemy apparently neglected to lower his sights, and bullets 'began going over us, and we saw them firing wildly and beginning to run'. A fight at close quarters ensued. Blaksley had two horses shot out from under him and had to fight on foot. He witnessed 'a scene of terror as it is quite impossible to describe', with Senussites 'running in all directions, shrieking and yelling and throwing away their arms and belongings; the Yeomen after them, sticking them through the backs and slashing right and left with their swords. The whole thing was a marvelous instance of the awful terror inspired by galloping horses and steel.'[5]

In this cavalry charge with drawn swords, the 'irregulars' of the Yeomanry demonstrated raw courage. The official history characterized their exploits as 'the outstanding event of the campaign' and noted that 'the Senussi never again stood to await a British attack'.[6] Unlike the fighting in the increasingly artillery-dominated and moonscape terrain of the western front, this cavalry charge with cold steel represented a reversion to nineteenth-century warfare with its emphasis on the man and his weapon. The fighting conformed to an earlier romanticized view of warfare, with warfare up close and

personal as soldiers looked each other in the eye. 'Isn't this splendid?' Souter's aide-de-camp exclaimed as the Dorsets closed on the
Senussites. Souter responded, 'Yes, I have waited twenty-four years
for this.'[7] This brave charge, which caused a ripple of excitement
throughout the Yeomanry, was not without its cost. The Dorsets suffered heavy losses, with dead and wounded amounting to one-third
of the attacking force. Five officers and twenty-seven men were
killed.[8] Blaksley was the only uninjured officer in his squadron. But
it had been a near thing. He had a bullet through his field glasses
case and another through his tunic.

Although the Senussi revolt never materialized into a serious
threat to the Nile Valley, it represented one more concern for the
British commander in Egypt, Lieutenant General Sir John Maxwell.
To rescue the faltering British effort in Mesopotamia, he had to
send many of his Indian troops to that theatre. That still left him
with some 60,000 troops, but most of these were Dominion soldiers from Australia and New Zealand who had been organized
into temporary battalions for training. In November 1915, as the
official history noted, 'the Force in Egypt was almost reduced to the
functions of a training and reinforcement camp'.[9] Fearing that the
Turks might launch a major offensive against the Suez Canal with
upward of 250,000 troops, Maxwell asked the War Office for twelve
infantry divisions, a cavalry division, and twenty batteries of heavy
and siege artillery. Additionally, he asked for two divisions to maintain
communications and domestic peace in Egypt, and three infantry
brigades with cavalry and artillery to defend the western border. The
War Office reduced this estimate, but not by much.[10]

Egypt, as the centre of operations in the Mediterranean, was rapidly transformed into a base teeming with men and equipment. In
mid-December, two Territorial Divisions, the 53rd and 54th, arrived
from the Dardanelles, and more were on the way from the eastern
Mediterranean and from Britain. In addition to the British infantry divisions, mounted divisions and Yeomanry brigades, there were
drafts designated for the new theatre in Salonika, and partially trained
Dominion troops. This 'jumble of units and personnel', in the words
of General Sir William Robertson, constituted 'an unwieldy mass

of well over 300,000 men'.[11] Because the Nile Delta was irrigated, swarming with mosquitoes, and extensively cultivated, these troops were usually quartered in encampments in vacant desert land close to Egyptian cities where water was available.

The fate of these British and Dominion forces in Egypt was largely in the hands of two officers: Robertson, a plain-spoken, direct and practical soldier, who became the new Chief of the Imperial General Staff in December 1915 with enhanced powers that made him the government's sole military adviser on strategy; and the man he replaced, General Sir Archibald Murray, who was sent to Egypt to command the large force being assembled to defend the canal. Maxwell retained command of the force in Egypt, but his responsibilities were now generally limited to the defence of the western border and the maintenance of internal order.

'Wully', as he was affectionately known, had advanced from a lowly private to become the professional head of the British Army as CIGS. His advancement was all the more remarkable because of his humble origins. Without money or social position, and for the most part self-educated, he was also the first to demonstrate that a private in the British Army could have a marshal's baton in his knapsack. He had made a habit of filling Murray's shoes. Before becoming CIGS, Robertson had succeeded Murray in turn as Chief of General Staff, Aldershot, Director of Military Training, and Chief of the Staff of the British Expeditionary Force. 'I seem to have done a good deal of spade work for a more forceful character who by his very ruggedness got more done than I could',[12] Murray later confessed.

Earlier, while serving as the British Expeditionary Force's chief of staff, Robertson had opposed the diversion of the Empire's limited resources to such theatres as Gallipoli, Salonika and Mesopotamia. 'Here we can beat the German', Robertson wrote to the king's equerry, Clive Wigram. 'No more d——n silly eccentric Dardanelles fiascos, pretty well doomed to failure & in no circumstances likely to help in decisive result. Fancy our fighting on a front from Calais to Constantinople.'[13] The defence of Egypt, unlike the Dardanelles or Mesopotamia ventures, was by no means a 'sideshow' to imperial strategical concerns. Its loss would be a disaster of the first magnitude.

Not only would the Suez Canal be lost, the Turko-German menace would now extend to Africa. Robertson recognized the strategic significance of Egypt, but he correctly believed that military authorities in Egypt and the War Office greatly inflated the Turkish menace. 'Think of the preparations', he prophetically wrote to Sir Charles E. Callwell, then serving as director of military operations in the War Office; 'we should have to make if we were marching some 700 miles, to be followed by 150 miles or so across the desert'.[14] At best, Robertson believed that the Turks might concentrate 100,000 men against the British in the Egyptian theatre. He was right.[15]

When Robertson became CIGS, he informed Murray, who was about to depart for Egypt to take command of the forces defending the canal, that France was the primary theatre for British operations and that divisions sent to or formed in Egypt constituted the strategical reserve for the Empire.[16] After Maxwell was brought home and Murray had been given total control of operations in Egypt, Robertson made it clear to him that the Egyptian theatre was totally subordinate to the expanding British effort against the main body of the German army. 'We want *men* badly', he bluntly asserted. 'Can't get the recruits we need. Men, men.' In plain terms, Robertson's policy was 'to keep Egypt reasonably secure. To keep a reserve in Egypt for India as long as it seems likely to be required. To get everybody else to France.'[17]

Murray faithfully complied with his chief's wishes. By July he had shipped out some 240,000 troops, including nine divisions, three independent infantry brigades, and nine batteries of heavy artillery. Most of these men went to France. In addition to a sizable body of mounted troops, Murray was left with what the War Office considered his least effective divisions. They were all Territorial Divisions, the 42nd, the 52nd, the 53rd, and the 54th. Once the unworkable system of dual command, with Murray in control of the canal's defences and Maxwell in charge of everything else in Egypt, had been ended with Maxwell's recall in March 1916, Murray renamed the British forces in Egypt the Egyptian Expeditionary Force, or EEF.

Although Robertson emphasized to Murray that France was Britain's primary theatre, Lord Kitchener, the Secretary of State for

War, had told him that he must 'maintain as active a defence as possible' to keep the Turks from establishing themselves within artillery range of the canal.[18] Murray consequently extended his defences some 11,000 yards east of the vital waterway. Another line of defence was established between this line and the canal. A third line of defence on the eastern side took the form of fortified bridgeheads. In addition to the many trenches that had to be dug and wired, railways, roads and pipelines had to be constructed.[19] A 'swept track' was maintained along the eastern bank of the canal by mules dragging a wide bundle of branches each evening. The next morning, patrols checked for any footprints that might suggest that the enemy had infiltrated the defences, perhaps with a mine to place in the canal. The extensive defence of the canal would not have been possible without the employment of native labour. But British soldiers were expected to do their part as well.

W.T. Massey, who served as the official correspondent for London newspapers, described the difficulty of constructing defences in the desert. 'To make a trench three feet wide', he wrote, 'you had to open some fifteen feet of ground, put in battens with canvas backs and anchor them, and then refill the spaces behind with the excavated soil. And when that was done a tiny rent in the canvas allowed sand to filter through at such a rate that a portion of the trench would be filled in twenty-four hours. Sandbagging after the trench was cut, and building of redoubts, was another phase of hard work.'[20]

M.R.L. Fleming, serving in the 160th Brigade, 53rd Division, quickly discovered the problems that sand presented his shovel:

Mile upon mile of rolling sand hills, a burning expanse unrelieved by tree or bush – such was our new home, some miles east of the canal. The Brigade was spread over a thirteen mile front, in a series of defended posts located on commanding sand dunes. Here it spent countless hours of toil, digging and sand-bagging – and then destroying the fruits of hard labour, and starting all over again. Never was there such a pointless waste of time, temper, and energy. The heat was intense and the flies were a pest.[21]

Sergeant William Barron, 1/4th Northamptonshire Regiment, 162nd Brigade, 54th (East Anglian) Division, described his daily routine to one of his loved ones in one of these redoubts. In April 1916, he lived with some 100 men in a dozen tents in the middle of a network of trenches called Round House Post. 'The camp was roused at 3.45a.m.', he wrote, to start

> ...work at 4 o'clock, carry on until half past five then we used to knock off for half an hour for gun fire, which meant a cup of tea and some bully beef stew, and in that half hour we had to clean our tents, and lay our blankets out in the sun to air. At six o'clock we started work again, and carried on until eight o'clock, when it was too hot to be outside ones tent let alone working, then we had our breakfast, just fancy finished a days work before breakfast, at least finished until 4 o'clock in the afternoon when we went and done another hours work, but in between nine o'clock in the morning and four in the afternoon it was almost too hot to breathe and we used to strip naked and lay in the tent, trying to keep cool, but even then we simply poured out sweat and our skin blistered, yes it was hot, enough for fowls to lay hard boiled eggs all day long.[22]

Defenders of the Suez Canal lived in dread of a Khamsin, the extremely hot and dust-laden wind that blows from March to April in Egypt. Bluett, who later became a member of the Egyptian Camel Transport Corps, watched a Khamsin develop and engulf his artillery unit. 'One evening the whole sky was aflame with lurid light', he wrote in his memoir, 'and we missed the revivifying breeze. In its place came a hot wind from the south-east, and although the sun was setting we could feel the sickly heat increasing momentarily. Presently, far over the eastern desert could be seen a gauzy cloud of immense size traveling towards us at a tremendous pace. In a few moments we were in the midst of an inferno of swirling sand and suffocating heat.' The impact of this blast of heat on Bluett and his comrades was dramatic:

> Men rushed blindly for their tents and swathed their heads in shirts or blankets in order to keep out as well as might be the flying particles of

sand. For three days it raged. Little work was possible beyond watering and feeding the horses. The short walk from the horse-lines to the watering-troughs was sheer torment, for the hot wind came down the slope like blasts from a furnace. It did literally turn the stomach. Many a man staggering blindly along with his three or four horses would pause, vomit violently and carry on.[23]

Summer followed the Khamsin season. At General Headquarters at Ismailia, which was surrounded by trees and gardens, the recorded temperatures ranged from 114 to 117 degrees during a four-day period in June, and this was in the shade. One can only imagine what it was like for front-line soldiers who, unable to work during the midday hours, sought refuge in an unlined bell tent. 'Another sweltering day of heat, a regular heat wave according to the papers (I'm glad they have discovered it is a heat wave!!!) is passing over Egypt. Temperature in one of our tents was 120 degrees guaranteed to make most people "perspire freely"',[24] was the wry comment of Lieutenant A.M. McGrigor of the 1/1st Gloucestershire (Royal G. Hussars) Yeomanry, 5th Mounted Brigade, who was stationed at Ballah near the canal. Some soldiers earned the ire of their superiors by cutting off the sleeves of their shirts. Shorts were reduced to little more than bathing suits.

Flies also inflicted misery on the soldiers. Bertram George, who served with the Dorset Yeomanry, wrote home that 'there are three sounds in Egypt which never cease – the creaking of the water-wheels, the song of the frogs, and the buzz of flies… Letter writing is an impossibility in the evening for as soon as the sun goes down, if a lamp is lighted, the air all round is thick with little grey sand-flies which bite disgustingly.'[25]

Preparing defences with nothing but empty desert within sight produced boredom. Sir Randolf Baker, a cavalry officer with the Dorset Yeomanry, wrote to his sister: 'Egypt seems likely to be extremely dull all the summer, as far as one can judge, & I am very keen to try & get to France, or elsewhere.'[26] Constant drills and fatigue duty in the oppressive heat also demoralized many. Some took out their frustration on the Egyptians. While recovering in the hospital from 'a touch of the sun', a disenchanted young subaltern from the Essex Yeomanry Horse Artillery currently serving with the Scottish Territorial Field Artillery, E.N. Buxton, wrote to one of his sisters: 'I now look upon Arabs no longer as picturesque, but as loathsome scum. There is still a certain amount to admire in the sunsets which are very fine but otherwise this is a land of filth, garbage, flies and dust.'[27]

The command appreciated that military inactivity and the extremely arduous and demanding fatigue duties sapped troop morale. Passes were generously granted, and Cairo, Alexandria, Ismailia and Port Said became crowded with troops of all ranks. Port Said was the most accessible city to servicemen in the canal zone, but the cosmopolitan city of Cairo was the first choice of many soldiers. 'Imagine a huge Eastern town, with its queer old streets, queer old shops, picturesque inhabitants, mosques, flies and filth', J. Wilson, who served in the 179th Company, Machine Gun Corps, 60th Division, recorded in his diary; 'and imagine big bits of it bodily cut out, and big bits of London, and big bits of Brighton bodily transplanted there; and imagine the result left to take its natural course for some years. That is what Cairo is like, as nearly as I can describe it.'[28] Cairo's antiquity and history also had its attractions for many. 'We all realised that we were in a country steeped in Ancient history and, as it transpired, we were able to obtain some well-deserved leave', recalled L.J. Matthews of the 5th Siege Company, Royal Monmouth Field Company, Royal Engineers, 74th (Yeomanry) Division. 'Small parties of us, whose interests were similar, were able to see something of Cairo, the pyramids and the Sphinx.'[29]

R.C. Case, a junior Royal Engineer officer, 313th Field Company, 60th Division, enthusiastically wrote to his mother: 'I am having 74 hours of the best trip of my life. Just think! This trip would have cost me somewhere about £200 in civil life, certainly not less, and here am I now, doing it for about £2 railway fare and 12/– per day inclusive hotel fee, exclusive of drinks only.'[30] Case was staying in the famous Shepheard's Hotel, which was the favourite of almost every officer who served in Egypt and Palestine. Geoffrey Inchbald, a junior officer in the Imperial Camel Corps, recalled that Shepheard's Hotel maintained:

...the highest possible standard of living throughout the entire war, and it would be an understatement to say that we made the most of it... There were at least three bars, one of which was presided over by a gentleman called Hannibal, and was alleged to be the second largest in the world... There were also two enormous dining-rooms and the food was absolutely superb in its own right, and not simply by contrast with what we had been consuming during the last few months.[31]

Cairo's atmosphere could be magical to a soldier seeking relief from the desert. While sitting on the verandah of Shepheard's Hotel, Major Vivian Gilbert, the commander of a machine gun company in the 180th Brigade, 60th Division, recalled:

...sipping strong black coffee and gazing at the every-changing panorama of the passing crowds in the streets. In the distance I could see the lighted lanterns twinkling in the trees of Ezbekia Gardens. Carriages drawn by fast-stepping Desert ponies with glistening sil-vered harness, flashed by with a jingling of bells and a cracking of whips. Now and then a luxurious limousine, bearing some beauty of the hareem, but faintly seen, veiled and mysterious, would glide through the traffic, silently. Native guides, water-sellers and vendors of Oriental merchandise, mingled with soldiers in smart summer khaki drill uniforms, their shorts exposing bare knees burnt brown by the sun.[32]

No other British theatre of operations, of course, provided such sightseeing opportunities: Heliopolis, the Citadel, the magnificent Barrage Gardens, and, of course, the famous Sphinx and the pyramids. 'I don't profess to be a romantic sort of person', the engineer Case wrote home, 'and reckon that it takes something pretty considerable to impress me, but I must confess that the sight of these pyramids with the sphinx, wild desert surroundings, the pyramids of Memphis, the Nile and the great city of Cairo in the background, impressed me more than anything I have ever experienced before. The whole thing is absolutely awe-inspiring, and to one who realises the work entailed, a description is almost impossible.'[33]

Not every soldier was so impressed. Many in the ranks did not have the means or the education to enjoy the best that Cairo and its environs had to offer. Some found little conventional entertainment available. 'I cannot remember that anything was done to keep the troops amused', Inchbald recalled, 'and we were left very much to our own devices. There were one or two theatres and music halls, including the Kursaal, but we found the performances very dull and conducted in pretty well every language except English.'[34] Lance-Corporal R. Loudon, a signaller with the 1/4th Royal Scots, 156th Brigade, 52nd Division, recalled that he 'went occasionally with some others, but kept to the main thoroughfares, since the meaner streets seemed to consist of miserable slum dwellings. I thought that Cairo was a most unattractive place... soldiers were continually pestered by beggars or by men and boys offering to sell cheap articles of jewelry, etc. We were advised always to go in groups, as solitary soldiers might be robbed or even murdered and thrown into the Nile if they strayed too far.' Loudon also objected to Cairo's night life, with its 'nude dancers' and 'other disagreeable haunts'.[35]

Other soldiers, of course, had a contrary view. Cairo had attractions for young warriors of more earthy instincts. It was, in the words of A. W. Fletcher, who served with the Lincolnshire Yeomanry, 'a city blessed with grandeur unequalled in the world yet packed with all the lust and vice conceivable'.[36] To be sure, prostitution was hardly unique to Egypt. A red light district could be found in London and other large cities. Nonetheless, the War Office feared that young and unsophisticated British lads sent abroad would be corrupted. Secretary of State for War Lord Kitchener, for example, placed an appeal in the active service pay books of soldiers dispatched to France that included this warning: 'In this new experience you may find temptations both in wine and women. You must entirely resist both temptations and while treating women with perfect courtesy, you should avoid any intimacy.' As the former commander in chief of the Egyptian army, Kitchener anticipated even greater temptations for British soldiers dispatched to Egypt with its reputation for vice and sensuality.

This view of Egypt as a den of iniquity was overdrawn. The presence of tens of thousands of boisterous young men, many of whom were away from home for the first time, fostered a booming trade in alcohol, drugs such as cocaine and hashish, and prostitution in Egypt's cities. Although prostitution was officially sanctioned by the Egyptian government, it might be argued that the widespread and visible prostitution was as much a result of the extensive British military presence as it was the result of local custom.[37] The Melbourne doctor James W. Barrett, who worked to reduce the instance of venereal disease in both Dominion and British troops, found that Egyptian prostitutes only differed 'from prostitutes elsewhere in that the quarters are dirtier and that the women are practically of all nationalities, except English. The quarter in which they live is evil-smelling, and is provided with narrow streets and objectionable places of entertainment. It contains a considerable infusion of eastern musicians and the like, and is plentifully supplied with pimps of the worst class.'[38]

Private F.V. Blunt of the 2/15th London Regiment (Civil Service Rifles), 179th Brigade, 60th Division, experienced one form of exotic entertainment when he joined other troops in a Cairo restaurant that featured belly dancers. 'I had never seen anything like it before', the former junior civil servant recorded in his pocket diary:

> The women were bare from the waist up except for necklaces and trinkets etc. They stick out their tummies and seem to be able to make their stomachs shake, ripple and move up and down like jelly. It is just amazing how they are able to move their stomach about and at the same time shake their bottom and their tits. One of the women had long pendulous tits that she seemed to be able to throw almost over her shoulders. They were given great applause from the soldiers.[39]

Alcohol was also readily available, with cities such as Port Said having a bar on every corner. The Dominion troops, called the 'fucking five bobbers' by envious British soldiers who were paid about one-fifth less per day, drove up prices. This did not deter many British soldiers from drinking themselves into oblivion. Some dealers were involved in sharp practices. J. Thompson, a gunner in the Royal Field Artillery, 210th Brigade, 42nd Division, recalled that in 1915, some Greek merchants emptied genuine Scotch whisky bottles by 'piercing the bottom with a red hot wire. Then withdrawing the genuine liquid and replacing it with a native spirit called Arak – a very dangerous 'fire water.'... Several of my comrades were seriously ill through drinking this poison.'[40] To curtail widespread drunkenness, army authorities in Port Said forbade the sale of alcohol, first between 10p.m. and 5a.m., and later between the hours of 1 to 3p.m. and 7 to 9p.m. This reduced the consumption of alcohol, but not by much. The next stop for many drunken soldiers was the red light district.

Doug Calcutt was sober when he visited the Alexandria quarter inhabited by the licensed prostitutes. According to his diary, he was motivated by curiosity rather than by any desire to satisfy a sexual urge. He ignored the conspicuous signs that read, 'Out of bounds to all troops. By Order. G.O.C. Alexandria district' and entered 'a conglomeration of little narrow streets' filled with 'a jostling throng of troops from up the line'. What he next observed disgusted him. 'The women and girls sit on the steps in some houses in all sorts of vulgar attitudes. In others where there is no front to the house – like a room with one wall let down they sit on the step up. They call after you to come here dearie, and are abusive if you don't. Swearing and using the most filthy language. They frequently expose their persons as a sort of proof of bona fides and brandish their Doctor's Certificates.' (These certificates, incidentally, offered little security. Although they might be marked 'Saine', the prostitute was often not free from venereal disease.) If soldiers ignored these entreaties, another approach was 'to steal your cap and run upstairs with it'. Scantily dressed women also 'threw their arms round the necks of the unwary who ventured too near. They shout (like all natives do) that "Kan Kan" is going for 1/2 piastre and generally endeavour to excite one.' Calcutt records that he was unimpressed by this crude approach. Nor did he find the prostitutes attractive:

> The poor things are jaded and heavy eyed and look worn out. Any beauty they had has been replaced by a painted *animal* sensual face. The animal look in some of them is awful. Some have visible signs of recent nervous exhaustion such as a sticky perspiration. I watched

several 'Kan Kan' parties formed and the door closed on them. There are not many black women: about half and half. I went in one place. *Not because I was excited in the least.* The thing is not clever sensuality at all. Repulsive bestiality more aptly describes it. The average English man when he thinks of 'Eastern sensuality' conjures up, if he conjures up anything, something much more seductive. This is crude in the extreme. A boy all in a perspiration is sitting on a bed playing with himself to excite his worn out passion while a little girl stands outside exhorting the crowd in *unadulterated* language to come in and see for one piastre them have sexual intercourse. When she gets enough the doors are closed.

Calcutt portrays the soldiers as being hesitant at first. 'They want to go in', he wrote,

but are afraid to confess it and wait till someone sets the ball rolling. Dirty rags and cigarette ends lay on the floor, and smoke filled the atmosphere. The troops although they have paid to come in seem hardly interested. Some are a trifle tipsy. They express disapproval of the played out boy and maul the girl about. (She is alone in the room with ten men.) They have their intercourse on the sofa and it is a very disappointing affair, and the Tommies crowd round and assist them and interfere and pass disparaging remarks. It lasts about one minute and being fully clothed in this case nothing is visible. They shout their disapproval and so she consents to 'Kan Kan' with a cigarette which she does.

Rather than being aroused, Calcutt was 'BORED'. It was all so '*crude* and brazen'.[41] After departing the quarter inhabited by prostitutes, Calcutt noted that he went to get some supper at the YMCA. To give soldiers healthier outlets, many excellent clubs had been established in Alexandria and elsewhere. Although Calcutt did not say so, he might have gone to the popular Esbekieh Soldiers' Club, which was established by the YMCA. Many other soldiers chose these soldiers' clubs over the grubbier side of Alexandria and other cities. Blunt, although later intrigued by belly dancers, was 'frightened' by his first contact with pimps and prostitutes in Cairo. He and his friends 'were only too happy to get away from it and back to the cleaner areas and the British clubs – Church, Army, YMCA, etc'. 'Be the kind of man your mother thinks you are', was the rule he hoped to live by.[42]

At these clubs, Blunt and Calcutt could have picked up 'Women: A Word to Men' or 'A Warning to Men Going Abroad', YMCA publications that were a part of the moral campaign against venereal disease. Self-restraint, although the best defence against venereal disease, was often not possible for many young, sex-starved soldiers. Doctor Barrett discovered that 'a very large number of men either find the sexual appetite overpowering or deliberately indulge, and unless some form of prophylaxis is adopted many infections are certain. Some of the men were quite candid and stated they intended to indulge, despite generals, doctors, and chaplains, and with or without prophylaxis, though they preferred to be safe.'[43]

From 1916 to 1918, there were 31,051 admissions to hospitals in Egypt for venereal disease. Approximately half of these cases, 14,153, or 75.31 per 1,000 troops, occurred in 1916 when the British front remained close to the cities of Egypt. During this same period, 18.2 cases per 1,000 troops in France were recorded.[44] In other words, British soldiers in Egypt in 1916 were contacting venereal disease at a rate four times greater than those in France. When a soldier was discovered with venereal disease, he was housed in a hospital where strict military discipline was imposed, with a noncommissioned officer being placed in charge of each hut or tent. Some doctors thought that the patient would recover faster in a military environment. This approach also made it clear to every soldier that he could not escape the army by contracting venereal disease. A soldier recuperating (it usually took about two months) was put on half pay and lost his field pay. This money was not remitted, as was the case with other illnesses when the patient was released. Family allowances were also stopped while VD treatment was being administered, a practice that surely created an uncomfortable situation for married men.[45]

Many men, whether they practised restraint or not, yearned for companionship with a woman who spoke their language and shared their culture. Miss Dorothy ('Dolly') Williams, who worked during the war in a munitions plant, saved some of her wartime letters, including one from Jack, a soldier with the 160th Light Trench Mortar, 53rd Division. 'Just fancy', he wrote, 'I have been abroad now over 2 yrs 4 months & not had the pleasure of speaking to or taking a girl for a walk.' Jack underscored his plight as he put down his pen: 'Well I think I must close now as my *wife* is in bed (if you can call it so, 1 blanket on the ground not bad eh) & wants me to keep her warm, but it is only a Palestine wife, another Sussex boy & we are both jacks so there is nothing doing.'[46]

A common complaint for those who served in the EEF was the near impossibility of getting home leave, especially for those who were unmarried. 'Furlough' was thus defined in the trench newspaper, the *Middlesex Yeomanry Magazine,* as 'an obsolete word which applied to an old degradin' practice, incredible in the recent days of a sturdier soldiering, whereby men who had served so many years abroad were actually allowed to re-visit their homes and even openly associate again for a while with their parents'.[47]

Even a wound did not represent a ticket to Blighty. 'If hit on the front near Home then the wounded do get a chance for Blighty, but here... of course we know of the times on the other fronts, but the risks are none the worse, we fight with the same tools against the same enemy & at the same time never have a chance of a spell in "Blighty"',[48] lamented Sergeant A.V. Young, 2/17th London Regiment (Poplar and Stepney), 180th Brigade, 60th Division, during the last year of the war.

The future commander in chief of the EEF, General Edmund Allenby, who missed his own wife terribly and eventually arranged for her to come to Cairo, expressed concern about the consequences of his men's exile from British women. Shortly after he took command, he wrote to Robertson requesting home leave for his men who had been away from Britain for more than two years. 'The number would be considerable; but a lot of them are becoming tired and stale, and I think that the consequent improvement in moral tone and contentness would compensate for the temporary diminution in effective strength.'[49] Faced with a mounting shipping crisis and manpower shortages, however, the War Office turned his request down.

The sentiments of Dolly's friend Jack reflect the sense of longing, even desperation, found in soldiers' correspondence with women back home. Lieutenant Buxton, who had attended Cambridge after graduating from Harrow, was charged with the censorship of his men's letters. He was amazed by how many of them proposed marriage, not just to one woman, but to several. 'There is a awful lot of the most barefaced sentimental tosh', he wrote one of his sisters, 'and one wonders sometimes how some of them can have the face to offer marriage to about 10 girls at the same time, with the most beautifully expressed sentiments.'[50]

For those who had girlfriends back home, absence did not always make the heart fonder. John Bateman Beer, who served with the 2/22nd London Regiment (Queen's), 181st Brigade, 60th Division, was surely dismayed when he read the first sentence of a letter he received in October 1917 from his girl Ivy. 'Dear Jack', she wrote, 'For the last month I have been endeavouring to pluck up sufficient courage to write and tell you that everything must be over between us.' The letter continued:

> No doubt you will think me awfully unkind and perhaps fickle to write like this while you are away, but this matter has worried me a great deal, and I have been halting between two opinions, as to whether it would be kinder to let you know now, and let myself be called unfaithful, or to wait until you come home, although knowing all the time in my heart that I was untrue. When you went away, and I told you that I loved you best, I really meant it Jack, but such a lot seems to have happened since then... I would not hurt you dear unless I could help it, but unfortunately we cannot control our own feelings. Will you believe me when I say that I am very sorry, for I am, more so than perhaps you think. Anyway, forgive me if you can, and I trust that you will still let us be friends, whatever happens.[51]

Jack was not prepared to think of Ivy as a 'friend' after she had thrown him over for another man, and refused even to reply. He contemplated bachelorhood, but he admitted to his father in a letter that 'not seeing a woman for such a long time, when I get back I may alter my opinion'. At any rate, as he wrote in this same letter, I am 'not going to worry my head about it, as in the Army there is plenty to worry over'.[52] Indeed. Several weeks later he was wounded by an artillery shell at Beersheba during 3rd Gaza.

Married men worried about the survival of their marriages. An older family man, Captain O.P. Boord, 1st Garrison Battalion, Devonshire Regiment, who had rejoined in 1915 after serving for over a decade in the prewar Territorials, was sought out by his men to discuss their situation. 'We have frequent and dreadful tragedies here – so many of our men come to us to say that their wives have gone off with other men, sold up the house & left the children to shift for themselves – it all sounds too dreadful especially when the men have sent all their money home to their wives',[53] Boord informed his mother in 1916.

Many members of the EEF had more than personal matters to think about in 1917. In an attempt to pry open the door to Palestine and Jerusalem, the EEF attacked the fortress town of Gaza on three separate occasions in 1917 in the heaviest fighting yet seen in this theatre. To reach Gaza, the EEF first had to cross a great wilderness, the Sinai Desert. This advance represented an impressive feat of endurance as well as engineering.

3

Clearing the Sinai

On Christmas Day 1916, with British troops occupying El Arish, Brigadier General Guy Payan Dawnay described the accomplishments of the Eastern Force, of which he was chief of staff: 'It really has been an extraordinary "campaign", this one in Sinai', he wrote to his wife:

> It necessitated the fitting out of much the biggest desert column that there has ever been, with actually *tens* of thousands of camels. No wheels practically; camels, camels AND camels! Then we have had to lay a railway 100 miles over a howling wilderness for the supply of the troops, the camels being used to carry on the supplies etc. in front of railhead. Finally we have had to lay a great pipe-line to carry water to the forces – the water being pumped up the pipeline from the Sweet Water Canal on the west side of the Suez Canal.[1]

The Sinai, some 120 miles wide from east to west along its Mediterranean coast, presented many challenges to the British soldier. A Tommy writing home is supposed to have described this desolate and monotonous landscape as follows: 'Dear brother', he wrote, 'we are now in the desert. If you want to know what a desert is like, it's miles and miles of sweet damn all.'

The decision to cross the Sinai was Murray's. He wanted to shake up the men under his command who had become complacent during their static defence of the Suez Canal. His chief of staff, Major General Sir Arthur Lynden-Bell, explained to the War Office the situation that he and Murray had found when they arrived in Egypt: 'The great difficulty in Egypt has been to produce an atmosphere of war. Up to the time of our arrival the whole idea in Egypt appeared to be amusement and having a good time, and the state of Cairo and Alexandria was a positive scandal, thousands of officers hanging around the hotels… We have taken this matter in hand, and have now issued orders that all officers are to join their units forthwith.'[2]

The argument for abandoning a mostly passive defence of the canal that carried weight with Robertson was Murray's contention that an advance along the northern or coastal route to El Arish would neutralize any serious Turkish threat to the canal and release the large number of soldiers presently defending it. Once established at El Arish, the British could use a mobile force to attack the flank of any Turkish force that advanced along the central route. Additionally, the central route could be made more precarious for the Turks by destroying the storage tanks and cisterns that had supplied them with water during their daring attack on the canal in 1915.

But no British advance to El Arish was possible without camels, the only practicable means of transport across the soft sand of the Sinai, which was almost impassable for wheeled vehicles, even those fitted with special sand wheels, six-inch iron rims bolted to ordinary tyres. The field artillery had 'ped-rails', or thin blocks of flat wood chained to their wheels that distributed the weight and reduced the sinking of the wheel. As Lynden-Bell told Freddie Maurice, the Director of Military Operations in the War Office, 'The whole matter of taking the offensive depends entirely on the number of camels we can collect.'[3] British officers were sent to the Delta and abroad to purchase healthy camels – not an easy task in Egypt, where many camels were infected with mange. Tens of thousands were ultimately employed by the Egyptian Expeditionary Force (EEF), making this camel force the largest ever assembled.

Camels were war winners in desert warfare, but they were difficult beasts to manage. A native proverb was that Allah had created the world and all its animals, then turned to man and said, 'Now try your hand'. The camel was the result. Most camels used for transport were males. During the breeding season, usually from March to December, these males were likely to go mad, or *magnoon*. A member of the Imperial Camel Corps Brigade, A. S. Benbow, described in a letter to his wife what happened when a camel made a curious bubbling noise, known as 'blowing his bubble'. 'His tongue appears to become inflated', Benbow wrote, 'and is forced out of his mouth at the side of his face covered with saliva and froth, his neck being forced back against the front part of the hump for a few seconds, at the end of which the contortion ends and he prepares to attack you.'[4] British soldiers, not to mention the native camel drivers, lost limbs, and some were killed when attacked by a camel in this condition.

A camel, however, did not have to go *magnoon* to be a menace. In a letter home, Lieutenant J. W. McPherson, a member of the Camel Transport Corps, gives a vivid description of his close call with their powerful jaws:

> I noticed a brute giving sidelong glances from bloodshot eyes and warned the Adjutant not to come too near him. I had hardly spoken when he left the water and came for me open-mouthed. As I turned the horse, his jaws met so near my bare knee that he covered it with foam. I was splendidly mounted, but the horse could not get sufficient pace on at once, and the camel missing me again fixed his teeth in the pony's flank and hung on, literally the incarnation of grim death. My poor beast reared, tried to bolt and finally foundered in a pool of blood, quite done for; then the camel turned his attention to a native, picked him up by the head and shook him till his neck broke.[5]

Depending on their type, camels led by a driver could travel at a pace of from two to three miles an hour. They carried a variety of supplies, but their most precious cargo was water and wounded men. The camel had a pack saddle with wooden crossbars placed on his back, thus allowing it to provide the soldier with what might be his only supply of water. On each side, a metal tank about the size of a suitcase (called a *fantasse*) holding about twelve gallons of water was lashed. To convey wounded men across the sand by camel, ambulance saddles of two types were devised. Some of the most badly wounded were laid down in *cacolets,* a sort of trough with a sunscreen. Others sat on something akin to a chair that was also attached on each side of the saddle. Lives were saved, but a camel's long-legged movement made this method of transportation an ordeal for the wounded. W.G. Cadenhead, a machine gunner who served with the 1/3rd Scottish Horse, 1st Dismounted Brigade, before joining the Imperial Camel Corps, had painful memories of his jerky and swaying ride after being wounded at 1st Gaza: 'Intense pain, mostly from this movement seemed to cause complete unconsciousness for much of the subsequent journey over the desert until we came to a rail-head.'[6] When available, sand carts rather than *cacolets* were used for soldiers with abdominal wounds, fracture of the thigh, and similar wounds.

Drivers were required as well as camels. Camels could be purchased, but could Egyptian peasants (*fellahin*) be so easily found to do the army's work? On the eve of Turkey's entry into the First World War London instructed General Maxwell to assume military control of Egypt. He did so, telling Egyptians that the purpose of martial law was to defend the country and promising that Britain 'accepted the sole burden of the war' and would not call 'upon the Egyptian people for aid'.[7] This promise was broken as the war widened in Egypt. The defence of the canal, and especially the crossing of the Sinai, were vast logistical and engineering projects that required a large labour force. If Egyptians were employed in digging trenches, laying the required broad-gauge railway lines and water pipes, and loading supplies, many British soldiers would be spared this back-breaking labour and would be available to fight. Tens of thousands of camel drivers were also needed.

The resulting Egyptian Labour Corps (ELC) and its offspring the Camel Transport Corps (CTC) became essential ingredients in the war against the Turks. The fellahin were organized into companies and subjected to military discipline. The pay was low, the discipline often harsh, and the clothing simple. The official ELC uniform consisted of khaki shorts and a smock with the letters 'ELC' in red on the chest. The hatless and usually barefoot camel drivers in the CTC were identified by the thin sky-blue outer garment that they wore.

The best workers came from the southern provinces of Egypt, but many of them refused to sign a contract for more than three months. Nor would they agree to return to work until their savings had been depleted. When the Directorate of Military Labour turned to the Nile Delta for workers, it found the peasants there just as reluctant to work for the military. The authorities were thus forced to resort to forms of compulsion and extend the terms of service to six months.

The difficulty of recruiting Egyptians to assist in Turkey's defeat is perhaps best illustrated by the history of the CTC. Lieutenant Colonel G.E. Badcock, the assistant director of transport for the EEF, was not far from the truth when he wrote, 'The first recruits were volunteers which is to say that of every three, one came to avoid the police, one was sent by the Police, and one was a respectable wage-earner.'[8] A company in the CTC initially consisted of 1,168 Egyptians, 2,020 camels, and twenty horses. British officers included a company commander, an adjutant, sectional officers, and a number of noncommissioned officers. Discipline was maintained by native overseers, the *reises* and *bash reises,* who received nine and twelve piastres respectively. The driver, or 'naffer', as many soldiers referred to him, received seven piastres. The overseer, who assumed the role of a sergeant in this paramilitary organization, exercised his authority with a giant buffalo- or rhinoceros-hide whip. It was a punishable offence for a British soldier to strike a native, but it appears that this was almost never enforced. Besides, the native overseer, under the direction of British officers, was under no such restriction and was quick to use his whip. According to Badcock, a majority of these *reises* obtained 'their rank at the Recruiting Station by the previous purchase of a whip'.[9] Not surprisingly, entry into the CTC quickly became a revolving door, with some 170,000 Egyptian drivers serving, most of them only briefly.

The papers of British personnel serving in the EEF provide a revealing glimpse of the army's relationship with the fellahin. This is especially true in the case of two lieutenants: McPherson, the survivor of the camel attack previously described, who served with the CTC, and E.K. Venables, who was posted to the ELC.

McPherson, who was fluent in several languages, including Arabic, joined the CTC in February 1916 after recovering from wounds received at Gallipoli. His first responsibility was collecting camels shipped from the Sudan. The usual practice was for the army to inform the high commissioner how many camels were needed. This order then went down the line from the governor general of the Sudan to the governors of the provinces to the sheiks and then to every clan and subclan, informing them how many camels were needed and where they were to be sent.

The colonel in command of the CTC told Lieutenant McPherson to take the train south to the last station. At Shellal, at the first cataract, he was expected to collect camels sent from the Sudan and, in the words of the colonel, 'obtain by any means necessary' the men to look after them. Upon his arrival, McPherson quickly discovered that this latter assignment was no easy matter. 'I hunted for recruits, but all in vain – the natives muttered something about war and the sea and shook their heads.' Undeterred, he visited the local mudir, or lord lieutenant, at Assuan, who offered to furnish him with 'press gangs'.

McPherson, hoping that this would not be necessary, tried another tack. He asked for the services of a money payer, or *sarraf,* and plunged into the bazaar of Assuan and the tents of the Bisharin, promising anyone temporary work at seven piastres a day and the right to quit at any time. He also promised anyone willing to formally enroll for service anywhere half a sovereign (or fifty piastres) and seven piastres a day with rations. 'No one swallowed the latter bait', McPherson ruefully commented, but he acquired enough temporary workers to care for his camels, in large part because the natives of the region were 'horribly poor' and 'their mouths watered at the sight of this wealth and feasting'.

After several days of treks into the desert to exercise the camels and some drills, McPherson tried again. He called upon the *sarraf,* and banknotes and silver were piled on a table in front of the assembled natives. This time, they took the bait. One hundred men stepped forward to collect the king's half-sovereign and affix a seal or thumb mark. Each new recruit then had a lead seal fastened round his wrist.

One is reminded of the sharp practices of military recruiters in the eighteenth century as described by Candide, who was tricked into becoming a soldier in the Bulgarian army. Many of the fellahin did not comprehend that they had, in effect, put themselves under army discipline by taking the king's half-sovereign. As McPherson noted, 'Things were now on a military basis and I held my little Courts Martial when necessary. Cases were tried and if necessary, the accused punished summarily by a small fine or a mild flogging.'

McPherson's treatment of one camel driver, who was not only absent from his guard post but found drunk in Assuan, was anything but mild. McPherson considered the man's behaviour a case of serious insubordination. He arranged his recruits in a crescent and had the prisoner stripped. He next selected a 'trusty Sudanese boy' to administer twenty-five lashes with a rhinoceros-hide whip. Before the first blow was delivered, a man dressed in European clothes stepped forward and informed McPherson in perfect English, 'you shall not flog this man, it is brutal and illegal.' When McPherson asked for his identity, the man replied, 'I am Dr Talaat Bey and I shall report this to your Colonel.' He then tried to address the increasingly agitated crowd in Arabic. McPherson stopped him short with the threat: 'If you utter another syllable in Arabic or Ethiopian, I will have *you* stripped and give you *forty* lashes. If by word or sign you incite these men to insubordination or interfere with the execution of my orders I shall shoot you on the spot. If you have anything to say, say it to me in English or Turkish or German, and if you intend to disobey me, write your report first and I promise you it shall be forwarded with my report of your death.' With the doctor silenced, McPherson ordered the flogging to begin. The first twenty lashes reduced the prisoner's back to a bloody pulp. Dr Talaat then intervened again: 'I beg a thousand pardons, but any further laceration of these parts will produce a condition defying medical treatment.' McPherson response was, 'Very well, turn him up and let him have the remaining five on his feet.'[10]

A more sympathetic, and indeed truer, side of McPherson was revealed when his company began a desert march at dawn on July 21 1916, from Heliopolis, the City of the Sun, which was not far from

Cairo. With the Turks now threatening in the Sinai, his company's destination was the British front, which was now about twenty-five miles east of the canal. On July 23, still on the western side of the canal, his company reached the outskirts of the ancient city of Bilbeis. McPherson expected a halt because camels were not to be marched in desert conditions during the intense summer heat of the midday hours between 9a.m. and 4p.m. unless an emergency existed. After a brief rest, however, the company commander, called by McPherson 'a cocksure idiot without judgment or common sense', decided to push on.

This order was tantamount to murder for some of the camel drivers. 'The heat was most intense and the sand burnt and cracked the natives' feet', McPherson wrote. 'Half of them were unprovided with water bottles in spite of the reports and urgent requests for them from the Section Officers for months past. It was a pitiful sight, the poor devils fainting with thirst, heat and weariness, falling out or plodding on blindly.' One British officer went mad and attempted to kill himself. McPherson did what he could, sharing his water and allowing one of his exhausted drivers to mount one of his camels and ride for a while. The company commander's reaction was quite different. When he saw men trying to mount their camels, he had them pulled down and flogged. When the four-mile procession stopped for the night, McPherson opened one of his *fantatis* and poured water down the throats of his men as 'they lay half dead on the ground'. Only two men consequently died in his section. Other sections suffered much greater losses in what McPherson termed a 'fool's march'.[11]

Just as the camel drivers in the CTC conveyed water to thirsty troops in the Sinai, the pipe and rail that brought this water forward from the Sweet Water Canal could not have been laid without the efforts of their hard-working counterparts in the ELC. The building of a standard-gauge railway (four feet, eight and a half inches) across the Sinai began in February 1916. The first stage was a twenty-five-mile stretch from the canal to the district of Qatiya, which was at the western end of a series of oases of brackish water. Napoleon had used Qatiya in 1799 as a base for his advance across the desert to Palestine. Egyptian State Railways provided much of the material, including its own railway tracks, which were pulled up. Some locomotives and their engineers were shipped from England. 'It was rather curious', Major Vivian Gilbert, the machine gun company commander, comments, 'to see these engines, with their own drivers who had accompanied them to Egypt, calmly shunting and backing in the sidings at Kantara just as though they were in Eastleigh or Waterloo Stations.'[12]

Unlike the Ottoman Empire, Britain, as a rich and powerful industrial nation, had the means to make a methodical advance across this barren wasteland. The ELC became a vital cog in the EEF as it built more than fought its way across the desert to the borders of Palestine. Thousands of native labourers, assisted by British sappers, pushed the line forward. 'As the ground was levelled', according to Lieutenant E.K. Venables, the commander of the 39th Company, ELC, 'rails were bought up on trucks over the lines already completed: a sort of enlarged meccano outfit in sections already bolted on to the iron crossbars.'[13] Native labour unloaded the rails and laid new track. A similar approach was taken with water pipes when they were laid next to rail lines. Pipes, weighing as much as half a ton each, were unloaded one by one as the train moved slowly along the track. 'Thoroughly enjoying this new game', the official history suggested, the Egyptians became 'very expert at it'.[14]

Because Egyptians often sang (really chanted) as they worked, many soldiers assumed that they were 'wonderfully cheerful and light-hearted souls'.[15] If one understood Arabic, the reality was quite the opposite. 'Kam Lehloh, Kam Yaum?', which translates as 'How many days, how many nights?', could well have served as the anthem of the ELC. A work party began this chant by asking this question, meaning how much longer would they have to work before returning to their homes and loved ones. A soloist would respond with a prediction, perhaps 100 years, which would be greeted with much wailing and wringing of hands. The group would then repeat the question, and the soloist with each response reduced the number of years of service left. His final response would be 'one day, one night', and his fellow workers would clap their hands with pleasure. And the song was over.

Sometimes screams of pain rather than the sound of song was heard from the 'gyppo', as he was called by the British. 'Oh, what a life', wrote a junior Royal Engineer officer, 'my wretched sappers working intensively 5 hours this morning and 5 hours yesterday, digging and sandbagging and sawing and cursing; Egyptian Labour Corps the same, Reises cursing and reviling, flaying chunks out of yelling dagoes with their shambocks.'[16]

Hard labour and the overseer's whip were not the only concerns for Egyptian workers. Frequently they were placed in harm's way. Venables, whose previous experience had been with a field ambulance unit of the Royal Army Medical Corps – known in some quarters as 'Rob All My Comrades' – had been posted to the ELC in April 1916. He had the usual racial notions of his generation, but he also had great respect for the hard-working Egyptians and treated them humanely. In his account of the ELC, 'They Also Served', he described his workers under enemy attack. 'One morning', he wrote, 'an Austrian plane flew over, and at my signal to stop work and keep still, all the squads lay down, any injunction against looking skyward being unnecessary, as dusky faces were not a visible mark as white troops would be.' This enemy aircraft, however, was not on a bombing raid. Rather, it was a spotter for artillery. When shells began to fall, Venables succeeded in keeping his men calm 'until a shell exploded among the steadiest squads; this was too much, they jumped up and unwisely ran away back over open ground, leaving a few men slightly wounded by splinters'. Soon the rest of the workers 'followed the example of the first escapees, rearward, helter-skelter, anywhere away from that whining and banging'. Venables, on horseback, then began to collect 'fugitives over a space of anything up to fifty square kilometres'.[17] Once collected, Venables made sure that the men under his supervision were given rest, food, and water.

No punishment was meted out. This, however, was not always the case, for the British often resorted to strict military discipline when camel drivers found themselves in a combat zone as they carried water and supplies to soldiers and transferred the wounded to the rear. McPherson described a situation in which he believed that he had no choice but to use force. In pursuit of the Turks after the battle of Romani, some of his new recruits bolted when attacked by an enemy aircraft. 'My Brigade guard of Tommies had orders to shoot such, but I asked them to fire high, and then they marched up the fugitives at the bayonet point, and I had them stripped and flogged and their position and the double danger they ran explained.'[18] On another occasion, when he was very much in sympathy with the plight of his drivers, he again resorted to coercion. On the eve of the First Battle of Gaza in February 1917, he was given an order to advance eastward from Romani. This order came when the enrolment period for most of his drivers had expired. To make matters worse, the most important Muslim feast of the year was about to begin. As McPherson admitted, 'It would have been hard enough to have been kept at Romani during the feast, even had they been allowed light duty and permitted to feast and keep up their traditional ceremonies, but to have to march out at dawn eastward to toil and perhaps death was more than their patient hearts could bear.' Most of his men refused to saddle up. Instead, they demanded to be paid and discharged. When one of the men made a threatening move toward him, McPherson, discovering that his service revolver was fouled with sand, hit the man over the head twice with his weapon, rendering him 'senseless in a pool of blood'. British troops then appeared on the scene. McPherson's company moved out on schedule.[19]

With the public unaware that the enlistment of native labour was seldom 'voluntary' and that discipline was frequently harsh, the army's use of native labour did not create a stir. Massey, the EEF's official newspaper correspondent, gave the home front a sanitized version. 'The happy, singing Egyptians', he wrote, 'were willing helpers of British troops. They were handsomely paid, far above the labour rates in Egypt, were better fed than at home, and had a good allowances of leave.'[20] The army's treatment of the fellahin, however, shocked some British soldiers when they arrived in Egypt. 'The treatment of these Egyptians is a scandal', W. Knott, a conscientious objector who served in the Field Ambulance, believed. 'They talk about modern civilization and abolishing slavery yet these men have task masters paid by the British Government to whip them like dogs with long leather whips. Even the British and Australians kick and bully them unmercifully. Let us take the beam from our eyes before talking about Germany and her allies.'[21]

Many newly arrived troops tended to agree with Knott when they witnessed the harsh treatment of native labour. But soon these same soldiers decided that the mores of western society did not apply to the apparently primitive and simple fellahin. 'To sum up', concluded Captain Boord, 'they are children from birth to the grave, and must be treated as such.'[22] Spare the paddle and spoil the child was General Edmund Allenby's approach when he later succeeded Murray as commander in chief. Egyptians should have been protected from the lash because native personnel were subject to the Army Act, which did not permit flogging. Allenby wanted the War Office to change this. 'Everyone who knows the country considers power of flogging to be necessary', he argued in a letter to the War Office. 'The general behaviour of the Egyptian Labour Corps is very good; but there are now and then cases for the lash.'[23] Although Allenby failed to get this flogging of native labour legalized, it continued nonetheless.

Nor was it possible for many Europeans to believe that the life of the simple gyppo had the same value as that of a European. L.J. Matthews of the 5th Siege Company, Royal Monmouth Field Company, Royal Engineers, 74th Division, provided an example of this thinking. After the Third Battle of Gaza, members of the ELC were ordered to clean up the battlefield. Matthews believed that the disastrous consequences were the responsibility of the native labourer rather than of the military authorities. 'Once again', he recalled, 'they demonstrated their stupidity and carelessness, for although they had had previous experience and were warned against unexploded shells ands grenades, they still picked up grenades, shook them in their excitement and killed themselves. We kept well down whenever we saw what was likely to happen.'[24]

At the war's conclusion, the bodies of many fellahin lay interred from the Suez Canal to Megiddo. Badcock, the assistant director of transport for the EEF, sought to write a proper epitaph for those who served in the CTC, but his words could equally have applied to the ELC: 'Tried by extremes of heat and cold, always his own worst enemy, not accounting bravery a virtue or cowardice a crime, scourged by fever, cheerful, miserable, quarrelsome, useless, wonderful men, their name is for ever written *honoris causa* in the records of the War.'[25] Babcock gave these humble Egyptians credit for their vital contribution to victory, but his words also reflect the clash of cultures and the racial values that were prevalent at the beginning of the twentieth century.

The British advance across the desert began at Kantara, a small village containing a mosque and a few mud houses. Kantara was the starting point for perhaps the oldest caravan route in the world, stretching across the Sinai until it reached El Arish on the Mediterranean and then continuing north to Gaza and Palestine. In 1916–1918, this gateway to the desert grew along with the British military effort against the Turks. In 1916, Kantara resembled, according to A.E. Williams, a private in the Army Cyclist Corps, 'a western cow-town. Tents, marquees and wooden shacks stretched far out across the sandy waste'.[26] By the end of the war, it was more like a modern metropolis, with macadamized roads, electric lights, miles of railway sidings, and workshops, cinemas, theatres, churches, clubs (including a fine YMCA establishment), workshops, and even a golf course. By late 1917, it had almost certainly become the largest British base camp in any theatre. Its modern train station represented two very different worlds. The train going west had comfortable carriages, including a dining car, and passed green fields and canals on its way to the cities of Egypt. If you boarded a train on the Kantara Military Railway, you were desert bound. 'Going eastwards', Martin S. Briggs, a sanitation officer, opined, 'was always depressing for any but the most bloodthirsty.'[27]

The 5th Mounted (Yeomanry) Brigade (Warwickshire Yeomanry, Worcestershire Yeomanry, and Gloucestershire Hussars) under Brigadier General E.A. Wiggin acted as a screen to protect the advance of the sweating, labouring army of workers as it approached Romani. Encouraged by their success against the Senussites at Agagiya, the Yeomanry were eager for battle. Their officers, however, were inexperienced and new to desert warfare. 'They rode gaily out into the desert to 'have a crack' at an enemy whom they respected as a man but despised as a soldier… a sharper contrast than that between the desert of northern Sinai and the soft and gracious English country-side is scarcely to be discovered in the world. But the strangeness of their surroundings only heightened the zest of the yeomanry for campaigning', noted H.S. Gullett.[28]

When the resourceful commander Kress von Kressenstein, the architect of the Turkish raid on the canal in 1915, learned that the British were laying pipe and rail east of Kantara, he responded with a raid by some 3,500 men against Yeomanry. The Turks surprised the outnumbered and outgunned 5th Mounted Brigade that had been distributed in small and isolated pockets among the oases in the Qatiya district. The affair at Qatiya, the Yeomanry's first important engagement against the Turks in the Sinai, resulted in the total loss of three and a half Yeomanry squadrons. By any definition, it had been a disaster for the Yeomanry. In the view of Major General E.W.C. Chaytor, the commander of the New Zealand Mounted Rifles, the defeat was largely due to incompetent leadership. The Turks had not been kept under observation, and no attempt had been made to prepare defensive positions with a clear field of fire. According to Chaytor, camps at Hamisah and Romani had been quickly abandoned although the Turks had not come within miles of them. The Yeomanry withdrawal was tinged with panic; the rail-way construction force, uninformed of their withdrawal, had at first identified them as the enemy as they approached.[29] Coming on the heels of their successful cavalry charge in February at Agagiya in the western desert, this defeat was a bitter pill to swallow. The 5th Mounted Brigade had to be withdrawn to the canal for reorganization because of its heavy losses. Their place at the front was taken by the ANZAC Mounted Division, which had been formed in March under the command of Major General Harry Chauvel.

A lull in the fighting followed the affair at Qatiya. Kress von Kressenstein held his hand while waiting for critical German techni-cal support that included antiaircraft artillery, heavy artillery, aircraft, and machine gun and trench-mortar companies. Given this respite, the British reoccupied the Qatiya district and pushed their railway to Romani, which was reached in May. The 52nd (Lowland) Division was then sent forward to dig in along a line of commanding sand dunes that ran from the coast at Mahamdiyah for about seven miles to Katib Gannit, an especially imposing sand dune that towered above its neighbours. A formidable series of redoubts in the shape of a fishhook, sustained by rail, bolstered by wire and artillery, and defended by machine gunners and riflemen, soon emerged.

The EEF now had the advantage if Kress chose to launch an attack against the canal defences. British cavalry was greatly superior to the enemy, and its infantry at Romani was positioned in prepared defences. What appeared to be a weakness – the termination of the British entrenchments at Katip Gannit – actually served as an enticement to the Turks to concentrate their forces in an extremely precarious position. The soft and heavy sand of the tangled mass of sand dunes in this area made the construction of defences almost impossible. Marching around or over these waterless dunes in the heat of the summer was also extremely taxing and slow, about one mile an hour, for either infantry or cavalry. If the Turks concentrated their main strength against the British right, becoming spent in the process, Murray planned a battle of annihilation by rounding his exposed left flank with his mounted forces and achieving a modern-day Cannae.

But would the Turks fight on ground so favourable to the British? Kress showed no sign during the first half of July that he intended to attack, and it began to appear that no Turkish offensive could be expected until the milder conditions of winter. On July 19, however, there was great excitement at General Headquarters (GHQ) when British air reconnaissance reported that the Sinai 'Desert Force' of about 16,000, which included a crack Anatolian division, was on the move. After coming within striking distance of Romani, however, Kress halted his troops and began to entrench in the Oghratina oasis area. A puzzled and disappointed Murray wired Robertson on the evening of July 22 that the Turkish plan might be only to block the British advance to El Arish. If so, Murray professed to have no answer. He admitted that he should attack the Turks before their defences were completed. But he hesitated. 'I fear I cannot march ten to fifteen miles over a heavy sand country and attack an entrenched enemy.

My men could not do it as one operation and to take two days over it would give the enemy every advantage... My weak battalions are not strong enough to justify me in running the great risk which would be entailed to EGYPT if unsuccessful in the operation.'[30] According to Captain Orlo C. Willliams, a cipher officer at GHQ, Murray's limp response infuriated other staff officers.[31] It concerned Robertson as well.

The next day, the Chief of the Imperial General Staff wired Murray that he opposed a passive policy that allowed the Turks time to prepare a strong defensive position and reminded him that British policy was to deny the Turks control of the oases in the Qatiya district. He also pointedly noted, 'I am not clear why the water in this oasis is ample for the Turks but not for us.'[32] Robertson's puzzlement is understandable, but British soldiers, unaccustomed to the saline water, especially in the almost unbearable heat of the summer, could not drink the local water. Even their horses suffered when they drank it.

Murray subsequently made preparations for an offensive that was scheduled for August 13. Kress, however, had only been waiting for his big guns to catch up with his army. The ability of the Turks to bring these artillery pieces forward represented a remarkable achievement. Tracks had been dug in the sand and packed with brushwood to support the wheels of the gun carriages. In other places, boards had been laid for the wheels, then picked up and used again. Kress did not intend to cross the canal. Rather, he planned to establish a fortified position opposite Kantara and disrupt traffic on the canal with his heavy artillery.[33]

On August 4, massed Turkish infantry, shouting 'Allah, Allah', attacked at 1a.m. on the British right among the soft sand dunes, just as Murray had hoped.[34] The weight of the attack fell on a large sand dune that the British called Mount Meredith. By late afternoon, it seemed clear that the Turks had lost. The skeleton force of mounted troops on the right flank of the British line, who bore the brunt of the attack, bent but did not break. The Australians and New Zealanders were clearly the heroes of the day, but they also received support from the 5th Mounted Brigade that had recently returned to the front. The 52nd Division had not been heavily engaged, and the 42nd Division, which had been held in reserve, was marching to the sound of the guns. Within twenty-four hours, the British were able to concentrate 50,000 men in the Romani area, giving them more than a three-to-one advantage over the Turkish forces. Unless Kress rapidly extracted his exhausted and thirsty men from the battlefield, his force was in danger of being destroyed.

Lieutenant Joe McPherson was among the British troops who had been rushed to the front. On the morning of August 4, he was assigned to furnish water for the Worcestershire Yeomanry, 5th Mounted Brigade. Protected by a cavalry escort, he marched across the battlefield. 'Shells and bullets whistling over us, the rattle of machine guns, and rifle fire, and the roar of artillery made that obvious to me', he wrote in a letter to his brother Dougal. 'Can the camels manage a beeline across the hills?' he was asked by an officer, because the Worcesters were 'absolutely without water and every minute is precious'. As he navigated a steep sand hill, his camels halted before a precipitous drop. His view of the battle taking place below was one that he would never forget:

> A mass of the enemy were intercepted and our cavalry were charging them until they surrendered. A Taube was being shrapnelled and the shells burst apparently close to it, a snake-like vaporous spiral descending from each towards the earth. Suddenly hell opened beneath our feet, out of the peaceful palm grove came shot and shell – not in our direction, and our troops responded with terrible effect. A hail of shrapnel crashed into the trees and a fusilade opened upon it. Men rushed out and attempted to climb and remained dead framed on the sand. Horses and camels burst out and fell spouting blood. The same happened at a very tiny oasis a few hundred yards away.

McPherson was fascinated by what he saw: 'It was so theatrical and dramatic that I felt rather like the occupant of a stage box at the fifth Act of a tragedy.'

McPherson was observing the fierce battle swirling on and around Mount Royston, a sand dune about the height of Katib Gannit and

Mount Meredith. Later in the day, New Zealanders and Yeomanry, assisted in the last stages by infantry from the 127th Brigade, 42nd Division, captured this prominent dune. As thirsty and battle-weary soldiers descended Mount Royston after dusk, McPherson attempted to ration his meagre supply of water. He remarked, 'It was sad to see how the men drunk with blood and mad with thirst wasted the precious stuff in their eagerness to drink, and their officers seemed powerless to keep discipline at this stage.'[35]

With their water supply exhausted, McPherson's supply camels joined the victors of Mount Royston in a withdrawal of about four miles to Pelusium Station, which had been a beehive of activity throughout the day. Captain O. Teichman, a medical officer of the Worcesters, described 'what seemed in the dark to be indescribable confusion – mounted troops coming in to water, infantry detraining and marching out, busy ASC [Army Service Corps] depots, camel convoys loading up, ammunition columns on the move, wounded arriving in sand-carts, and large columns of prisoners being marched in'.[36] At midnight, after fifteen and a half hours in the saddle and twenty-one hours without sleep, with only a few biscuits to nibble on, McPherson had a meal of tea and bully beef before trying, without much success, to get some sleep.

From his vantage point in the defences just to the right of Katip Gannit, Lieutenant P.G. Sneath, who had been appointed as a trench mortar officer to the 155th and 158th Brigades, 52 (Lowland) Division, witnessed the mopping-up operation that began the next morning. Just after Sneath and his comrades had been ordered down from their 'stand-to' at dawn, a soldier stood on the parapet and began waving his arms as if he had gone mad. Fearing that a sniper might kill him, Sneath knocked the man to the ground. He then peered through a periscope to discern the object of his great excitement. He recalled:

> An Australian Light Horse patrol was approaching the post with a batch of prisoners… As they approached Turks could be seen rising from behind the cover of scrub and sand dunes as far as the eye could see. They were throwing down their rifles and holding up their

hands. Some were waving white flags in token of surrender. They were coming into all the posts on our left in large numbers as it was opposite these posts that the main body had concentrated for the frontal attack which never took place. The Australian Light Horse were rounding them up like sheep.

The pursuit was on. As Sneath watched:

...a mass of fresh cavalry passed through the line between the posts and started the pursuit of the units that were in retreat, followed a few hours later by infantry which had come up overnight to reinforce the posts... The infantry pressed on in rear of the cavalry as fast as the heavy going would permit and prevented the Turks from rallying. Isolated groups put up a forlorn rearguard action some seven miles in front of our line, but the action was short lived. All day lines of our infantry in extended order combed the desert for wounded and the few remaining snipers. Many of the latter got away but there were few surviving wounded, as even a slightly wounded man cannot survive many hours in the pitiless sun without water.[37]

McPherson was also involved in the pursuit on August 5. At 10a.m., his camels moved out from Pelusium Station, this time to supply water to the 127th Brigade, composed of the Manchester regiments in the 42nd Division, which had been assigned to support the cavalry. The advance over the soft, heavy sand in the intense heat was too much for the infantry. Their boots sank into it, were partially buried, and had to be dragged out. Exhausted from the previous day's fighting and burdened with equipment, many Tommies collapsed in a delirious state. Some died. McPherson 'mounted many... jaded infantrymen, and some of the natives on our already burdened and tired camels, but many of these riders had to give place to poor chaps in extremis. These lay about the battlefield, many in the attitudes of death, but for the most part unwounded and simply dying of thirst and fatigue in the burning sand under a fiery sun. Many were tied apathetic and helpless on the camels.' That night, when he bivouacked with the 127th Brigade, he 'personally served out three quarters of a pint to all my own men and to innumerable Tommies, and had to cover some of these with my revolver to prevent their taking it wholesale'.[38]

On the evening of the next day, August 6, when the 127th Brigade finally struggled into Qatiya, it was discovered that 800 men had collapsed in the two-day march from Pelusium Station.[39] The 125th, 155th and 157th Brigades also had many men fall victim to thirst and the blazing sun. Gunner J. Thompson, who served with the 210th Brigade, Royal Field Artillery, 42nd Division, recalled what happened when survivors of this march approached the few palm trees of the Qatiya oasis. 'Rumour quickly passed that water lay within 2 feet of the surface, and distressing scenes were witnessed of men, mad with thirst, desperately digging with trenching tools and even their bare hands, in a vain attempt to find it. Fortunately, the camels arrived an hour later bringing an allowance of one pint for each man.'[40] The foot soldiers' pursuit was over, for it was now clear that to continue to use them in support of the cavalry would result in a death march for many men.

Casualty figures greatly favoured the EEF in the battle of Romani: 1,130 to the Turks' 5,500 to 6,000. Only 202 officers and other ranks had been killed. The Australian and New Zealand mounted troops, who had been involved in the heaviest fighting, had sustained eighty-seven per cent of the EEF's casualties. The Australasian Light Horsemen had been magnificent, and the victory belonged to them. But the Yeomanry had fought well when called on, and it was not the infantryman's fault that he could not plough through the sand in the furnacelike conditions to engage the enemy during the pursuit. The rugged Anatolian Turk, unburdened with heavy equipment and familiar with desert conditions, moved with surprising speed. As Lynden-Bell informed the War Office: 'The Territorial troops did jolly well, though a number of them were very young and had not seen any previous fighting. The one trouble with these fellows is that they cannot march over the sand in this temperature, and in this respect the old Turco has a great advantage over us, because his infantry can move about three times as fast as ours.'[41] He could have added, as Murray admitted,[42] that mounted troops were equally unable to catch up with the retreating Turkish infantry. L. Pollock, a trooper in the Australian Light Horse, provided a succinct comment on the cavalry's failure: 'We followed them up for a period of about seventy-two hours and we had to disengage from further action on account of water for the horses. The horses were exhausted. The men were exhausted and that was that. We couldn't go any further.'[43]

Although the Turk had been defeated at Romani and would never again be in a position to impede the British advance across the Sinai, more had been expected. Murray, it must be recalled, sought the total destruction of Kress's forces. The Turks were operating at a great distance from their bases and were greatly inferior in numbers; they had all of the disadvantages. GHQ, in the words of Lynden-Bell, remained dumbfounded that the Turks had 'committed themselves to the extreme folly of attacking the position at Romani'.[44] Yet Kress withdrew the greater part of his exhausted force without being enveloped. Then, fighting several skilful rear-guard actions, he succeeded in withdrawing to El Arish.

Murray blamed Lieutenant General Herbert A. Lawrence, the commander of Section No.3 of the canal defences that included Romani, for the escape of the Turks. As the battle developed, GHQ concluded that Lawrence and his chief of staff, Brigadier General H.E. Street, were 'not making use of their opportunities and want ginger'. This led to a flurry of activity. Dawnay, Murray's chief of staff, talked with Street, but no agreement could be reached. Murray then called in other officers to consider 'the means for gingering up No. 3 section'. The upshot was that Dawnay was sent to Kantara at 4a.m., August 5, with 'letters from C. in C., one of which was to be dealt out according to the situation'.[45]

Murray's intervention in the conduct of operations had little effect. After the battle, 'a bitterly disappointed' Murray sent Lawrence a private note accusing him of 'timidity' and 'of magnifying dangers & difficulties'. In Murray's view, Lawrence lacked the 'spirit of offensive' and had been 'impervious' to his orders, carrying 'out the letter but not the spirit of his instructions'.[46] Lawrence was finished after this letter and was soon on his way back to London. 'I think the climate has affected old Lawrence and his staff officer, Street, and I must try to get both of them away on leave for a bit',[47] Lynden-Bell informed the War Office.

In reality, both Murray and Lawrence were too removed from the battle to make prompt decisions about a counterstroke as the battle evolved. Murray was at GHQ at Ismailia, and Lawrence remained at Kantara, some twenty-five miles from the front, before moving his battle headquarters to Romani on the 6th. The telephone was a poor substitute for being close to the battlefield. From their distant locations, they were not always cognizant of the local conditions facing the troops and were inclined to see their units as pins on a map. Many of their men, however, were as spent as the Turks. While battle-weary and exhausted soldiers of the 127th Brigade marched late in the evening to reach the Pelusium Station to receive water, Murray talked through the night about their field commander Lawrence not having 'ginger'. It is little wonder that the 127th Brigade and other units were unable to respond to their subsequent marching orders at 4a.m. the next morning.

Even if the infantry had advanced on schedule and the cavalry had been deployed promptly and aggressively, desert conditions made a 'perfect' battle difficult. The infantry, new to desert warfare, simply could not keep up with mounted troops. If the cavalry, whose exhaustion mirrored that of the Turks, had succeeded in getting around the enemy's left flank as planned, it would have confronted a superior force without infantry support. The outnumbered troopers might have been overwhelmed if forced to fight dismounted.[48] The Turks, although beaten, conducted an orderly withdrawal and retained their fighting spirit. Almost to a man, the members of the EEF praised the pluck and endurance of the Turks at Romani. 'I have no word to say against the Turk', Buxton, a subaltern with the Yeomanry, wrote to his mother. 'He fought like a man and a gentleman, and though we chased him out of it, he is by no means routed into rabble, and when we go and dig him out, I think we shall find him as game as ever.'[49]

With Lawrence and Street both 'degummed', Murray created the so-called Eastern Force, with its GHQ at Ismailia, to conduct future operations. Major General Sir Charles Dobell was chosen to command this force. This new arrangement, which moved Murray's headquarters from Ismailia to Cairo, had the disadvantage of putting even greater distance between the commander in chief and his troops as they advanced across the desert.

After the battle of Romani, construction work in the Sinai intensified. The railway now moved forward at an average rate of fifteen miles a month. The laying of pipe, however, stalled until the twelve-inch pipe that Murray now wanted was available. Once this pipe arrived from the United States in September and October, the Royal Engineers and native labourers raced to catch up with the railway. Workers also built a 'chicken-wire' road made from close mesh wire net parallel to the rail line. This wire had been intended to prevent sand from caving in the trenches of the canal defences. With the army moving eastward, it was put to another use. Three rolls of this chicken wire were unrolled side by side and held down by wire staples driven into the ground. This created a surface that was superior to the soft sand on which four men could march abreast.

The desert campaign proved to be an endurance test for many soldiers. W. Knott, a conscientious objector who served in a non-combatant role as a member of the 32nd Field Ambulance, 10th Division, provided a poignant description of infantry marching as many as twelve miles a day:

> To see them trudging through the soft, burning sand, sometimes over a wire road which they themselves have laid to make the going a little easier, carrying rifle and equipment weighing seventy pounds, with the relentless sun blazing down on the shimmering desert, and little water to drink; to see them in camp sleeping on sand, breathing sand, eating it with every morsel of food, ears and eyes full of it when the 'Khamsin' blows – all this, if it does not make campaigning in Egypt the awful and infinitely perilous business which it is on other fronts does make it the supreme test of a man's endurance.[50]

When soldiers pitched camp, it was without the bell tents that had been left behind at Romani. Troops made do in holes dug in the sand covered with a ground sheet to keep out the sun at midday; during frigid desert nights, they covered themselves with a single blanket.

A thirst that could not be satisfied was a lasting memory for many. 'Very few of us realise what thirst really is', recalled Albert R. Surry, a signaller with the 161st Brigade, 54th Division. 'What a dreadful effect it has upon human nature unless one has been through that agony. It is impossible to realize the depths a man will sink to endeavour to appease the terrible horror of thirst.'[51] Nearly fifty years after serving with the 42nd Division in the Sinai, one veteran, gunner J. Thompson, confessed that the 'sight of a leaking tap' made him 'squirm'. In his account of desert service, he wrote of his 'daily obsession' with water. 'Men, especially infantrymen were collapsing daily', he recalled, 'although fatalities were surprisingly few. Men soon learned however the vital necessity of conserving the bulk of their water until after the period of high noon. Actually this was now made an order and a man was "on a charge" if his water-ration was touched before midday. During the whole of the crossing, the personal daily water ration never exceeded a water bottle full, about 2¼ pints.'[52] When not in combat, each soldier had a ration of one gallon, but between one-half and three-quarters of this water was allocated to the cookhouse for tea and cooking and for his personal hygiene.

The months of September, October and November passed without any major military activity. But this changed when the railway was pushed to within twenty miles of El Arish, putting that village and another Turkish outpost at Magdhaba within striking distance. After El Arish had been secured and connected by railway, the next objective would become Rafah on the border of Palestine. But once the Eastern Force ejected the Turk from Egypt, what should its next move be?

On December 10 Murray wired Robertson that he believed that 'important results might be secured by an advance by us from Arish into Syria'. Once at Rafah, Murray hoped that circumstances would permit him to advance on Beersheba where 'enemy's main concentration appears to be. Occupation of this place would, moreover, have advantage of placing me on a railway. At Beersheba I should be only 70 miles from Hejaz line, against which my aircraft could co-operate daily. Further, I cannot but think our appearance at Beersheba would result in a rising of Arab population in southern Syria, who are known to be very disaffected towards Turks.'[53] Three days earlier, Murray had appointed Lieutenant General Sir Philip Chetwode commander of the vanguard of the Eastern Force. His mobile force was given the name 'Desert Column', and it initially consisted of the Anzac Mounted Division, the Imperial Camel Corps Brigade (composed of eighteen companies, six of which were Yeoman), and the 42nd and 52nd divisions. Chetwode, who had been educated at Eton, had been a superb athlete in track and field. He entered the army through the militia and had earlier commanded cavalry on the western front, where he had been criticized for being overly cautious in pursuing the retreating Germans after the First Battle of the Marne. The first impression he made was not always a good one. According to Cyril Falls, 'superficially, Chetwode was all that Americans most dislike in Britons and that many Britons dislike in their own countrymen'. But Falls adds that 'he was highly capable, and above all, inspired confidence'.[54]

On December 21, mounted troops, eager to escape the desert, surrounded El Arish after a night march, only to discover that the Turks had fled. The next day, the infantry of the 52nd division occupied El Arish, to be joined by Chetwode, who arrived by boat. Chetwode immediately ordered another night march by Chauvel's troopers to capture Magdhaba, some twenty-five miles south-east of El Arish. On December 23, this encircled Turkish garrison surrendered. With the loss of only 146 men, twenty-two of them killed, the British bagged 1,282 prisoners.

Chauvel's troopers, most of whom had had little or no sleep for three nights, then returned to El Arish. Many fell asleep in their saddles. Horses collided with other horses in the darkness and dust thrown up by the moving column. The exhausted troopers' minds began to play tricks on them. Although they rode across barren countryside, many later claimed to have ridden past well-lit streets with tall buildings and curiously shaped animals. Chauvel himself was not immune to hallucinations. He suddenly galloped away from the column, only to return later. His sheepish explanation was that he imagined he was in pursuit of a fox on a fox hunt.[55]

By January 4, the railway reached El Arish. The only Turkish garrison remaining in Egyptian territory was near the Palestine frontier at El Magruntein, just south-west of Rafah. On January 8, as night fell, the ANZAC Mounted Division (minus one brigade), the 5th Mounted Brigade (Yeomanry), and the new Imperial Camel Corps Brigade rode out of El Arish. The long column, illuminated by the moon, presented a striking picture as it moved across the desert. 'Here come the Light Horse', observed C. Guy Powles:

> ...with their emu plumes waving – here the quiet grim New Zealanders – here Yeomanry in helmets, from many countries – and on the road itself go by the guns with their Scotch and English crews – and away out on the flank stretching out mile after mile into the black darkness of night come the camels, riding in sections four abreast. There are Australians among them and Yeomen from the British Isles and our own New Zealanders, and following them a band of tall, silent, swarthy Sikhs on huge Indian camels. These are the Hong Kong and Singapore Mountain Battery, who so ably serve the Camel Brigade. And lastly, far behind, softly and slowly and calmly, come long streams of laden camels led by Egyptians bare-footed in the sand.[56]

Although the Turks were dug in at El Magruntein and the open terrain favoured them, the British won another one-day battle in heavy fighting. With bayonets fixed and revolvers cocked, with the artillery thundering its support in the background, dismounted troopers rushed the Turkish defences. Just when it appeared that the British would have to break off the attack and retire, white flags began to appear in the enemy trenches. British losses numbered seventy-one killed and 415 wounded. Some 200 of the enemy were killed and another 1,635 survived to be taken prisoner. The Desert Column had used its mobility to encircle and destroy the last two remaining enemy positions in Egypt. But the margin of victory had been slight at both Magdhaba and Rafah, as the action at El Magruntein is commonly called. In both actions, the commanders had decided to break off the battle almost at the precise moment that Turkish resistance collapsed.[57]

Chetwode's appointment as commander of the Desert Column and the subsequent ejection of the Turks from Egypt coincided with important political changes in London: David Lloyd George, determined to give British grand strategy a new look, replaced Herbert H. Asquith as prime minister in December 1916. The dynamic Welshman had a nineteenth-century liberal's distaste for the Turks and sought to make the destruction of the Turkish Empire a central war objective.[58] Of more immediate concern, he wanted a clear-cut military success to bolster morale on the home front. When Robertson inquired whether the conquest of Beersheba would serve that purpose, Lloyd George demurred. He wanted Jerusalem. Robertson wanted Murray to be active on his front – but not that active. One method he used to control his commanders in the peripheral theatres such as Mesopotamia, Salonika and Egypt was through personal messages not seen by the ministers.

On December 13, Robertson's alter ego on the Imperial General Staff, Freddie Maurice, wrote to Lynden-Bell. 'The Prime Minister is very anxious, naturally, for some success to enliven the winter gloom which has settled upon England, and he looks to you to get it for him. He talks somewhat vaguely of a campaign in Palestine, and I think has at the back of his mind the hope of a triumphant entry into Jerusalem.' But Maurice, reflecting the views of Robertson, suggested that Murray should not aim beyond Beersheba during the winter and warned him about being 'led into a goose chase which will interfere with the main theatre'.[59]

The other ministers also wished to avoid a risky policy, and on December 15 Robertson sent Murray his official orders. Although he was expected to keep the Turks busy on his front, his primary mission remained 'unchanged, that is to say, it is the defence of Egypt. You will be informed if and when the War Cabinet changes this policy.'[60] Surprising events beyond Murray's theatre during the next few weeks, however, encouraged the government to expand his mission and make his front, albeit briefly, the focus of British military operations. The result proved to be a disaster for British arms – two defeats within a month – and the demoralization of an army largely composed of Territorial divisions and the Yeomanry.

4

Johnny Turk Triumphant

In late March 1917 the Eastern Force was on the move, advancing in stages along the coastal road toward Gaza, whose very name meant *fortress*. The infantry began its march as darkness approached to avoid the prying eyes of Turkish aircraft. 'The sensations of the march were rather peculiar', Captain E.T.Townsend, 1/5 Highland Light Infantry, 157th Brigade, 52nd (Lowlands) Division, reported to his parents in a letter. 'A glorious sunset with a cool breeze blowing gave way to a darkness very slightly lightened by a mere slip of moon. The air grew dead and a thick pall of dust from the light sand soil hung round us, hotter now than 1/2 hr. ago when the pleasant breeze dispersed the "stour" – worse this than marching in pure sand. All round us, marching 10,000 men and many hundred camels. The men sing, a pipe band plays, now far off, now 3 yds. behind me, the one a wail, the other an inspiring screech, the loads rattle, the beasts themselves emit their horrid bubbling gurgle, the crickets sing, a voice cries "Stick it – Bill, there's a pub round the corner!" Another – "What about that ham & eggs supper."'[1]

A.V. Benbow, who was now a member of the newly created Imperial Camel Corps Brigade, includes a vivid description in his diary of the advance of the mounted forces. In three great columns, they covered the coastal plains before Gaza: 'On the left a column of cavalry, in the centre the Camel Corps and on the right the Transport Corps, with their loads of stores and blue-gowned camel-drivers, the Red Cross Unit with their dozens of white hooded red crossed wagons drawn by six or eight mules a piece, and all the camels, each carrying a stretcher, better known as cacolets, slung on either side of their backs.'[2]

The resulting First Battle of Gaza was the greatest test yet for the Egyptian Expeditionary Force (EEF) and its commander in chief, Archie Murray, the son of a landed proprietor. Cultured, reserved and intelligent, Murray was considered a brilliant staff officer before the war. However, after being selected as the chief of staff of the British Expeditionary Force, he had been unable to cope, especially during the stressful period of the British retreat from Mons. He simply did not have the physical stamina, once fainting at an inn at St Quentin on August 26. Sir John French, the commander in chief of the BEF, had taken advantage of a medical leave by Murray to replace him in January 1915.[3] Murray had next served as the Deputy Chief of the Imperial General Staff (CIGS) and then as CIGS in the War Office. His new position in London did not make the same physical demands as service in the field. But some senior officers continued to question his fitness to lead.

When 'Wully' Robertson replaced him as CIGS, Murray was given command of British forces in Egypt. Here at last Murray enjoyed success. In 1916, although the War Office took many of his divisions from him, the achievements of other British commanders in the outlying theatres in 1916 paled in comparison with his. He brought the Senussi revolt under control, seized the strategical initiative from the Turks at Romani, and cleared the Sinai of the enemy with a methodical advance of rail and pipe to the borders of Palestine. His obsession with detail and smothering involvement in staff work irritated some at General Headquarters (GHQ). 'He *is* like a certain silly type of schoolmaster who can't show interest in his boys without annoying them',[4] was Captain Orlo C. Williams's characterization. Yet his mastery of details, which included a demand for twelve-inch water pipes, was vital to the EEF's success in coping with desert conditions.

But would successful staff work translate into victory in a major battle? The Turks could hardly have been more co-operative with

Murray's bold plan of envelopment and annihilation at Romani, but the execution had been flawed, and Murray bore some of the responsibility for the command and control problems. His lack of physical stamina made him more a 'staff' than 'field' leader, a real weakness on the EEF's front where battles were short, generally decisive, and limited in area and scale when compared with the massive and prolonged offensives in France, where attritional strategy prevailed. In these and other respects, Murray's theatre represented a return to Napoleonic warfare in which a great captain of war might impose his genius and personality on the outcome of a battle. The opportunity to break the enemy might be missed unless the responsible commander had close (even visible) contact with the battlefield. Murray's remoteness, especially after GHQ relocated at Cairo, also undermined his rapport with the ranks. His visits to the front were infrequent, and while on inspection tours, he seldom strayed far from his train, in part because of the brutal desert conditions that affected his fragile physical condition. His luxurious train, equipped with a dining car, further removed him from the desert life of the rank and file. 'Some travelling in the chief's train, my dear! Sleeping carriage for each officer – food, drinks and smokes of the most sumptuous and all for free',[5] an impressed Dawnay reported to his wife.

Lloyd George, who had difficulty discovering a general whom he thought competent or imaginative, later condemned Murray in his memoirs for lacking drive and for being overly cautious. Murray's later complaint that he was provided insufficient support in men, heavy artillery and aircraft in his attempt to take Gaza – although he outnumbered the Turks two to one – would seem to confirm this interpretation. But this view deserves some modification. Murray was painfully aware that some senior officers continued to question his fitness for command, and he felt he had something to prove. Certainly he was offended when, despite his successes in 1916, he was not promoted to general or given any recognition in the January 1917 *Gazette*. He was, in fact, the only theatre commander who did not appear in the *Gazette*. This was, however, later modified and Murray somewhat mollified when the government conferred upon him the GCMG,[6] or Knight Grand Cross of the Order of St Michael and St George.

The signals that he had been receiving from London about his mission had been mixed because of the fluid nature of the war against Turkey and the secondary nature of his theatre of operations. His most recent instructions reached him on January 11. He was expected to fight local battles to tie down Turkish troops and strengthen his essentially defensive position on the Palestinian border. These instructions represented a compromise that Robertson had reached with Lloyd George's new government. Preparations for a resumption of the offensive in France and an escalating shipping crisis stretched British military resources to the breaking point. Robertson thus did not want to commit to a forward policy in Palestine. He buttressed this advice to the government with a practical argument: A railway to both Gaza and Beersheba could not be completed before April, when the oppressive summer heat made a successful campaign to take Jerusalem unlikely. As a sop to the ministers, Wully promised that his staff would prepare for a large-scale offensive on Murray's front next winter, when local conditions might be more favourable.[7]

Although Murray requested two additional infantry divisions for his front, he was now asked to relinquish yet another one for Haig's use. He chose the 42nd Division, which left him with three Territorial Divisions, the 52nd, 53rd and 54th. To compensate him for his losses, the War Office promised 'a rather hotchpotch of units', which included twelve white Territorial battalions from Aden and India, native Indian battalions and Soudanese battalions.[8] For his part, Murray immediately began to constitute a new division, the 74th, from dismounted Yeomanry regiments in Egypt. The loss of the 42nd Division forced Murray to reorganize his forces once again. The Eastern Force, commanded by Dobell, now consisted of two mounted divisions, the Imperial Mounted Division and the ANZAC Mounted Division, the Imperial Camel Corps Brigade, and three infantry divisions, the 52nd, 53rd and 54th. Its mobile arm, a mix of infantry and cavalry, called the Desert Column and led by Chetwode, consisted of the two mounted divisions, two Light Car Patrols, and the 53rd Division.

Initially the Eastern Force planned an attack against a Turkish force dug in at Wali Sheikh Nuran, which was west of Shellal on the

Wadi Ghazze. Kress von Kressenstein, however, deemed his forces too weak to defend this forward position. On March 5 1917, he abruptly withdrew them to the Gaza-Beersheba line. Murray described the new situation to his friend, Charles À. Court Repington, the influential and well-connected military correspondent for the *Times*. 'I had hoped that they would remain and let me attack them as soon as my railway reached Rafa, but when the line reached Sheikh Zowaiid, within about 10 or 12 miles of Rafa, they retreated, and are now on the line Gaza – Tel el Sharia – Beersheba with about 33,000 men, either on that line or to the south of Jerusalem', he wrote. 'On this line they are for the present outside my striking radius, so I have to wait until the railway is fully established at Rafa before I can strike.'[9] Confidence ran high in the Eastern Force. The fear was not that the Turks would stand and fight, but that they would once again retreat. 'I do not believe they will stand on the line Gaza-Beersheba', Murray continued in his letter to Repington. 'They have a holy fear of our cavalry and, as they cannot place both flanks on an obstacle, fear the result of a general engagement.'[10] As late as March 23, this was also the view of Dawnay, Dobell's talented chief of staff. An intercepted Turkish message on the 19th revealed that the Turks planned to shut down their wireless station in Gaza and establish their headquarters in Jerusalem.[11]

To keep the Turks from escaping battle once again, Dobell, the commander of the Eastern Force, got Murray's approval for a lightening strike, or *coup de main,* against Gaza. As Dobell's Chief of the General Staff (CGS), Dawnay put it this way: 'Our chance of achieving any effective success lies in the probability that he may not suspect us of being able to develop sufficient strength against him anywhere with sufficient rapidity… In undertaking the advance against Gaza, therefore, the chief consideration seems to be the necessity for moving forward in the greatest possible force with the greatest possible suddenness – the whole force moving forward simultaneously and more or less concentrated.'[12]

This aggressive plan had its dangers. To achieve surprise, the attack had to be launched from a railhead that was still some fifteen miles from Gaza. This magnified the importance of water. If Gaza were taken within twenty-four hours, its plentiful wells would serve as a source of water that could be supplemented by supplies from British ships. But this tight time frame weighed heavily on the minds of those who executed this plan. As Murray once wrote in reference to Lieutenant General F.S. Maude's advance up the Tigris River to Baghdad: 'I long for Joe Maude's Tigris, and shall probably end this campaign with water on the brain.'[13]

A second disadvantage was that the British had poor intelligence about the ground over which they would fight. 'Our information, both as to the enemy and roads, is at present very vague; also to the extent and character of his works', Chetwode wrote Dawnay.'Having drawn a cordon round Gaza and other places, our agents find great difficulty in getting through.'[14] Chetwode, protected by a cavalry screen, did, however, make numerous personal reconnaissances in the Gaza area and later claimed that he 'knew the ground intimately'. The responsible infantry commanders at 1st Gaza, A.G. Dallas and Dobell, however, made no attempt to get a firsthand look at the terrain.[15] This was ominous. The Turks knew how to dig. Dawnay had earlier been greatly impressed by abandoned Turkish defences that he had inspected at Maghdaba. 'You can't see them at all till you absolutely walk into them', he wrote to his wife. 'Our artillery could never pick them up.'[16] An unexpected obstacle, especially on the south-east perimeter of Gaza's defences, were thick cactus hedges as high as ten feet and every bit as formidable as barbed wire.

The numbers, however, favoured the British: estimates of the troops that Kress von Kressenstein might deploy ranged from 13,600 to 16,000.[17] Chetwode's Desert Column, a mixture of infantry and mounted troops, was assigned the task of capturing Gaza. Its mounted troops, some 11,000 men, would surround Gaza to prevent its defenders from escaping and to block possible Turkish reinforcements advancing from the direction of Beersheba. Its infantry complement, the 53rd Division, led by Major General A.G. Dallas, which included the 161st Brigade from the 54th Division, constituted a force of roughly 12,000 rifles, thirty-six field guns, and six 60-pounders, was expected to secure Ali Muntar, a 300-foot knoll that dominated the city, and push on into the town. An additional 16,000 men commanded by Dobell were deployed as follows: two brigades of the 52nd Division were held in reserve, and the 54th Division was positioned to the south-east of Gaza to support the mounted forces in blocking Turkish reinforcements.

On March 26, mounted troops enveloped Gaza with no major hitch. Matters did not go as smoothly for the infantry, who had had little sleep since they had begun their staged advance from Rafah to Khan Yunis on March 24. Although their packs had been lightened by the removal of haversacks and ground sheets, they carried extra rations and bandoliers of ammunition, along with a second water bottle. Leaving Khan Yunis under a beautiful blood-red sunset on March 25, the 53rd division reached its first obstacle at about 2.45a.m. – the Wadi Ghazze, a sandy riverbed with steep mud cliffs on both banks. This wadi (or river), which was fed by many tributaries, was mostly dry except when its banks overflowed with storm water. After most of the soldiers had navigated the Wadi Ghazze, a dense fog rolled in from the sea, reducing visibility to twenty yards.

The command structure established for the approaching battle was as follows. Murray had come by train to El Arish, where he kept in touch with Dobell through the telephonic and telegraphic exchange that had been established at Rafah. With no troops under his direct command, his influence on the ebb and flow of the battle was destined to be minimal. Dobell and Chetwode established their headquarters alongside each other in the open on the west bank of the Wadi Ghazze near In Seirat, creating what amounted to a joint headquarters for the Eastern Force, the equivalent of an army, and the Desert Column, the equivalent of a corps. That Chetwode was practically in Dobell's pocket was an uncomfortable situation for both men, especially for the cavalryman. In retrospect, a better command arrangement would have been for Dobell to direct the infantry and Chetwode the mounted forces, with separate headquarters located closer to the action on the east side of the Wadi Ghazze.

By 10:30a.m. the mounted troops had enveloped Gaza. The 53rd Division under Dallas, although it had reached its assembly points by 8a.m., had not yet begun its assault against Ali Muntar. Some soldiers slept while they waited. Because Dallas did not know the ground, crucial time was lost in reconnoitring unfamiliar terrain, a task made more difficult by the morning fog. Dallas unwisely went forward to reconnoitre without either his brigadiers or artillery commanders. This delayed and, because of confused communications, hampered the issuing of orders to his troops and the positioning of his artillery. When the attack began, Dallas was also away from his headquarters for hours at a time without leaving a junior officer who knew his whereabouts.[18] A frustrated Chetwode bombarded Dallas with messages to get a move on, but to no avail.

Finally, around noon, the battle was joined. 'The day was frightfully hot, the sun blinding our eyes as it reflected off the sand', Marchant wrote in his diary. From his vantage point with the 160th Brigade to the left of Ali Muntar, signaller Marchant recorded the action in his diary: 'On the right we could see the men advancing several miles among the low hills, at first with little firing but increasing as they got nearer, to a great intensity of shot and shell. The enemy resisted very fiercely all through the day, and for a long time held up the attackers, but towards evening we advanced rapidly, and our men could be seen swarming all over Ali Muntar, and edging towards the town.'[19]

Another perspective is provided by an Australian trooper with the Desert Column who witnessed the assault of Ali Muntar through field glasses. 'The poor Welshmen, coming up the open slopes towards the redoubts were utterly exposed to machine-gun and rifle-fire', Ion L. Idriess wrote:

> Shrapnel had merged in a writhing white cloud over the advancing men. They plodded out of a haze of earth and smoke only to disappear into another barrage. It was pitifully sublime. When within close rifle-range line after line lay down and fire in turn. And thus they were slowly but so steadily advancing, under terrific fire. Every yard must have seemed death to them. We could see in between the smoke-wreaths that when each line jumped up, it left big gaps. Some thousands of the poor chaps bled on Ali Muntar that day.[20]

The 53rd Division, which included the 161st Brigade of the 54th Division, took Ali Muntar despite the failings of its leadership. It displayed sheer grit and proved itself the equal of any Regular or New Army division. Its assault had involved no aircraft, tanks or chemical warfare. Artillery support, compared with any attack on the western front in 1917, was thin and poorly co-ordinated because of the virtual collapse of command and control at Dallas's headquarters.[21] After days of marching under a blazing sun with only a few hours' sleep and heavily laden, the infantry had advanced across open territory, through a maze of cactus hedges, and then up a steep hill against an entrenched and well-concealed enemy supported by machine guns and artillery.

Field Marshal Lord Wavell pays the Territorials the highest compliment when he uses them as an example of what was possible for infantry in modern warfare. 'It is an action worth remembering', he wrote, 'when tempted to believe that infantry to-day are powerless against a prepared position unless they are convoyed by tanks or be supported by an overwhelming mass of artillery.'[22] But the price had been high. The battlefield was littered with British dead and wounded as the sun set.

Although victory was within the grasp of the conquerors of Ali Muntar, this, alas, was not the view at In Seriat as dusk approached. Turkish reinforcements were observed moving to the sound of battle. 'From one position we could see 12 miles away at first, and gradually approaching, the dust clouds made by the enemy's columns!',[23] Dawnay later wrote to his wife. Chetwode, unaware that the British were driving the Turks off the entire Ali Muntar ridge and that many of the mounted brigades had been able to water their horses at pools during the day,[24] feared that what he termed 'the corridor' through which his cavalry might escape was getting too narrow. Dobell agreed, and the cavalry was ordered to withdraw. The decision to break off the battle came at almost the precise moment that Major von Tiller, the German commandant in Gaza, accepted defeat. With Ali Muntar in British hands and cavalry penetrating the streets of the town, he ordered his wireless station blown up and papers destroyed in anticipation of the town's capture. Meanwhile, Kress von Kressenstein, believing that Gaza had fallen, ordered his advancing relief forces to halt for the night. In essence, all of the key commanders accepted defeat at the same time.[25]

The troops had been poorly served by their leadership. Chetwode and Dobell had remained remote from the action on the western side of the Wadi Ghazze. Hampered by a lack of staff (Dobell amazingly had only three general staff officers under him), they had been unable to conduct operations with the telephone, telegraph and heliograph. The belief that Gaza had to be taken before dusk because of the water situation pressured them into a hasty decision. Although Dallas had not wanted to break off the battle, he failed utterly in directing either his brigades or artillery. His brigadiers later made it clear to Chetwode that they would never again go into battle with him as their commander.[26]

The cavalry's withdrawal had a domino effect on the infantry. The 53rd Division now had its flank exposed. Chetwode consequently phoned Dallas and told him that he must withdraw his force where it could join hands with the 54th Division to his right. Dallas protested but had no choice but to comply. Unaware that the 54th Division had been ordered to close up with his division, he overreacted and withdrew his force to approximately his starting point for the attack on Ali Muntar.[27] As the generals consulted, argued, and issued orders that had little to do with reality, the heroes of Ali Muntar abandoned their hard-won position. Frustration, anger and disbelief were common emotions as the 53rd Division fell back. In the bitter words of their divisional historian, 'they considered they had captured Gaza, and that they had been dragged, like a dog on a leash, from their prize'.[28]

Although Dallas had telegraphed Desert Column headquarters the new position he was taking up, it was not until 5a.m. that Chetwode understood that the 53rd Division had withdrawn from all the territory it had won the previous day. He immediately ordered an advance to see if a reoccupation of the Ali Muntar Ridge was possible. Two brigades, the 160th and 161st, were sent forward. The latter brigade, from the 54th Division, had been attached to the 53rd Division for the battle. The brigade, commanded by Lieutenant Colonel W. Marriott-Dodington, actually reoccupied the ruins of the mosque overlooking Gaza. But the Turks were now heavily reinforced, and they counterattacked.

Major V.H. Bailey, an artillery officer, served as a galloper for the headquarters of the 54th (East Anglian) Division. He was sent by Major General S.W. Hare, the commander of the 54th, to deliver a message to Dodington ordering him to retire. 'When I got there', he recalled, 'Dodington said he wanted to take me up to his front so I could tell the General why he *would not* obey the order.' With his men on Ali Muntar, he stressed, '"I command the whole situation. Tell the General I'm staying here." So I galloped two miles back and told the General. He was very upset… He finally said to me, "Go back, and tell Dodington this. For reasons of which you know nothing, it is essential you retire at once." Back I went and delivered the message to Dodington. He said to me, "Do you know what's behind all this? I can only think of one thing, that there's been some fearful disaster in France and the whole force here is being withdrawn."'[29]

The retirement was tinged with some panic. From his position, signaller Marchant observed: 'In the afternoon they were seen to be retiring, and whole Battns were dispersed in all directions. Some Lewis gunners came right across the plain to our position, bringing their gun with them. We could get no communication with hdgtrs and so could not learn their exact movements… Towards evening, through the telescope, we could see Turks and Bedouins roaming over fort Ali Muntar stripping and robbing our dead and wounded.'[30]

With the Turks once again in control of Ali Muntar, the Eastern Force's position became precarious. The bungled attempt to join the 53rd and 54th divisions had placed the divisions back to back and vulnerable to a counterattack. An attempt to reform the line near the east bank of the Wadi Ghazze did not improve the situation much; and the hot wind of a Khamsin that had begun the previous day continued to blow. Dobell conferred with Murray by telephone, recommending a complete withdrawal across the Wadi Ghazze. Murray, according to the official history, 'reluctantly' concurred. By 4a.m., on March 28, the Eastern Force, near exhaustion, was across the Wadi Ghazze, leaving behind the unmistakable footprints of a defeated army. 'Everywhere one saw evidence of our hurried retreat, every unit striving to cross the Wadi as quickly as possible', Captain O.

Teichman wrote.[31] Some 500 soldiers were missing and another 523 were dead. The 53rd Division and the 161st Essex Brigade had taken most of the some 4,000 casualties.[32] So concluded the EEF's first attempt to take Gaza.

Confusion at the top made it even more difficult than usual for ordinary soldiers to understand what was happening in their particular sectors. One moment they were ordered forward into the teeth of heavy enemy fire; the next minute, for reasons that seemed equally obscure, they were hastily withdrawn, relinquishing ground for which they had paid dearly with their blood. R.J. Carless, a signaller, later remarked: 'We went back a short way for the night much to our disappointment as the objective had been reached but the disappointment and dismay and bewilderment was all the greater next morning when we found we had got to do it all over again.'[33]

Brigadier General W.J.C. Butler took the extraordinary step of assembling the battalions of his 160th Brigade after 1st Gaza and offering an explanation to the men. The 160th Brigade had seen little action on the 26th, and as darkness approached, Butler had yet to receive any instructions from Dallas or his staff. 'I had received no orders', Butler told his men:

> ...and could get in communication with no one. I asked the officer commanding artillery the quickest time in which he could get his guns across the wadi in case of a retirement, and he said, owing to the heavy state of the ground there, it would be impossible to retire under four hours. As all that time was impossible to be given, I resolved to take the matter into my own hands and withdraw the Battn after dark, and take up a defensive position in front of the guns, which we did.

The exhausted members of the 160th Brigade had reached their new position around 5a.m., only to do an immediate about-face. Butler, unable to establish communications with division headquarters, ordered his men forward to resume their original position, only to retire once again to the Wadi Ghazze. At midnight, new orders were received that were to be sent across the wadi by 2400 hours. 'As you can see this was impossible', Butler explained:

...as it was already that time, and that half the Battn was sound asleep and nothing was ready. I am sorry to say that the men were very slow in rousing themselves, and it was necessary for me to use my whip and wake some of them up, after they had been called over a quarter of an hour. We succeeded however in eventually rousing the Battn and start preparing to move. It was a severe tax on everyone's strength, but we succeeded in crossing the wadi by 0230 on the morning of the 28th.[34]

Robertson and the ministers also deserved an explanation of the debacle of 1st Gaza, but one was not forthcoming from GHQ. Dobell had informed Murray that he had 'failed',[35] and Murray himself recorded in his desk diary that the results of the first day had been 'only fairly successful' and those of the second day 'disappointing'.[36] Yet Murray sent a glowing report of the battle to London. 'On the 26th and 27th we were heavily engaged east of the Ghazze with a force of about 20,000 of the enemy', he cabled. 'We inflicted very heavy losses on him; I estimate his casualties at between 6,000 and 7,000 men, and we have in addition taken 900 prisoners including General Commanding and whole Divisional Staff of 53rd Turkish Division.'[37] This led to extravagant claims by the press with newspaper placards in the streets of London proclaiming 'A Brilliant British Victory' and '20,000 Turks Defeated'.

The Eastern Force knew better, and its confidence in its leadership was further undermined when Dobell issued a special order on April 1 in which he praised their 'gallantry, devotion and determination'. Dobell tried to reassure his men, without success. 'It is to be borne in mind', he explained, 'that the essential object in all fighting is to damage, diminish and defeat the enemy's forces, rather than to gain or retain a particular locality. In this essential object the troops engaged at Gaza were most fully successful.'[38] Lynden-Bell was equally positive in his letters to the War Office.[39] In an effort to disguise this British defeat, both Dobell and Lynden-Bell resorted to the grim language of attrition so common to the stalemated western front where strategical objectives had taken second place to wearing down the other side's army.

Neither Lynden-Bell's nor Murray's analysis of the failure to capture Gaza satisfied Robertson. With Turkish accounts proclaiming victory, he demanded details. Murray's carefully crafted response was notable for its obfuscation. In private Murray criticized his commanders, telling Captain Williams, a member of his staff, 'Dobell has never commanded a big force, Hare has never fought a division, Dallas has never fought a division except as a staff officer, Chetwode is the only one who has experience.' He had been 'within an ace of taking things into his own hands'. And what would Murray have done differently if he had been able to control the battle? With the advantage of hindsight, he said he would have ordered the 53rd Division to hold its position, resuming the attack with fresh troops in the morning. Or he would have 'left a bolt hole out of Gaza by which von Tiller could have escaped: instead of which he first *netted* all the holes with his cavalry, and then withdrew *all* the nets'.[40] This was Monday morning quarterbacking at its worst. From his distant perch at El Arish, Murray would have had an even worse grip on the battle than his generals in the field.

Murray argued that his motive in not giving 'away his higher commanders & their weakness' was to give 'all possible praise' to the troops who had fought 'magnificently'.[41] This was not the first time that Murray had whitewashed the failures of commanding officers to give credit to the troops. He had behaved in a similar fashion when he was the CGS for the BEF in 1914.[42] But one suspects that he was much more interested in protecting his reputation than that of his men in his description of 1st Gaza.

Murray's fuller response to Robertson's queries included many dubious claims. In his make-believe battle, the enemy had suffered heavy losses and the Desert Column had at no time been 'harassed or hard pressed', its attack just falling short 'of a complete disaster to the enemy'. Murray described accurately the situation at 6p.m. on March 26: 'Position of our 53rd Division at dusk on high ground, Ali Muntar, just south of Gaza, with some troops in the Turkish defences. 54th Division on prolonging ridge to Sheikh Abbas. Wadi Ghazze and right flank made secure by 52nd Division. Primary object attained.'[43] But he gave no hint that irresolute and confused leadership had thrown victory away at this critical moment.

The author of the history of the 53rd Division had the best rejoinder to Murray's excuse that the morning fog had delayed the infantry assault and had been largely responsible for the failure to take Gaza: 'It might be said that the real accidents of the day, which robbed the troops of the fruits of their victory, were not so much the result of the sea fog in the morning as the fog of war amongst the higher command in the evening.'[44] Soldiers of all ranks were disgusted by Murray's complacent and misleading description of the battle. Many agree with the Turkish note dropped from an aeroplane: 'You beat us at communiqués, but we beat you at Gaza.' As Captain Williams noted in his diary: 'The curious thing about the recent fighting at Gaza is that, while the Chief and CGS are pleased, the troops think it was a rotten show, & leading was very bad.'[45] If not for military censorship, many angry soldiers would have told the truth to loved ones back home. 'I am afraid one is obliged by the censor to write the dullest possible letters' Sir Randolf Baker, the commander of the 1/1st Dorset Yeomanry, 6th Mounted Brigade, Imperial Mounted Division, wrote his mother, 'when there is so much one could say & would like to. I expect you will have realized from the official communiqués something of what we are doing. When we meet again, I shall have much to tell you of the real thing as we saw it.'[46]

Murray's self-proclaimed 'successful' operation in combination with other events suggested that Turkey was on its last legs. Maude's forces had occupied Baghdad on March 11, depriving the Turks of their most favourable base of operations in Mesopotamia and Persia. As the Turks retreated from Persia, the Russians pursued them along a 250-mile front. Arab unrest was on the rise in Arabia, and the Turkish threat to Mecca had dissipated. A general staff review of the war, dated March 20, described a Turkish army that was 'steadily deteriorating'.[47] Lord Milner expressed the growing optimism of the War Cabinet about the war in the Turkish theatres in a letter to Lloyd George: 'As things are, the Turk is crumbling... Having got him on the run should we not keep him on the run?'[48]

Prodded by Lloyd George, the general staff had been considering all aspects of a campaign to knock Turkey out of the war. In great secrecy, two important appreciations had been produced that emphasized political as well as military aspects of a British offensive in Murray's theatre. First, the general staff circulated in January a twenty-one-page appreciation, 'NOTE ON OUR FUTURE MILITARY POLICY IN THE EVENT OF THE FAILURE OF THE ENTENTE POWERS TO OBTAIN A DECISION IN THE MAIN THEATRES DURING THE COMING SUMMER'. Though unsigned, the author was probably Lieutenant General George M.W. Macdonogh, the brilliant director of military intelligence in the War Office, who kept in touch with the Foreign Office and frequently prepared appreciations on war aims and peace negotiations.[49]

Britain, according to the author of this appreciation, had three major war objectives: the maintenance of her maritime supremacy, the preservation of the balance of power in Europe, and the security of Egypt, India, and the Persian Gulf. If Germany's armies were not vanquished in 1917, pressure for a negotiated peace might become irresistible. In that event, Germany might gain a decent peace by withdrawing from Belgium and northern France. Such a peace might not be disastrous to maintaining British naval supremacy and the European balance of power, but it would leave untouched the serious German threat to Britain's position in the Middle East. 'From Aleppo they [Germany] could operate against Armenia, towards Mesopotamia or towards Syria and Egypt. Russia could probably spare few troops from her Western front, and her communications in Armenia and Persia would be very difficult. In these conditions the maintenance of adequate garrisons for the defence of Mesopotamia and Egypt would place an intolerable strain upon our resources.' Aleppo, the junction of the Syrian, Anatolian and Tigris railways, as well as of all the primary roads connecting Syria and Mesopotamia with Asia Minor, was the key to defending Britain's position in the Middle East. Although Aleppo was roughly 375 miles from the Egyptian border, Murray's forces were much better positioned to take it than the British forces in Mesopotamia.[50]

Previously London had placed primary emphasis on Egypt's defence. This general staff memorandum, however, portended a forward policy that took British forces well beyond the borders of Egypt into Palestine and Syria for political and strategical considerations. London's primary emphasis remained the defeat of its chief strategical rival, Germany. But what if the German army could not be defeated and British allies such as Russia wavered? In that event, the Turkish theatres served as an insurance policy for the British Empire.

But did Britain have the resources to wage two great campaigns simultaneously, one in France and the other in the Middle East? Robertson did not think so. He pointed out that Britain's available naval and military resources limited what British arms could achieve in this outlying theatre. His appreciation, circulated in February, addressed the specifics of a forward policy on Murray's front. Robertson believed that it might be possible to concentrate by the autumn, when the weather made a campaign possible, six infantry divisions, two mounted divisions, and the Imperial Camel Brigade. In addition, troops were required to police Egypt's western frontier and maintain internal order. Robertson thought such a force strong enough to capture Jerusalem and secure the line Jaffa-Jerusalem-Jericho. But a rapid advance from this position to threaten Aleppo depended on the navy's ability to establish bases at Jaffa, Haifa, and Beirut; and the admiralty, when consulted, could not promise to secure these bases because of its serious shipping shortages and the continued threat posed by U-boats. 'Failing sea transport', Robertson emphasized, 'no very rapid progress north of Jerusalem can be expected owing to our dependence on the railway. In this latter case we must not expect much assistance from the tribes in rear of the Turkish lines, and consequently the Turks will only retire as military pressure compels them.' This, in all likelihood, would mean that the best Murray could hope for was to occupy Palestine and hold the most favourable line for the defence of that country. In his February 22 memorandum, Robertson also emphasized that any offensive to take Jerusalem must be delayed until the autumn.[51]

Pressure from the civilians and Murray's misleading assessment of 1st Gaza encouraged Robertson to abandon this timetable. As he later told Sir James E. Edmonds, the compiler of the official history, 'The early telegrams about the first battle of Gaza affected the action of the General Staff very much indeed.'[52] On March 30, Robertson asked for and got the War Cabinet's permission to instruct Murray to 'develop his recent success to the fullest possible extent and to adopt a more offensive role in general'.[53]

General Headquarters of the EEF had been hoisted by its own petard. After returning to GHQ in Cairo, Murray and Lynden-Bell continued to put the best possible face on the results of 1st Gaza. When Robertson warned GHQ against raising public expectations through extravagant claims, Lynden-Bell wrote to Maurice that 'all the news now coming in from Turkish sources, deserters, etc goes to show that our success was even greater than we said, but I shall not say another word about these operations in our communiqués for fear of still further raising extravagant hopes'.[54] GHQ continued to argue that the failure of the *coup de main* against Gaza actually worked in the EEF's favour. 'We were so afraid that the enemy would withdraw northward into Palestine and that we should have to go chivying them about without bringing off any decisive result until we arrived at a strong position somewhere on the line Jaffa-Jerusalem', Lynden-Bell told Maurice. 'So that it suits us admirably that they have done exactly what we wanted and collected in our immediate front near Gaza. I feel quite certain that if we had not attacked on the 26th we should not have induced them to hold Gaza as they are doing now.'[55]

Murray had become a victim of the expectations he had created in London. His reputation now hinged on a decisive victory. Nothing else would satisfy the government, which desperately needed to boost home morale. In a letter to Lynden-Bell, Maurice emphasized the 'political arguments'. He wrote, 'the Government feels that its hands must be strengthened as much as possible by military successes, and the moral prestige of a success in Palestine would be very great on the public mind'. Jerusalem's capture would raise British spirits just as it demoralized the Turks. 'There is a great deal of very real discontent in Constantinople, and Enver's position has been much shaken by the loss of Baghdad', Maurice stressed. 'If you can get Jerusalem it should pretty near finish the Young Turk party.'[56]

The War Office believed that the maximum Turkish force that could be assembled and supplied in southern Palestine was around 30,000 men. According to official Turkish sources, the Turkish defences on the Gaza-Beersheba line were, in fact, manned by only about 18,000 men.[57] This meant that in addition to its overwhelming superiority in mounted forces, the Eastern Force still had a fifty per cent advantage in infantry. As the EEF's recent encounter with Johnny Turk demonstrated, however, superior numbers did not guarantee a victory. The Turks were at their best when dug in, and the waterless environment around Gaza continued to pose many difficulties for the attackers.

During the three weeks that separated the 1st and 2nd Gaza, both armies busily prepared for the next battle, with the Turks extending and strengthening their defences while the British massed their available forces near the front and extended their railway to within five miles of the Wadi Ghazzi.

GHQ and the Eastern Force's leadership were now out of step. Because of pressure from London, Murray wanted to resume the offensive immediately, and he thought that Dobell's preparations were taking too long. 'Sir C. D. [Charles Dobell] & his staff did not escape suspicion from above of lack of push. It was more than suggested to begin with that three weeks was too long for preparation', recalled Dobell's chief of staff Dawnay. Things came to a head during the second week of April. First, Dawnay refused to guarantee the victory that GHQ demanded. In a letter to Lynden-Bell, he 'expressed the view that as far as a real victory in the forthcoming battle was concerned it "would be not more than about an even money chance"'. GHQ's response to this cautionary note, according to Dawnay, 'was instantaneous; viz. a personal cypher wire to Sir C. D. inviting him to send me home on the score of "lost nerve"'.[58]

Dobell refused to sacrifice his valuable chief of staff, telling Murray and Lynden-Bell that he could not promise the victory that they and London wanted and expected. 'His force was not over strong, especially in artillery (guns and shells) & the Turkish position was strong enough to give the enemy's forces a pretty even chance.' In the ensuing discussions, Dobell introduced an alternative plan prepared by his chief of staff Dawnay: an attack against the Turkish flank at Beersheba (essentially the same plan successfully employed in breaking the Turkish front at 3rd Gaza). But Dawnay admitted that abandoning a frontal assault would delay the offensive for at least six weeks, and even then, the British might not have sufficient force to successfully complete this flanking operation. The prospect of further delay was critical to Murray. 'He certainly could not wait so long, in view of what was expected of him', he insisted, and he ordered Dobell to complete his preparations for an offensive no later than April 17.[59] Dobell now had only one option: a direct assault against the strongest Turkish defences in Palestine.

First Gaza had been designed as a cutting operation that emphasized speed and surprise and gave the mounted forces a key role, with only one infantry division, the 53rd, assigned the task of taking Gaza. This time, Dobell's plan included three infantry divisions, the 52nd, 53rd and 54th, with the recently formed 74th (composed of dismounted Yeomanry regiments) in reserve. The Desert Column, which no longer included infantry, was expected to protect the British right flank and exploit any breakthrough by the infantry. This approach was familiar to any British officer who had served with the British Expeditionary Force in France. With no flanks to turn, Haig in 1916 attempted to break through the German defensive system into open country where his cavalry could be deployed. Every available weapon had been utilized to shepherd the infantry across no-man's-land on the Somme. High explosive shells proved to be the most effective weapon against dug-in and wired positions, although poison gas, tanks, and aeroplanes had also been used during Haig's prolonged offensive.

In sum, a small-scale and abbreviated version of a typical western front attack was planned to take Gaza. Unfortunately, Murray lacked the necessary technical support for an assault against barbed wire and machine guns. In the blunt assessment of S.F. Mott (who had replaced the discredited Dallas as commander of the 53rd Division), 'There never appeared to be anything in the conception of the plan beyond brute force without the adequate artillery to carry it through.'[60]

The British had only 170 pieces of artillery, and of these, only sixteen were medium and over. Air power was insufficient, with only twenty-five serviceable aeroplanes available. Chemical warfare and tanks, both of which the Turks had never experienced in this theatre, seemed to offer the best chance of a successful frontal assault. The British had first used tanks in France in September 1916; eight had subsequently been shipped to Egypt, the only theatre outside of Europe to receive this promising new weapon. These tanks, which arrived in January 1917, were not of the latest type and had been used for instructional purposes. Yet GHQ was excited about their possibilities. In March, Murray and Lynden-Bell witnessed a practice demonstration. 'We saw them attack a position, and the sand though fairly heavy, did not interfere with them in the least. They buzzed along most satisfactorily, and if we can only get the Turks to stand I feel they will frighten them out of their lives', Lynden-Bell reported to the War Office.[61]

As the generals looked over their maps and made their plans, British camps were alive with preparation for the greatest battle yet fought in this theatre. For the first time in the campaign, a nucleus of officers and other ranks were held back from the assaulting forces to provide for their reorganization after heavy losses. The infantry had hitherto experienced the essentially desert and mobile warfare of Romani and 1st Gaza, but this offensive against a strong Turkish defensive system promised to be different. Unbloodied men were more likely to have a romantic version of combat. The aristocratic Lieutenant E.N. Buxton, a graduate of Harrow, serves as a good example of someone who had yet to be initiated into the nightmarish experience of trench warfare. 'My belief is that life is measured, not by space but by intensity', he wrote to one of his sisters. 'When men greatly care for a great cause, they are living life, at its intensest, so far as it can be lived in this world, and they must carry over into their further existence a tremendous store of vitality, to launch them further on their new stage. So, if I die well I have no fear of my start in the next stage. My only fear is to die badly.'[62] A fellow signaller who occupied a trench with Marchant was more prosaic. As the guns of the preliminary bombardment boomed in the background, he talked 'of his home life and of his religious views. Although he did not say so', Marchant later recalled, 'I realised afterwards that he knew his time had come. As it happened I partnered him during most of the following day, and he was shot towards the evening.'[63]

Religion was also on Lieutenant J.W. McPherson's mind as he attended Mass on the coastal plain before Gaza, which was teeming with infantry and mounted troops moving to the front. 'Thousands of cavalry rode past us to protect our right flank, limbers, guns, G.S. wagons etc. clattered past smothering us in dust and lines of infantry marching as far as the eye could see came slogging along', he wrote in some awe. 'Two regimental bands were playing, one at a C. of E. service not far off, and a kilted crowd were skirling (is that the right word?) not far off either on the bagpipes.' As he sat in the boiling sun with his helmet on, the priest began the service 'accompanied by no other music than the above except that some gun or other supplied nearly every stop of the organ… The crump, crump, crump of trench mortar shells and the rattle of machine guns supplied the drums and kettle drums.' After a brief sermon, the priest began Mass. 'Suddenly he said "I'm sorry I couldn't hear all your confessions, but don't be shy, boys, I'll give you two minutes to dispose your hearts and then you shall all (who wish) come up for the Blessed Sacrament – if I stopped to hear about half your sins, many of you would be dying in them."'[64]

The climax of 2nd Gaza occurred on April 19, when the British attacked along a 15,000-yard front. An ineffective preliminary bombardment, supported by warships, opened at 5.30a.m. An artillery officer, Major General S.C.U. Smith, acidly described it as follows: 'This bombardment was the most futile thing possible resulting, as I had stated, only in warning the enemy of the point of attack and in gross waste of ammunition. The fire trenches were the object of the bombardment and to think that any intelligent enemy will hold his front line trenches in strength when there is no threat of an infantry attack was ridiculous – considering the distance apart of the opposing forces.'[65]

At 7:15a.m., the 53rd Division began its advance in extended order across the sand hills of the coast. Although the 53rd jumped off fifteen minutes earlier than the 52nd Division to its immediate right, its progress was slow. Soldiers of the 53rd wore wire sand shoes with a flat sole of thick wire made like a tennis racket, tied to their boots with laces, to keep them from sinking into the soft, deep sand. Sand was not the only reason for the deliberate advance. According to Marchant, soldiers carried 'extra heavy packs, being loaded with sandbags and tools for reversing the trench when taken, instruments, and 200 rounds of ammunition. We also had above our packs the tunic as it was too hot to wear it.' Marchant remembered 'the dead lying about seemed to be piled high with kit'. Machine guns, rifles, and artillery rained lead on the men. 'It was a deafening rattle with men falling on all sides', Marchant noted. 'We all spent what moments we could spare in bandaging wounds of others, most of them being full of sand, the flesh being much torn by the use of dum-dum (filed down) or explosive bullets... The tanks were dropping out one by one, the deep sand proving too much for them... About 1600 the barrage suddenly lifted and the order to charge was given. The two Battns immediately rushed forward shouting and heaving Mill's grenades.' Despite heavy casualties, the infantry captured Samson Ridge with the bayonet. 'I can honestly say', Marchant wrote, 'the whole advance was carried out with great coolness and courage, no man wavering at any time. Death and torture was all around them, yet was passed with a casual glance, or a quick application of a field dressing. It seemed commonplace, part of the job to be expected. Many men were killed after being wounded, or again wounded before they were got away. Most of our officers and NCOs became casualties, and at the end the Battn was commanded by a 2nd Lt.'[66] And this was the same division that had conquered Ali Muntar in March, only to be withdrawn when victory was within its grasp because of a confused and indecisive higher command. McPherson was attached to the sappers of the 155th Brigade, 52nd Division. He described the action when he and the sappers came within sight of the enemy's fortifications:

> The first attacking party had failed and were in full retreat, but rallied on meeting the advancing K.O.S.B. [King's Own Scottish Borderers] troops and both parties attacked again. It looked like simple murder for our men. Relatively few fell to the shrapnel and H.E., but the rifle fire and machine guns punished them terribly. The 53rd Division

should have been attacking on the right, but for some reason they had not come up, and our poor chaps were exposed to an additional enfilading fire. On making their final charge, the Turks stood up and received them with hand grenades, fleeing then to another line of trenches. Our poor chaps occupied the trench for a time, but under an enfilading fire, and then the Turks attacked with fixed bayonets, killing or capturing nearly every man.[67]

The authors of the official history, so protective of the higher command's reputation at 1st and 2nd Gaza, do a disservice to the men of the 53rd Division. 'But it appears', the official history suggested, 'that the men of the 53rd Division still felt the effects of their losses, disappointments and fatigue in the battle fought three weeks earlier, for their advance, even up to Samson Ridge, had been much slower than that of the other two divisions. They had, however, suffered upwards of six hundred casualties, chiefly in carrying Samson Ridge.'[68] Yet the capture of Samson Ridge represented the only real success for British arms on April 19.

Rather than raise questions about the 53rd Division's courage and determination, the official history might have emphasized the impossible task given another division, the 54th. Major Bailey, who served as a liaison officer between the 54th and 52nd Divisions, witnessed an extraordinary discussion on the evening of April 18 between General Hare and his artillery commander Brigadier H.G. Sandilands. For two hours, the men argued over the scheduled attack at 7.30a.m. the next morning by the 54th. 'Seriously and very firmly', Sandilands 'begged' Hare to 'withdraw the order'. The 54th was expected to advance some 2,000 yards over what the artilleryman Bailey described as 'perfectly open grass-land, quite flat and as smooth as a lawn'. Sandilands told Hare, '"I have not got the ammunition for it. Even at one round per gun per minute, I shall have nothing left to fight a battle with. By the error of the gun, I can't guarantee to drop a single shell into the single line of trenches over 2,000 yards away. All we shall do is to keep them awake and ready, and when the infantry start to move forward they will just be mown down in swathes. It is just murder."' Hare listened but insisted that his hands were tied. '"I can't alter the order now"', he said.[69]

The 54th's attack went off as scheduled, with predictable results. The enemy's artillery had not been silenced, and Turkish machine gunners were still at their posts. The advancing Tommies had no chance. Three battalions in the 163rd Brigade lost 1,500 men and all of their company commanders. When Hare inspected the battlefield the next day, Bailey observed that 'tears were streaming down his face'.[70] Hare's predicament was a difficult one. History has not been kind to irresolute or pessimistic commanders. Dallas, accused of losing his nerve at 1st Gaza, had been summarily dismissed. Because of his dire warnings to Hare, Sandilands was going to be sent home as well. Even if Hare had protested the order to attack, neither Dobell nor Murray, who had established his headquarters in his railway train at Khan Yunis and was in communication by telephone with Eastern Force headquarters, would have acquiesced.

Murray, now down to the last throw of the dice, was prepared to risk all. Despite the lack of progress on April 19, Murray called Dawnay a little after 3:30p.m. and wanted Dobell 'to put in his reserves to force a conclusion'. Dawnay, who saw no indication that the Turkish defences were about to crack, demurred and was supported by Dobell. Murray responded by telephoning a direct order to resume the attack at dawn on the next day 'and to press it to a decision'.[7] According to Dawnay, every divisional and artillery commander opposed a resumption of the attack and saw no prospect of success. This point of view was strongly represented to Dobell, when on Murray's instructions he conferred with his divisional commanders. Dobell, as the responsible commander, then canceled the attack, and Murray reluctantly confirmed it.[72]

The tanks had been a disappointment, chemical warfare even more so. The crews of the eight tanks had performed valiantly in almost impossible conditions. The fine sand clogged the tank's machinery, especially its treads, and the crews suffered terribly as temperatures rose to 200 degrees because of the red-hot engines and blistering sun. The other surprise weapon, poison gas, had no effect on the battlefield. The hot climate caused it to evaporate, and the strong winds dispersed it. Murray told the authors of the official history that 'the 3,000 gas shells' used had 'no more effect in that atmosphere than squibs would have had'.[73]

But the greatest weakness of the attack had been the failure of artillery to neutralize the enemy's artillery and to terrorize and pulverize its infantry. The naval guns were ineffective, and the Royal Artillery did not have either the shells or guns to adequately cover a front of some 15,000 yards. At the battle of Arras in France in April, the British had allocated one gun to every thirty-six feet of front; at 2nd Gaza, it was one gun per 100 yards of front. None of these weaknesses could be corrected overnight. In fact, there would be even fewer shells to support the offensive if it had been resumed on the 20th.

At 9a.m. on April 21, Dobell paid the price for canceling the offensive. He was ordered to appear at GHQ and was handed the draft telegram that Murray planned to send to London. 'It gave as the reason for my removal that the C-in-C considered, and had long felt, that I was ignorant', Dobell remembered. When the shaken Dobell returned to his headquarters, he received a call from Lynden-Bell asking if he would consent to a cable being sent explaining his recall on his 'poor health'. Dobell agreed, to his later regret. His terse and peremptory orders on April 23 to return home were even more insulting. 'You are directed to proceed forthwith to England and report to the War Office on arrival. You should report to the E.S.O., Port Said, before 4p.m. tomorrow for passage which has been arranged. Permission is given for your servant to accompany you. Acknowledge.'[74] Chetwode replaced him. 'This climate tells on everybody... He has not been himself for some time', Lynden-Bell wrote of Dobell, 'and on the 26th March, the day of the first Gaza fight, he got a very bad touch of the sun, and although he says he is all right it is quite clear to us all that he is absolutely abnormal and quite different to what he used to be. Chetwode will do very well, I am sure, and is sensible enough to wear an enormous thick hat.'[75]

Dobell unfairly became GHQ's scapegoat for the second failed attempt to take Gaza. Murray took no responsibility himself except to later argue that 'my own particular failing was that I had unselfishly reduced my forces too low, and sent away the best Divisions and best Divisional Commanders. If I had kept Joe Maude, Horne, and the 29th Division, history might have been different.'[76] Murray's attempt to rewrite history was grossly unfair to the Territorial divisions. Murray had convinced his government that the Turks were on their last legs, and then to save his reputation, he pushed forward a frontal assault without the technical means to succeed.

As reflected in the death toll and lack of progress, the offensive was an even greater failure than the first attempt to take Gaza. Official British casualties amounted to 6,444 and included 509 killed. The death total was actually much higher because 1,534 soldiers were listed as missing, although the Turks claimed to have captured only six officers and 266 other ranks.[77] Many of those listed as 'missing' were the wounded soon to join the dead. Many of the wounded were scattered in front of the British defences and could not be retrieved. It would be months before some of these bodies, many covered by sand, could be found.[78]

It was going to take more than 'an enormous thick hat' to save Murray and Lynden-Bell, the two men ultimately responsible for the debacle of 2nd Gaza. Both men were given hats before the end of the year, but they were 'bowler hats', army slang for the sacking of the upper ranks. The failure of the second attempt to take Gaza added to the gloom in London in April. At the beginning of the month, Turkey had seemed on the verge of crumbling because of British and Russian pressure, and the French were about to launch a great offensive with their commander in chief, Robert Georges Nivelle, promising a breakthrough in twenty-four to forty-eight hours. This promising military situation, however, changed almost overnight.

On April 18, the day before the Eastern Force's broad-front assault to capture Gaza, Robertson reported to the ministers that Nivelle's attack had not lived up to expectations and that French politicians were now leaning toward abandoning the offensive until US help arrived. News was even more ominous from the newly democratic government in Russia. Nicholas II's overthrow in mid-March had not led to a revitalization of that country – on the contrary. The best intelligence from Russia, Robertson said, was that there was now no possibility that Russia planned to attack either the Germans or Turks. Free from Russian pressure, the Turks might reinforce their efforts in Palestine and Mesopotamia.[79] A further development that had an impact on Britain's Turkish theatres was the dramatic success of Germany's resumption of unrestricted U-boat warfare. British ships were being sunk at an average of thirteen a day. The average in 1916 had been three a day. The secretary of the War Cabinet, Captain Maurice Hankey, even believed that the U-boat would 'probably ultimately compel us to withdraw our forces from Egypt'.[80]

To salvage the situation in Palestine, British leaders believed that new leadership of the Egyptian Expeditionary Force was vital. Murray's competence, rather than his stamina or health, was at issue. Lloyd George had actually wanted Murray replaced with an officer 'of the dashing type' before his second failure to take Gaza.[81] Although Robertson had persuaded him to hold his hand, the CIGS began to consider possible replacements, with Lieutenant General Lord Cavan, a first-rate corps commander in France, emerging as the front-runner.[82]

On April 23, the War Cabinet discussed Murray's future. The decision to remove him was unanimous.[83] Yet Murray was not officially informed of his dismissal until June 11. This delay of over six weeks reflected the importance that the government now attached to the Palestine theatre. Cavan did not emerge as Murray's successor despite Robertson's support. On March 12, 1917, Jan Christiaan Smuts, the South African soldier-politician, had arrived in London to attend the newly established Imperial War Cabinet, a committee to co-ordinate the Empire's war policy. Smuts, who was of Dutch stock, was heralded by the British press as one of the Empire's greatest soldiers. He had conducted a skilful guerilla campaign against the best British generals in the South African war. More recently, he had led Imperial forces operating in the German colony of East Africa.

The first British leader to view Smuts as the saviour in Britain's war with Turkey was Leopold S. Amery, an avid imperialist and geopolitical adviser to Lloyd George. As soon as Smuts arrived in Britain, Amery wrote to him. 'If I were dictator I should ask you to do it [succeed Murray] as the only leading soldier who has had experience of mobile warfare during this war and has not got trenches dug deep into his mind.'[84] However flattering this was to Smuts, it was premature. Murray had yet to make his first attack on Gaza.

Once the decision had been made to remove Murray, Lloyd George pressed Smuts to take his place. In the prime minister's view, Smuts was an obvious choice. He had shown drive and imagination as a field commander, and he also understood the geopolitical importance of Palestine to the security of the British Empire. But Smuts held back. Never one to think small – in 1918 he dared to suggest to Lloyd George that he should replace John J. Pershing as commander in chief of US forces in Europe – Smuts wanted an all-out effort against the Turks. Lloyd George had his eye on Jerusalem, but Smuts envisaged a distant advance into Syria that severed Turkey's vital communications and struck a mortal blow against the Turkish Empire. Murray had asked for two additional divisions before attacking Gaza. Smuts's plan included the landing of an army of 100,000 men at Haifa behind the Turkish front at Gaza-Beersheba. At this critical juncture in the war, with her European allies flagging, Britain had neither the men nor the ships to support such an ambitious plan. After consulting with Robertson, Smuts came to understand this.

On May 31, Smuts unequivocally turned down Lloyd George's offer to succeed Murray. 'I have been torn between this strong personal desire on the one hand to accept your offer and do my bit at the Front', he wrote, 'and on the other hand my equally strong conviction that our present military situation on all Fronts does not really justify an offensive campaign for the capture of Jerusalem and the occupation of Palestine, however highly desirable those objects may be.'[85] Smuts's decision left the door open to the soldier destined to lead imperial forces to a brilliant victory on the Turkish battlefields.

5

'Bloody Bull's Loose'

As the Eastern Force butted its head against the Gaza defences in April, General Sir Edmund Allenby's Third Army found itself in a similarly futile operation on the western front. The battle of Arras had got off to a promising start with the Canadians capturing Vimy Ridge. For a moment, it appeared that a gap could be torn in the German front that could be exploited by the cavalry. This had long been Haig's dream, and he was bitterly disappointed that Allenby, a cavalryman, could not deliver. It was not that Allenby did not make the effort. In fact, three of Allenby's generals protested over his head to Haig that his order for relentless pursuit against intact and extremely strong defences was reckless and did not justify the terrible losses.[1]

Allenby's direction of the battle of Arras tarnished his reputation and put his relationship with Haig in jeopardy. Smuts's rejection of the command of the Egyptian Expeditionary Force (EEF), however, gave Allenby the opportunity to achieve great things in Palestine. As noted earlier, Robertson had first considered Cavan as Murray's successor. But when he had broached the subject in April, he suspected that Haig would be reluctant to lose his able commander of the IV Corps.[2] It appears that Haig after Allenby's controversial leadership of the Third Army had no similar concern for losing him to a 'sideshow' in Palestine, a theatre where the editor of the official history has acidly remarked, 'all failures were consigned'.[3] A more charitable conclusion is that Robertson trusted Allenby, a fellow classmate at the Staff College in 1897, and thought him the best available man for the job. Robertson perhaps did not consider him earlier as Murray's replacement because of his vital role in the battle of Arras.

Allenby, the son of a country gentleman, fitted the image of a country squire. He had a robust constitution: he had spent his youth riding, shooting, fishing, and sailing. He was an undistinguished public school student, twice failing the entrance examination to enter Indian Civil Service. Yet he had no difficulty getting into and graduating from Sandhurst. Although he studied with Robertson and Murray at Staff College, he was more a field commander than general staff officer. Before the war, he had led and trained in turn a troop, a squadron, a regiment, a brigade, and a division.

Tall, with a strong, determined face, he appeared every inch a soldier. His dominating physical presence gave no hint of any shyness. Yet he once confided to a fellow officer that 'shyness had ruined his life'. He went on to admit that although he had 'tried desperately' to overcome this shyness, he had failed. He then recalled a meeting with Sir Douglas Haig. 'They were both so shy that neither of them could say one word. It was ludicrous but true and so they silently and mutually agreed never to be alone when they met.'[4] His abrupt manner was perhaps an attempt to hide this shyness. James E. Edmonds, a fellow student at Staff College, concluded that 'when later Allenby became a general, to our great amusement, he tried to play what he thought was the part and assumed a roughness of manner and an abruptness of speech which were not natural to him'.[5] His angry outbursts and abuse of subordinates earned him the unflattering nickname 'Bull'.

This was the unattractive Allenby – the martinet who once jumped a soldier in the trenches for wearing a cap instead of a steel helmet, only to discover that he was berating a corpse.[6] But there was also Allenby, the humanist with an inquiring and retentive mind. He especially loved nature and was conversant with music, literature and history. 'I discovered his musical tastes', wrote Major General Sir George de S. Barrow, the commander of the Yeomanry Mounted Division, 'by hearing him humming a bit out of Beethoven's "Emperor" Sonata during the retreat from Mons.'[7] Another officer remembers him as fascinating company while travelling in a motor car in Palestine. 'He would discourse on the habits of animals and birds and theorise on the mysterious life cycle of the salmon. Often he would break the thread of the discussion and speak about the biblical geography and history of the locality the car happened to be passing.'[8]

Allenby was truly a bundle of contradictions. Although he was often aloof and intimidating with fellow officers, he took a more personal interest in the rank and file than almost any modern British commander. He was cautious in his appreciation of the require-ments for future operations, and he was, if anything, overconfident and a risk-taker once the battle was joined. Perhaps the maxim that describes him best was one of his favourites: 'Once you have taken a decision, never look back on it'.[9]

On June 27, Allenby arrived in Egypt to be met by Lynden-Bell at Alexandria. Not surprisingly, General Headquarters (GHQ) anx-iously awaited its new commander in chief. 'All sorts of stories are going round about Allenby being a big & burly man of fierce address, who prefaces all his remarks with "What the bloody hell"',[10] the staff officer Orlo Williams scribbled in his diary. But when Lynden-Bell returned from his first meeting with his new chief, he pretended to swing a bat and told his staff, 'I've been playing with a pretty straight bat. The bowling isn't so bad. He seems quite reasonable.'[11]

Lynden-Bell was soon gleefully reporting to the War Office that Allenby 'has entirely endorsed all his predecessor's views on the situ-ation out here'.[12] This was true insofar as the EEF's technical and manpower requirement for victory in Palestine were concerned. But Allenby brought a new style and needed energy to GHQ. 'My word, he is a different man to Murray', noted Colonel Richard Meinertzhagen, an intelligence officer. 'His face is strong and almost boyish. His manner is brusque almost to rudeness, but I prefer it to the oil and butter of the society soldier.'[13]

On his first visit to GHQ, Allenby demonstrated that he was not Murray. When a senior member of the adjutant general's office brought him a stack of papers dealing with routine matters such as discipline and dress, he tossed them on the floor to make the point that he was not to be bothered with minor details that could be handled by junior officers. Allenby also interviewed all of the members of the staff he inherited, concluding that many of them were inexperienced.[14] The result was a thoroughgoing purge that eventually included Orlo C. Williams and Lynden-Bell.

Allenby also removed many petty requirements that served no useful purpose. Brigadier General J.T. Wigan, 7th Mounted Brigade, commenting on how the new commander in chief improved the morale of all ranks, wrote: 'Officers visiting Cairo, even in the hot weather had to wear breeches and boots or leggings at all times, both in the day time and at night. (I only mention this trivial matter amongst others, as an example of the many irksome and unnecessary irritating regulations made both for officers and other ranks, all of which were abolished very soon after the arrival of Sir E. Allenby.)'[15]

Because he believed that his place was at the front, Allenby established his headquarters near Khan Yunis in Palestine. As he told a medical officer, 'You know, General Headquarters' roots in Cairo and Ismailia are like alfalfa grass. They are getting too deep into the ground and want pulling up. Moreover, Staff Officers are like partridges: they are the better for being shot over.'[16] The bars and dining rooms of Shepheard's and other first-class Cairo hotels soon reflected the GHQ's new location. 'I have never seen such an array of brass gathered together as I found in the bars and dining-rooms on the first occasion', approvingly observed Geoffrey Inchbald, a junior officer with the Imperial Camel Corps, 'nor so few as on my second visit.'[17]

Allenby wasted little time in making his presence felt with the rank and file. He seemed to be everywhere as he moved by car and horse up and down the line. 'We were drawn up in line mounted on our camels', Inchbald recalled, 'when we saw a cloud of dust which heralded the approach of half a dozen horsemen proceeding at full gallop towards a point about a quarter of a mile to our front. Leading the posse was a gigantic man mounted on a gigantic horse, who could not possibly have been mistaken for anybody but our new commander-in-chief.'[18] His troops did not always live up to his high standards, so Allenby's unscheduled visits created apprehension. A coded message was soon devised: 'BBL' for 'Bloody Bull's Loose'. Once, when Allenby noticed a semaphorist waving these letters to a neighboring unit, he inquired what they meant. The signaller weakly responded that 'it referred to an agricultural mishap, "Bull broken loose."' Allenby almost certainly knew better, but he did not make an issue of it.[19]

When Allenby returned in late July from one of his inspection tours, he received a message feared by the parents of every soldier. His only son, Michael, a subaltern with the Royal Horse Artillery on the western front, had been killed by a fragment from an artillery shell. Allenby immediately wrote to his wife:

> My darling sweetheart, I wish I could be with you; but I know how brave you are; and you will be strong to bear this awful blow. You and Michael fill my thoughts, and I feel very near to you both. Every remembrance of him is a joy. From his birth to his death there is not a day that you or I would have wished changed or to have been lived otherwise than he lived it… Whenever he came to stay with me, he was always the same; a friend, on equal terms; and yet, unaffectedly, he always kissed me when we met and parted – as he did when a child.[20]

This tender letter reveals a man quite different from the one presented to the world by his tough exterior and brusque manner.

Combat in Palestine was much more personal than the static trench warfare of the western front, with its millions of combatants, remote commanders, and industrialized warfare, where death frequently came from an invisible hand, delivered by long-range artillery fire on roads and camps behind the lines or from poison gas and small arms fire on a churned-up battlefield with limited visibility. The British infantry and mounted forces in Palestine, however, fought essentially a war of movement with a very visible enemy. Their war with 'Johnny' Turk was as personal as it had been for British troops during the Napoleonic wars. The Tommies, no less than Wellington's troops, needed to know their commander. Allenby fulfilled this role brilliantly; few commanders in either world war were as well known to their troops or paid closer attention to their needs when not in battle. Of course, the scale of the war in Palestine, as compared with the western front, contributed to Allenby's extraordinary accessibility. But Murray, with the same opportunities, remained a distant commander. 'There was scarcely a man in the force who did not feel that he was a matter of personal interest to the C in C and the effect was miraculous. Such a complete contrast to the previous regime',[21] opines one EEF officer on the differences between Allenby and his predecessor.

Allenby's accessibility was clearly an important factor in creating a personal bond with his troops. But it would have meant little if a third attempt to take Gaza met the same fate as the first two. Unlike Murray, Allenby had the prospect of a substantial increase in men and equipment and a government determined to make his theatre second only to the western front. 'I told him in the presence of Sir William Robertson that he was to ask us for such reinforcements and supplies as he found necessary, and we would do our best to provide them', Lloyd George wrote in his memoirs. The prime minister pointedly informed Allenby: 'If you do not ask it will be your fault. If you do ask and do not get what you need it will be ours.' His mission: 'Jerusalem before Christmas'.[22]

A fundamental strategic question for Allenby's theatre is well put by the official history: 'Was there a half-way house between the Canal and Aleppo, and if so, where was it?'[23] While Lloyd George sought to accelerate the campaign in Palestine during the last half of 1917, Robertson applied the brakes. Robertson's initial position, which the War Cabinet approved, was to wait until Allenby assessed his situation before giving him an objective. But Lloyd George expected great things from Allenby, and the new commander of the EEF found himself in the middle of a tug-of-war between the prime minister and the government's military adviser, Robertson. This conflict over higher strategy ultimately threatened the survival of the government and led to Robertson's dismissal.[24]

After touring his front and consulting with Chetwode, on July 12, Allenby, via telegram, submitted his requirements for taking

Jerusalem. He put the strength of the Turkish force opposing him in southern Palestine at 46,000 rifles and 2,800 sabres. (This figure represented a serious breakdown in British intelligence because the enemy's rifle strength was actually much less.)[25] Assuming that substantial Turkish reinforcements were not sent to his front, Allenby estimated that he could conquer the Holy City with seven infantry divisions and three cavalry divisions. But he warned that he would need substantial reinforcements to advance further, and perhaps even to hold the Jaffa-Jerusalem line.

Robertson's response to Allenby's appreciation was prepared on July 19 1917, at the very moment that the ministers, after agonizing debate, approved Haig's plan to secure the Flanders coast, the so-called Passchendaele offensive. By default, Britain had become the mainstay of the anti-German coalition. The French Army had mutinied after Nivelle's failed offensive, the Russians seemed finished, the Italians were wavering, and serious US military assistance in Europe was at least a year away. In Asia, the British were even more dependent on their own resources to check German expansionism. Yet a greater commitment to the Palestinian theatre would put additional strain on Britain's depleted shipping, which also sustained British ventures in the Balkans and Mesopotamia. 'It is for the War Cabinet to say whether the political advantages to be gained by the occupation of Jerusalem and Southern Palestine are such as to justify our undertaking at this state of the war a new and great campaign with the consequent strain on our shipping and all other resources', Robertson succinctly informed the civilians. 'It is my present opinion that the purely military advantages to be gained would not justify the expenditure of force required and the risks incurred, though I do not say that this opinion may not be modified later.'[26]

Turkey, which had gained some relief from Russia's collapse, was still in a bad way. But help was on the way. Negotiations between Berlin and Constantinople resulted in the dispatch of a German force, the Asia Corps (also known as Pasha II). Its numbers, about 6,500 men, were not as important as the technical assistance it included: machine guns, artillery, mortars, aircraft, and mechanical transport. This new Turko-German force, commanded by the former head of the German General Staff, Field Marshal von Falkenhayn, was known as the Yildirim Army Group.[27] *Yildirim* means 'lightning', and this new force hoped to strike the British at Baghdad as if a thunderbolt from the sky. Robertson correctly dismissed as fantasy the rumours that Germany planned to send as many as 160,000 men to the Turkish theatres. Nonetheless, the Germans, and especially their technical assistance, might make things tricky for the British in the Middle East, especially for Maude, whose position at Baghdad was not as strong as Allenby's.

The government consequently wanted Allenby to be active on his front to prevent the enemy from concentrating on Mesopotamia. On August 10, the War Cabinet instructed Allenby 'to strike the Turks as hard as possible during the coming Autumn and Winter', but gave him no specific 'geographical' objective. Robertson included a personal, private note with these instructions: 'I think the Instructions will be clear to you. They simply amount to doing the best you can with what you have got; to giving the Turk as hard a knock as you can; and at the same time avoiding going too far forward and getting into a position from which you can neither advance nor go back and which might involve us in commitments which we could not properly meet having regard to other places and to our resources.'[28]

As the government discussed Allenby's role, all remained quiet on the Palestinian front. After their unsuccessful offensive in April, the British did not retire from Gaza. Instead, they held their position and dug in. Conditions were brutal. 'I shall never forget a scene I saw on April 25/17', Sergeant T.B. Minshall, 10th Battalion, 231st Brigade, 74th Division, wrote. 'We were working at full pressure trenching and wiring in the burning sun, the hot winds parched the men's lips and throats until some were overcome with the heat and had to be carried to our position. To see big strong men crying like little children for water, "precious water," was terrible.'[29]

In front of Gaza, the infantry built and maintained a series of trenches, separated from the Turks by distances ranging from 400 to 2,500 yards that extended from the sea, to Sheikh Abbas and a little beyond. From this point, the British front turned south and diverged from the Turkish line that ran south-east along the Gaza-Beersheba road. At one point, some nine miles separated the opposing forces. Rather than a continuous trench line, the defences in this sector consisted of fortified strong points. The Turks had strongly fortified two areas: the central position of Sheria, and Beersheba, which anchored the southern end of their front. The distance from fortress Gaza to Beersheba was roughly thirty miles.

Where the armies were in close touch, conditions resembled trench warfare in France. Front-line soldiers had little rest, even after dusk. At night men used the cover of darkness to repair and improve their trenches. They strung wire, widened communication trenches, buried cables, and constructed gun emplacements. Although there were no serious hostilities during this period, trenches were raided, and groups of soldiers fought each other in no-man's-land under exploding star shells and flares. The Turkish and British artillery did most of their deadly work at night. 'The bombardment around Gaza is furious of nights now, the big hills rumbling as if volcanoes were torturing their bellies. The small hills here us are all aquiver under the flashes of the guns',[30] trooper Ion L. Idriess remarked in his diary. 'The daytime was always a peaceful period in the front line. Between 10a.m. and 4p.m., the heat produced what the men called a "mirage," and rifle fire under such conditions was apt to be erratic', recalled Robert H. Goodsall, a Royal Field Artillery lieutenant attached to the 74th Division. 'By a sort of natural agreement, both sides shut down the war until the hours of dusk and darkness.'[31]

The Turks might take a break during daylight hours, but the fleas, lice, flies and other pests that bedevilled the soldiers did not. Captain E. Stanley Goodland of the 1/5th Somerset Light Infantry, 233rd Brigade, 75th Division, tried to explain trench conditions to his wife. 'I am sitting in my dug out now and its just 2 o/c in the morning – weve been heavily shelled all night and have had no rest – I cant sleep now, for we have an epidemic of fleas & mice in these trenches', he wrote. 'Last night when I woke up to do duty I was a mass of bites and I think nowhere on my body could you have put a 5 shilling bit without touching a spot – tonight its just as bad – its a horrid war – but thank God we can laugh at our misfortunes altho all night we scratch and curse.'[32]

Lice were even more common than fleas. Many soldiers had

brought wool underclothing with them from Britain. The War Office, in its infinite wisdom, also required them to wear a flannel 'spine pad' that was supposed to reduce incidents of heatstroke by protecting the spine from the sun. 'In Egypt', Marchant admits, 'we found the lice made it impossible to wear these things and this also applied to a flannel body belt issued to us, which it was a crime to leave off. Crime or no they soon disappeared for good.'[33] Although men put up a good fight against this invader, the lice invariably won.

The authorities did their bit by establishing delousing stations. Private F.V. Blunt, 2/15th London Regiment (Civil Service Rifles), 179th Brigade, 60th (London) Division, provided an amusing account of his first experience of having his uniform fumigated. 'A tarpaulin had been sunk in a deep hole and a shower consisting of a tin drum on the top of a wooden scaffold erected. We were all told to undress, several hundred, and put our clothes in bundles. I never saw such a display of male nakedness before', he wrote in his pocket diary. What happened next was surely predictable. 'The sight of so many varied "cocks" was the subject of much amusement and ribald comment', Blunt continued. 'The tarpaulin was filled with water and water was carried to the two shower tanks. Everyone had a dirty shower and a dirty wash which was appreciated. It was the first bath of any sort we had had for many weeks. While this was going on our clothes were placed in a big portable oven and literally baked. The oven baking was expected to kill the bugs and lice with which our clothes were infested.' Unfortunately, some eggs inevitably survived this baking process, and the soldier's body heat soon hatched them out. An itchy Blunt was soon writing in his diary, 'I am smothered with lice... Every morning and whenever there is a spare minute, everyone takes off their shirts and opens their trousers to hunt out lice... This louse hunting is quite a part of life.'[34]

Flies were almost as bad. 'Flies by the million pestering one whenever one stays still, flies in your drink, flies in your food, flies in your tent, flies wherever they can be most inconvenient and annoying',[35] Captain Case of the Royal Engineers wrote to his family. The ubiquitous fly contributed to soldiers' exhaustion. 'It was difficult to get much sleep in the daytime owing to the heat and the swarms of flies that intruded into our blanket bivouacs', Bernard Blaser recalled after the war. 'In order to get any sleep at all it was necessary to protect completely all bare parts of the body, using the square yard of mosquito netting which was issued to cover over the head, and a towel or spare shirt over arms and knees. Even then, by so wrapping up, the heat became the more trying and sleep improbable.'[36]

Flies were not just an irritant; they contributed to septic sores that put soldiers out of action temporarily. The causes of septic sores were several – lack of fresh vegetables, infected water, and bites from mosquitoes – but flies perhaps played the leading role in a cut or abrasion becoming septic. As Antony Bluett of the Egyptian Camel Transport Corps wrote, 'the slightest scratch turned septic… Sand would get into the wound; if it were cleansed and covered up, the dry, healing air of the desert had no chance; if it were left open the flies made a bivouac of it – and the result can be imagined. There were men who were never without a bandage on some part of their person for months on end, and it was a common sight to see a man going about his daily work literally swathed in bandages.'[37] Allenby responded by issuing wire gauze 'swatters' and ordering all soldiers, when not directly involved with the enemy, to spend fifteen minutes each day killing flies at sunset when they went to sleep. To protect their legs from abrasions and the resulting septic sores, he forced cavalrymen to wear long trousers.

Scorpions also stung soldiers who slept in the open under the stars, wrapped in their blankets. 'Often they were already in possession when blankets were unrolled for the night, and if not then, one was usually to be found in the morning nestling coyly in the folds', Bluett noted. 'The moment you touched him with a stick he elevated his poisonous battering-ram, which was as long as himself, and struck and struck again in an ecstasy of rage, until he actually poisoned himself and died from his own blows.'[38] In this strange land, the British encountered many other 'creeping, crawling things', as Blunt put it. 'The land round here abounds in lizards, spiders, beetles… saw a beautiful large spider, probably a tarantula, like beautiful coloured cotton wool, about four inches long',[39] he observed while training in the Wadi Ghazze.

Many soldiers detested the Sinai as they ploughed through its soft, heavy sand and experienced storms that filled their eyes, ears, nose, and mouth with sand and pricked their skin with what felt like red-hot needles. But the fine dust they found around Gaza was even worse. In a letter home, Lieutenant Case explained the difference. 'Sand one can put up with quite easily, for altho' unpleasant in one's food and in one's clothes, it is always clean and easy to shake away, but dust is absolutely filthy, it covers everything, and gets everywhere', he wrote. 'It will require all the will-power I possess to live in this filthy, vile dust fog for long, and not develop a temper like a demon.'[40]

Troops and horses on the move stirred up clouds of dust. 'Fellows cursing and swearing everywhere', a member of the 2/15th London Regiment (Civil Service Rifles), 179th Brigade, 60th Division, H.T. Pope, recorded in his diary. 'So thick was the dust that if a person had been shaking a cork mat in one's face it could not have been worse. It got in our nostrils and down our throats and covered every exposed portion of our bodies with thick dirt.'[41] Blaser, a scout and mapper with the London Scottish, 179th Brigade, 60th Division, provided a similar description. 'On we tramped, perspiring freely, the dust that rose about us clinging to our moist faces and bare knees until we presented a most humourous spectacle.' Blaser wrote the preceding passage after the war. At the time it surely was not as funny when this 'low-down, dirty-grey powder', as he called it, covered his face with a 'thick coating of mud'.[42]

J.O. Evans, who served in the 2/16th London Regiment (Queen's Westminster Rifles), 179th Brigade, 60th Division, described his piti-ful attempts to maintain some personal hygiene. 'A hole is scooped in the sand', he wrote to his mother, '& the ground sheet spread over it & pressed down into the hollow, into this is poured about 3 pints of waster, then stripping to the buff we do the best we can for ourselves, clad only in a sun helmet.'[43] If no water was available for bathing, soldiers used a towel to wipe down their perspiring bodies. 'After the sun has been busy for three or four weeks and everyone is mahogany-coloured, the smears unavoidably left by this process are not noticeable',[44] an artillery officer with the 2/22nd County of

London Howitzer Battery, 60th Division, remembered.

A soldier's morale was often no better than the food in his belly. The EEF's rations were notorious for their sameness and poor quality. In the field, Tommies often had to survive for long periods on iron rations: bully or pressed beef, sometimes mixed with onions by the cooks when they made stew, and army biscuits. These army biscuits, which were similar to a dog biscuit in texture, have been defined as 'a disciplinary food for "terriers". The grave of many a fine upstanding molar.'[45] Some soldiers made them softer by putting them in the embers of a fire. In addition to bully beef, soldiers on the march were sometimes given a tinned mixture of meat (largely gravy) and vegetable (mostly turnips and carrots). This stew was called Maconochie after its manufacturer and was widely derided by British soldiers in all theatres. Calcutt, a private in the 2/16th London Regiment (Queen's Westminster Rifles), 179th Brigade, 60th Division, noted an especially unpleasant characteristic of this tinned stew: 'One of the features of the night marches was the frightful stink. The Maconochie stew ration gave the troops flatulence of a particularly offensive nature', he wrote in his diary. 'So we marched along in air released by hundreds of men breaking wind.'[46]

According to the accounts of many who served in Egypt and Palestine, tea was the fuel that powered the British army. Soldiers at every opportunity drank tea, when they awoke (early morning tea was called 'gunfire'), during a long break on the march, and when they made camp. 'I have known many men in civilian life who seldom drank tea', Blaser asserts. 'Now they swear by it as a most refreshing beverage and valuable stimulant. I am one of them. It is necessary in order to appreciate tea fully to have marched beneath a scorching sun, your back aching to breaking-point under the weight of your pack, feet burning and painful, your tongue feeling too large for your mouth, and every drop of moisture appearing to have left your creaking body.'[47]

When not in the field, the soldiers' diet was improved somewhat by rice, peas, dates, porridge, jam, bread, meat, and bread pudding. 'Luxuries' such as sardines, pears, chocolate, sausages, milk, café au lait, cocoa and biscuits could be obtained at the divisional and battalion canteens, which were capitalized and administered by officers. These canteens boosted morale by supplementing the soldiers' bare-bones army rations and also gave officers an opportunity to show concern for the men. 'Rush the Canteen after dinner. We line up at 5.15 to wait till 6', Calcutt wrote. 'Sergeants come up and buy stuff when they like... Colonel Gordon Clark comes up and wants to know what all the men are waiting for. He is told "Serving Sergeants, Sir." "Sergeants be blowed" he says. "Serve the men." So the canteen opened at 5.30. Sausages, skipper sardines, chocolate, milk.'[48]

Soldiers also bought their beer in canteens, and Calcutt provided a graphic description of beer drinking in the desert. A long queue of some fifty yards had formed in front of the canteen. What Calcutt next observed explains why he did not join this queue:

> The beer comes in barrels. In order to cope with a barrel in desert tent conditions the beer is decanted out into, of all things, a latrine bucket from where it is ladled out into the men's mess tins. On receipt of the mess tin of beer the troops walk round and take their places at the end of the queue again. By the time they reach the head of the queue and are prepared to duck their heads to enter under the flap of the marquee they are ready to urinate into the buckets placed conveniently immediately outside the marquee. The similarity between the beer with a head on it inside the marquee and contents of the buckets outside would be too much for quite a number of people including me.[49]

With his troops settling into trench warfare, Allenby expressed concern. Through Lynden-Bell, he informed Chetwode, who had replaced Dobell as the commander of the Eastern Force, 'In the present phase of the operations it is only too easy, even for units in the front line, to become over-obsessed with trench methods, and in the case of troops temporarily further back their danger is even greater, and it is therefore of the greatest importance to keep them all fit and ready, by constant training and plenty of marching, for the more active conditions which we all look forward to seeing before long.'[50]

The trenches were initially manned by the infantry who had been engaged in 2nd Gaza, the 52nd, 53rd, 54th and 74th Divisions. In July the first of the promised reinforcements reached the front, the 60th Division, a second-line Territorial Division made up of Londoners, many of whom had been shop boys, clerks, and civil servants in civilian life. The 60th also included a large Cockney element. This was the 60th Division's third theatre of operations in twelve months: it had already served in France and the Balkans. 'If we had been asked yesterday', Case wrote to his family, '"Is it possible to discover a worse situated, a more inconvenient, or a more unholy spot in the world than your late rest camp in Macedonia?" We would have unanimously replied "No, it cannot be possible." Today, however, we have not only changed our minds, but we have actually found this spot, and more than that, we are encamped upon it.'[51] The 60th Division's trip to the front on the Kantara Military Railway had been a nightmare. Thirty men and their equipment had been stuffed like cattle into each railway car. 'We were one jumbled mass of arms and legs, equipment, rifles and pith helmets', Blaser recalled. 'It was out of the question to lie down, and as the train bumped and jolted we gradually settled amongst our surroundings, being so wedged in and entangled with other people and their belongings that it was almost impossible to move.'[52]

Because the 60th Division had only served in theatres dominated by trench warfare, it was singled out for extensive training in open warfare that emphasized long marches and exercises in waterless territory during the heat of the day. Men were limited to two water bottles. Their training in the Wadi Ghazze was unlike anything that the division members had previously experienced. Private F.V. Blunt, who served with the Civil Service Rifles, 179th Brigade, had been a civil servant in the office of the Surveyor of Taxes. Although he had been rejected for service several times because he was deemed 'underdeveloped', he bribed a sergeant at a lax recruiting station to pass him. The following excerpts from his diary are typical of the Londoners' reaction to the strenuous training:

On October 1: 'Had another attacking stunt early this morning. Only got in the way of another brigade on manoeuvres. Battalion marched back to our base camp at El Sharath in the full heat of the day. Nearly killed me… "Oh this war is a bugger."'

On October 4:'We went out again in the afternoon on a Brigade Field Day – attacking up the Wadi. Finished absolutely beat – never had a worse day in the army. Awful lot of "buggering about."'

On October 6:'Feeling jolly rotten from the effects of the exertions during the last two days. Absolutely fed up with everything.'[53]

Calcutt suggests that officers needed the training more than the rank and file. The following excerpts from his diary also reflect his cynicism, his dislike of war and army life, and the intense training he and his comrades in the 60th Division endured before 3rd Gaza:

On August 25:'An awful muck up it was. We should have been wiped out. The supporting wave *lost* the wave it was supporting. We attacked straight off after 1½ hours hard march, the attack being 1000 yards across heavy sand. Arrived absolutely whacked… Our officers *lost us* coming back. They cannot even find the way in day light.'

On September 22:'March all night, falling in holes, and over wire, and halting in gullies, and sitting down just as it is time to go on again. Very cold Get in an hour's sleep and wake up stiff, wet and cold… The Sun comes out and we are immediately bathed in perspiration.'

On September 24:'In the afternoon (help) we attack the blasted Wadi Guzzie again. Oh Lord, if they muck up actual attacks like they muck up these practice affairs, we shall all be dead before we get anywhere near the Turks.'

On October 4:'Up at one o'clock. Battle order, and move off, Fowler leads us in the dark to Wadi Guzzie quite successfully, Artillery fire, exhibition of wire cutting and barrage fire. High Explosive and Shrapnel at close quarters. London Scottish *said* to have two casualties… We go to within 50 yards of the wire, charge it subsequently in full pack up hill. Could hardly hold the rifle up, let alone kill Turks. Wire hardly cut at all and about 400 shells were fired.'

On October 5:'Usual thing, trudging up and down the hills in the Wadi. Machine guns firing and popping. We advance through them. Fire a few rounds. N.C.O.'s wind up as usual. When they are front they yell 'keep up in rear' and when they are in rear they yell "steady in front."'

On October 8: 'Wind up. Hurried on surprise parade at 7.45, and in spite of the fact that eight men were crimed yesterday for having incomplete packs Rumsey and I have nothing in much. Exhibition of wire cutting by the hand method. An awful washout. Standing up in front of a trench fiddling about with a pair of nippers. They would be dead... March to Brigade Headquarters and rehearse the attack on Beersheba... We take the place of the Turks to-day. But first we pretend to be in reserve. Hide in a garden facing the enemy. Civil Service Rifles attack in front of us and arrive after doubling up without sufficient strength to kill a louse. Let alone Turks. All grousing and grumbling in fine style. "Fuck the Army" being the prevailing sentiment.'

On October 12: 'We are bound for El Shellal. Breakfast in the dark. Bit of fat bacon, some got none. Bally awful march. Our Corporal afraid to halt at all! So we keep overtaking the Battalion, and then "Steady up." Oh, these "windy twits." Arrived, dash off for water. The Waddi all pipes and taps, and pumping houses, laid on from wells: *splendidly organised*. Somebody has brains evidently. We march in fours by the side of the camels. We miss the stunt, an attack. Water again in the afternoon. More marching in fours across the desert.'

On October 13: 'Up and off defending the Wadi. The Scottish attack. Would not half have caught it. One Scot comes staggering up the incline just in front of Captain Flower. "Up Fucking hill and down bloody dales," he groans. "Very aptly put" says Flower. By the by "Retire" is a forbidden word in the 60th Division now. What does that signify; a "death and glory" division. N.C.O.s Officers and men will be "run" if using the word.'[54]

The mounted divisions also rehearsed their role in the next big push: the exploitation of the extreme left of the Turkish front. They repeatedly rode to Beersheba, departing in the afternoon and arriving at dawn. The troopers during the heat of the day then conducted exercises and familiarized themselves with the ground over which they would attack. After completing this stunt, they returned to their base, hollow-eyed with exhaustion, filthy, and thirsty after a round trip of between sixty and seventy miles. Each trooper carried one quart of water, which he could replenish only once during this ordeal of some thirty-six hours.[55]

Mounted troops also were responsible for protecting infantry officers as they scouted the left flank of the Turkish front for the forthcoming attack. 'It fell to the lot of my Squadron, among others, to provide protection and to act generally in the capacity of Messrs. Cook & Son', recalled Major Lord Hampton, a squadron commander in the Worcestershire Yeomanry, 5th Mounted Brigade, Australian Mounted Division. 'It was a curious sight. As far as the eye could see the hills were dotted with Khaki figures carrying large scale maps and getting ever closer to the white chalk lines which marked the enemy's defences. The Turks sat in rows in or around their trenches and watched the proceedings with a considerable interest but, much to my relief, attempted little retaliation.'[56]

These cavalry treks on the open plain attracted the attention of enemy aircraft. Lieutenant C.H. Perkins delayed his plans to attend Cambridge to join the Yeomanry a month after the war erupted. He described one such air attack on his Royal Bucks Hussars. 'The lack of anti-aircraft guns was also unpleasant when the dust of the cavalry movement into "no man's land" prompted the appearance of Fritz in his German Taube planes', he recalled. 'They were clever to fly up and down for quite a time before dropping a bomb at intervals on the extended column of troops at "walk march" pace. One or two troops in the column would dismount and fire rifle volleys at the face in the cockpit with apparently no result, and I must say it was somewhat hard not to duck one's head as he came over.'[57] Another response by horse soldiers to this threat from the sky was to march in small irregular groups known as 'aeroplane formations'.

The intense heat, dust, scorpions, flies and lice made life miserable for most soldiers. The crash programme in desert and mobile warfare, which included night marches and early morning assaults, also took its toll on the men's morale. Many longed for home and civilian life. L.G. Moore, 2/15th London Regiment (Civil Service Rifles), 179th Brigade, 60th Division, wrote to his family: 'I wonder if the people at home ever realise what a glorious country England is? When you've seen nothing but sand and soldiers and sun for weeks you *do* get "fed-up" and long for the green fields and trees and even *rain* of Blighty. There is roughly about a day's march between each tree here and *they* aren't worth looking at.'[58] Moore never saw home or 'Blighty' again. He was killed on December 27 1917.

After a strenuous march in full pack, Calcutt was moved to denounce 'all politicians and war mongers' to an apparently appreciative audience. 'General approval of the denunciations', his diary entry reads. 'Papers full of articles showing up home grousers as compared with the cheerful Tommy. This is very skilful on the part of the Press.'[59] Calcutt was also unimpressed with a pep talk given by Major General J.S.M. Shea, an Irishman of energy and drive, who had been hand-picked by Allenby to command the 60th Division. Shea proved to be a fearless and first-rate commander who stayed close to the action, but Calcutt was unmoved by his oratorical efforts to 'gin' up his unit. On October 11, Calcutt stood at attention in his tunic. He had a 'dressed up feeling reminiscent of going to Church in a velveteen suit in boyhood days. We may look very clean but are really very sweaty and dirty.' After inspecting the troops, Shea said, 'Gather round me, gather round me – never mind any formation, just gather round.' In Calcutt's view, he then laid:

> 'it on with a trowel'. A whole lot of fulsome rubbish about what a fine lot of men he could see we were, full of determination, something about undying honour and glory, splendid regiment, how he loved us (he actually said this), how we were the division going into the worst part of the whole attack and how proud we should be, how it would be no picnic, and how when we were ready to drop we should think of our fine First Battalion and then stick it. He was sure we were cheerful and gave ready obedience to our Officers and finally with a choking voice, congratulated Gordon Clark on having such men under him.

Shea's speech was favourably received by most men, but Calcutt had had his fill of army discipline. 'The reality, of course, is that the men are horribly fed up', he wrote in his diary, 'not by hardships and fighting, but by the silly kidish mucking about on the part of the purile minded incompetents that pass for Officers (Quite good chaps really) and the nagging of the N.C.O.s who treat the men as if they were kids in a kindergarten school. I guarantee they do more damage to "morale" than anything the enemy has ever done.'[60]

Some soldiers didn't have the intensive training of the men of the 60th Division, but many were still being stretched to the breaking point by endless fatigues and drill. This was especially true in the ranks in the RFA. 'Harness cleaning every day, and the harness is getting worse instead of better, the men have to do transport and fatigues', a frustrated James C. Jones, 1/2nd Lowland Brigade, RFA, 52nd (Lowland) Division, wrote in his diary, 'and are expected to clean harness too, it's impossible to get it cleaned... I'm absolutely fed up, being kicked about from pillar to post; out on transport all day and on duty at night, and running a sub-section in the bargain, it's impossible for any man to do it; the least thing and we are put under arrest.'[61] The nineteen-year-old Jones seriously considered taking a drop in rank to private to escape the pressure.

The EEF's leadership also resorted to trench raids to keep their forces battle ready during this period of stalemate. Both the infantry and cavalry were used in these stunts. A.S. Benbow, 9th Company, Imperial Camel Brigade, provided a description of a raid on the Sana Redoubt in August that reflected the meticulous preparation for some of these raids to assure their success and to limit casualties. The British used aerial reconnaissance to build an exact replica of the Sana Redoubt. Benbow's unit then made repeated assaults against this position in darkness until they knew 'the layout almost perfectly'. Before the assault, Benbow blackened his face and, for identification purposes, he had a white pyramid-shaped piece of cloth sewn to the back of his tunic and broad white bands attached to his arms. Men in the first wave carried balls of string to guide those who followed them. Each man also received chewing gum and black tennis shoes. The chewing gum's purpose was something of a mystery. Some thought it was intended to keep their jaws from 'vibrating with terror'; others believed that it was to keep them from whispering or talking. Although the black tennis shoes proved a failure because the men advanced over dry and brittle patches of scrub that crackled under their feet, the attack was a complete success.[62]

Strict discipline, rigorous training, and trench raids during the last half of 1917 prepared the EEF for the difficult campaign ahead. But senior officers had to use the velvet glove as well as the mailed fist to nourish the Eastern Force's wounded spirits after its two unsuccessful attempts to take Gaza. Although distance and limited shipping made home leave virtually unobtainable, soldiers still needed to escape the war, if only for a few days. 'One can hardly describe the joys of being let loose after all these months of toil and hardships from almost a prison life when one's life & soul were not one's own',[63] wrote W.N. Hendry, 2/14th Regiment (London Scottish), 179th Brigade, 60th Division.

Major Arthur Frederick Stanley Clarke, 1/10th London Regiment, 162nd Brigade, 54th Division, remembers a visit that Allenby paid his brigade. As the commander in chief was about to depart, he commented to Major General S.W. Hare that the men looked fit but tired. The following exchange ensued:

> 'They have had no leave for over a year, Sir,' answered our General Hare.
> Explosion 'Why?'
> 'Not allowed by G.H.Q., Sir.'
> 'Oh!' Explosion finished.[64]

A week later, Clarke and his men were sent to a holiday camp on the sea.

Many soldiers could not afford a visit to Cairo or other Egyptian cities, so holiday camps had been established on the seacoast where it was possible for men to have their clothes fumigated and cleaned. For the first time in weeks, many soldiers also enjoyed feeling really clean because of ready access to the sea. Private John Bateman Beer, 2/22nd London Regiment, 181st Brigade, 60th Division, spent several days on what he called the 'Palestine Riveria', and he reported his experience in glowing terms to his mother and father. He delighted in the simple creature comforts that service in Palestine had denied him.

He was given a pair of pyjamas and a blanket and allowed to 'lounge about at one's leisure & it was quite a treat to go to bed in pyjamas in a Bell Tent near the sea… a tent nowadays being quite a high form of living, especially after living out in the open, in the desert with a shortage of water, this was just what was needed'. Although he ate army rations, it was 'served in Dining Hall with tables to eat our food from'. There was also 'a band to play to us during the day & evening, and also concert parties to entertain us. A library is at our disposal & bathing ad-lib.'[65] Such amenities represented heaven for a Tommy serving in Palestine.

Blaser fondly recalled the boyish games he played in the ocean. 'Bathing parades morning and evening were the order of the day', he wrote, 'when the whole Battalion would be in the water at once. Several cliques were formed, which waged an aquatic war against each other, the supreme sacrifice being made when one of the "enemy," approaching you from the rear or from below the surface, succeeded in giving you a severe ducking.'[66] Music and sports also provided some release from the monotony, work parties, and petty details of military life. Every brigade had a band. 'In the evening Rumsey & I make café au lait, smoke cigarettes, and lay on our backs under a tropical sky, Egyptian crescent moon and clear twinkling stars and listen to the Brigade band play Gilbert and Sullivan',[67] Calcutt wrote about one of his lighter moments. Divisional concert parties modelled themselves after music hall acts, featuring sketches and songs.

The 60th Division had the famous 'Roosters' and the 53rd Division, 'The Rare Welsh Bits'. The 54th's Divisional concert party debuted with a revue entitled 'The Fair Maid of Gaza', a parody on the opera *Sampson and Delilah*. Men took the role of women and dressed accordingly. The heroine's black silk stockings in *Sampson and Delilah* created, according to one observer, 'quite a stir'. 'Miss Woodin', of the 'Tanks' of the Middlesex Yeomanry, with his 'excellent and realistic make-up and truly feminine voice and mannerisms', was also a favourite.

Audience participation enlivened these concerts. Soldiers were frequently encouraged to sing along. The humour in the sketches, frequently irreverent and earthy, usually focused on the trials and tribulations facing ordinary soldiers. Men made fun of their officers and authority in general. The 'Tanks' performed a skit, 'The Trial of Private Curricomb', which lampooned regimental routine and the orderly room. The villain in the 54th Divisional concert was an assistant provost marshal. The audience joined in with catcalls, whistles, and cheers.[68]

The army provided other amusements for the soldiers, but often they had a purpose. This was especially true of sports that stressed competition and unit cohesion; tug-of-war, boxing, wrestling on horses and camels, rugby, soccer. The infantry played football wherever they fought in the First World War, from France to Mesopotamia to Palestine. This game was hugely popular with both players and spectators. But there were times in Palestine when the troops were just too exhausted to enjoy themselves. 'Troops being forcibly fed with football, and *have* to play', Calcutt recorded in his diary. 'After being out all night and only just returned. They wangle out of it. Football mad.'[69] Other contests, such as officers' donkey races and 'bint' races with soldiers dressed in feminine attire, provided comic relief.

Mounted troops enjoyed racing their horses and even camels. Large crowds attended these affairs, held on racecourses built behind the front. Betting was the great attraction. According to Bluett, 'there was even a totalisator for those, which meant everybody who could obtain an advance on his pay-book, who liked what is called in racing circles "a flutter"; and there were always several amateur "bookies" as well'.[70]

Despite these amusements for the troops, the realities of war were never distant. For its next great battle, the British force went through yet another reorganization. Allenby replaced the Eastern Force in August with three corps: the Desert Mounted Corps, commanded by Chauvel and made up of mounted forces; the XX Corps, commanded by Chetwode and composed of the 10th (Irish) Division, the 53rd (Welsh) Division, the 60th (London) Division, and the 74th (Yeomanry) Division; and the XXI Corps, commanded by Lieutenant General Edward Bulfin and made up of the 52nd (Lowland) Division, the 54th (East Anglian) Division, and the 75th Division, which was built from scratch in Egypt and was not complete until October. All of these troops, with the exception of the 10th, which was made up of both Regular and New Army, were either Territorial or Colonial.

Besides numbers, the War Office strengthened Allenby's forces in two other important ways: air power and artillery. Turkish domination of the air had been ended in the autumn when Allenby received a substantial number of Bristol fighters. Mastery of the air helped make it possible for Allenby to surprise the Turks at 3rd Gaza. And his additional artillery, which included a substantial increase in heavy pieces, gave him a total of 475 guns to the enemy's 300. His force of roughly 75,000 rifles and 17,000 sabres on the eve of 3rd Gaza increased the odds in his favour even more.[71] According to a recent reassessment of Turkish manpower, the Turks, depleted by sickness, may have had as few as 20,000 men along their whole front, giving the British an overwhelming advantage.[72]

Allenby thus had advantages possessed by no British general in France: a massive superiority in men and material, and an open flank to attack. Rather than repeat a frontal attack against Gaza, he embraced a plan formulated by Chetwode and Dawnay. In simple terms, it called for a holding attack on Gaza by the XXI Corps that emphasized artillery, with the primary thrust coming from the Desert Mounted Corps and the XX Corps against the Turkish left at Beersheba. After Beersheba's capture, the British hoped to roll up the Turkish left as it advanced north from Beersheba toward Gaza.[73]

Allenby emphasized deception and surprise. When his infantry deployed for the offensive, they left their camps intact to make any Turkish airman believe that they were still occupied. The intelligence officer Richard Meinertzhagen carried out the most successful deception to mask the EEF's intentions. On October 10, he made the following entry in his diary:

Spent today in deceiving the enemy. I have been busy lately compiling a dummy Staff Officer's notebook containing all sorts of nonsense about our plans and difficulties. Today I took it out to the country north-west of Beersheba with a view to passing it on to the enemy without exciting suspicion. After crossing the Wadi Ghuzzee I went in a north-westerly direction towards Sheria. I was well mounted and near Girheir I found a Turkish patrol who at once gave chase. I galloped away for a mile or so and then they pulled up, so I stopped, dismounted and had a shot at them at about 600 yards. That was too much for them and they at once resumed the chase, blazing away harmlessly all the time. Now was my chance, and in my effort to mount I loosened my haversack, field-glasses, water-bottle, dropped my rifle, previously stained with some fresh blood from my horse, and in fact did everything to make them believe I was hit and that my flight was disorderly.[74]

This ruse apparently worked, and the Turks were led to believe that the British planned to concentrate on Gaza.

Bayonets were sharpened and hair cut short as the day for the offensive approached. Calcutt got what he termed a 'Beersheba' hair-cut. 'All off. Look a murderous villain now', he noted in his diary. His kit for the assault included one extra water bottle, one gas mask, one telescopic sight in case, one bivy sheet, one pole, three pegs, two sandbags, 130 rounds of ammunition, one rifle, one tunic, one shirt, one cap comforter, one cardigan, two pairs of socks, one holdall and contents, emergency rations of bully beef and biscuits, rations for the day, and a mess tin. His private belongings, which included his diary, went into his gas helmet satchel. His bivy, or bivouac, was new issue and proved to be invaluable during the winter advance on Jerusalem. It consisted of a waterproof cloth about five feet six inches square. Buttons and buttonholes made it possible to fasten two squares together, creating a cramped shelter for two men.

Calcutt's 60th Division was part of the XX Corps on the Turkish left flank. Its training for open warfare resembled the training British soldiers had received before trench warfare had become the norm on the western front. Calcutt and his comrades had been taught to advance steadily in waves through shell and shot until held up by the enemy's fire; a firing line would then be built up as a prelude for the final assault. In Calcutt's words, the first wave would engage 'the enemy with Rifle, Lewis Gun, & Machine gun fire. The assault-ing parties to get within 500 yards. Smoke cloud then starts and 10 minutes afterwards heavy artillery which will last for 10 minutes.

Assault will take place under cover of heavy bombardment and machine gun barrage fire. Reorganise and consolidate.'[75]

Soldiers reacted in different ways to the prospect of resuming the offensive. When Blunt learned that his platoon was in the first wave, he gloomily noted in his diary: 'Looks as if we shall cop it on the actual day.'[76] On the other hand, Sergeant A.V. Young, who came from a soldier's family, was gung ho. 'Our Battn [2/17th London Regiment (Poplar and Stepney), 180th Brigade, 60th Division] is at last to be tried in open warfare, for the Turk is more likely to be licked by the bayonet than anything else', he wrote in his diary. 'We are to turn him out. For months we have had all trench warfare. The keenness for fighting returns, the fed-upness goes for all are eager for the fight. I have no thought of fear, only curiosity as to what hand to hand fighting will be like.'[77]

The British now had ample artillery and shells to support the infantry, especially against the Turkish fortifications at Gaza. The XXI Corps, given the role of pinning down the Turks at Gaza, had sixty-eight medium or heavy guns and howitzers for counterbattery work, or one to every sixty yards of the area to be assaulted, the same ratio that the British had on the Somme in July 1916. British and French naval guns, which included one 14-inch and two 10.8-inch guns, added to the weight of this tremendous bombardment. It was going to be the largest conducted during the war outside the European theatre.[78]

RFA officer Major Bailey, the aide de camp to Brigadier General G.W. Bildulph, CRA, 54th Division, helped prepare the schedule for the XXI Corps's preliminary bombardment. 'We are arranging our six days programme so that the whole of the front of our group is plastered all day and every day', he noted in his diary:

> Each Battery is allotted certain 1000 yd squares in which they are to engage targets at certain hours. Each battery is allotted those squares – within which are its bombardment targets in the final assault, in order that Registration of Targets may be perfected during the 6 days. Each Battery is also given certain hours each day and each night during which it will not fire, and during which its personnel *must* rest.

As well as the day programme, I am working out night firing orders
for each Battery for each night of the six days.[79]

A tremendous thunderstorm accompanied this merciless torrent of
steel and explosives on 'X-6 Day', October 27, the day the preliminary bombardment of the Gaza defences began. 'The heat was
tremendous and the wet awful', Bailey continued in his diary, 'and at
the batteries most of the gunners served their guns during the night
firing, clad only in towels.'[80]

A storm of a different kind awaited the Turkish defenders of
Beersheba, a force roughly the equivalent of a full-strength British
brigade (4,400 riflemen). The offensive against this town with its
precious supply of water had been set for October 31. In the days
just before this date, the plain across from the enemy's front had
been a beehive of activity at night. The mounted troops and infantry
moving south heard the rumbling and over their left shoulders could
see the flickering flashes of the big guns bombarding Gaza.

A compass and carefully placed lanterns provided directions. To
change directions, the directing flank of a brigade marched to a
lantern that had been positioned during daylight. The brigade then
halted until another lantern was placed and lit on its outer flank.
Once the brigade had been squared up between the two lanterns,
it was pointed in the right direction.[81] In daylight, troops hid themselves in the beds of the wadis. To prevent the zinc or copper water
tanks carried by the camels from glinting in the sun, they were
wrapped in blankets. The staff's meticulous attention to detail meant
that the concentration of the XX Corps and the Desert Mounted
Corps on the Turkish left went off almost without a hitch.

6

Breakout

On October 30, Blunt of the Civil Service Rifles and Calcutt of the Queen's Westminster Rifles, 179th Brigade, 60th Division, prepared for the final approach march to Beersheba. Their route took them across a wilderness of bare, rocky hills and numerous wadis. Allenby wanted the 60th Division, in league with the 74th Division, to pin down the Turks in the south-west defences of Beersheba while mounted forces stormed the town on its eastern side. Calcutt and Blunt were given tea and rum for the following day and their final haversack rations: five onions, one tin of bully, a slice of cooked bacon, some dates, and biscuits. They moved out after the sun set, which was quite early in the Palestinian winter, about 5p.m.

'We have orders read out to us and wait by the route to fall in in our place', Calcutt recorded in his diary. 'Miles of troops, and guns and horses and donkeys and camels and cavalry and limbers and luggage and weird shaped things of unknown purpose file by. The London Scottish with fixed bayonets. All trailing along in the dust towards one spot. Horses struggling with guns and blowing. Poor Tommy ladened up like a camel himself yet found time to pity the poor fucking horses.'[1]

Turkish snipers welcomed Blunt's battalion when it reached its deployment point, some 2,000 to 2,500 yards from the enemy's earthworks. Blunt, who had enlisted in March 1917, experienced his first shots fired in anger. 'Here we got our baptism of fire and a taste of fighting, wind up', Blunt wrote in his diary. 'Rifle fire opened up and enfiladed us from neighbouring hills. It was a rather terrifying experience in the dark hearing bullets whizzing about all over the place with no idea from where they came... The numerous little wadis and gullies made excellent cover and we were able to lay down and await the dawn in comparative safety. In spite of the rifle fire I managed to get a hour's sleep. Oh how I awaited the light of dawn – thinking, wondering and praying.'[2]

After a chilly night, the morning broke hot and airless. To neutralize the enemy's artillery and soften up his defences, the British had 116 artillery pieces along a front of some three miles, a much smaller concentration of artillery than at Gaza. Gunners had spent the night sandbagging their positions. H.J. Earney, a signaller with the 9th Mountain Brigade, RGA, XX Corps, worked frantically to dig a dugout and arrange sandbags. 'Never before had I felt so tired as I did at that time, yet my mind was alert and all through the day the same condition prevailed', he noted in his diary:

> I sat in the dugout, Hqrs telephone strapped to my ear and we waited for the signal to begin. We had not long to wait. The battery opened fire with ranging shots registering targets. A field battery just behind us also opened up, as also did several btys around. Every time a gun was fired a piece of our dug-out would fall in, usually down the back of the neck. Bullets whistled over the top of the dug-out and an occasional shrapnel burst unpleasantly near. At noon, all batteries having registered targets the signal for the bombardment was given. *Then* we heard the music of the guns. It was great – for us, but I guess not so for 'Johnnie.'[3]

Blunt, who anxiously waited throughout the morning to go 'over the top', observed with fascination the work of British gunners. His battalion could not advance until the commanding Hill 1070, which extended in front of the enemy's primary defensive position, had fallen. 'All the morning we were deafened by heavy artillery fire. It was intense and especially our bombardment of Hill 1070', he observed. 'We appeared to have a great superiority over the Turks in heavy guns. Our London Scottish machine gunners were putting up a good show over the near ridges, with their Lewis guns.' As he lay on the ground under the boiling sun, Blunt asked himself if he were frightened. He could not give a proper answer. 'All I knew', he reflected, 'was that over the ridge in front of us were the Turkish lines and these had to be taken.'[4]

During the preliminary bombardment, Calcutt's company took cover in a gully fronting a British battery where Turkish counter-battery work soon placed him in danger. His diary entry for this day is tinged with panic. 'High explosive is bursting between us and the guns. Shrapnel comes over. Bursts above us and rains down on us. Steady stream of wounds. Young Morrison, elbow. Brown, arm. Low, head, and so on and so on. We ought to move back to our old position. Stupid to be in front of these guns which are banging away all the time, kicking up hells delight, and drawing fire which we are a catching.'

Calcutt soon embraced the hard, stony ground even more tightly. British rather than Turkish guns now threatened him:

Our guns give a bang followed by another and we are smothered with flying bits. A PREMATURE BURST from our guns 200 yards away. Cries of that's got us. Several casualties. One fellow (Rogers) jaw all blown to fragments. Blood spurting from nose. Gives one or two heaves. Is bound up but expires and is carried away. High explosive bursting lower down near the guns does not get them and they continue to bark in our ears. We [are] getting not only the report but the hungry rasp of the flame. Ground and stones and tunics spattered with blood but we still stay in front of the guns! I take cover behind my spare water bottle and gas helmet so far as head is concerned...We wonder how things are going. We have heard the bombardment and the machine guns, and the Stokes gun barrage of ten minutes which was to precede the assault by the 15th and 14th so presumably the dominating hill on our left, Hill 1070, has come off all right. It is now about 12 o'clock.[5]

Fifteen minutes later, Blunt went over the top with the Civil Service Rifles.

I was in the front of the first assaulting wave as platoon runner to Sergeant Boasted. We were in a little wadi behind a ridge. It was necessary to get over the ridge, and off the skyline as quickly as possible. Once over the ridge it was a rush down the valley and a charge up the opposite ridge where the Turkish trenches were at the top. Over the ridge I noticed at once that there were scattered groups of machine gunners... in emplacements of rocks and shallow trench. They were out there to keep a protecting fire on the Turkish trenches. To me they seemed to be right in the open and in suicide position. They had been out there since early morning and had suffered many casualties. I felt they had been real heroes. Once over the ridge we all rushed down the slope past the machine gunners. Bullets were falling everywhere. Several of our lads were hit and I noticed one or two bowled over. In the excitement I didn't have the 'wind up' one little bit. I just went on running, yelling, cheering and shouting out the Sergeant's orders at the top of my voice. Every minute I was expecting a bullet to get me but my good luck stuck to me. I did get my rifle and a finger grazed with a bullet but nothing more serious. When we got to the Turkish trenches we jumped straight in and shot or bayoneted or took prisoner all that were there. I was lucky, the section of trench I jumped in was empty. On either side I could hear shooting and fighting but it was soon all over... We advanced about 300 yards beyond the trenches where we worked 'like hell' with our entrenching tools digging ourselves in.[6]

With the Turkish guns silenced, Blunt and his buddies searched for war souvenirs and plundered the Turkish quartermaster stores to put together an acceptable meal, quenching their thirst with hot cocoa. Blunt wrapped himself in captured Turkish overcoats that evening, grateful and somewhat surprised to be alive, and slept soundly.

By 1:30p.m., the entire Turkish position between the Khalasa road and the Wadi Saba had been taken. Losses had been modest – 136 killed, 1,010 wounded. The British had the advantage in men and firepower, and the Turkish defences had been thinly manned and poorly wired. Nonetheless, the capture of the Turkish trenches represented a considerable accomplishment for the waves of assaulting infantry from the 60th and 74th divisions who advanced across open ground against modern weaponry. It was not a case of the artillery rather than the infantry conquering the enemy's defences. The artillery's support had been a fraction of what was thought necessary to breach German lines in France.

Captain Case, whose Royal Engineers unit had been renamed the 522nd London Field Company in February 1917, later pondered what led his fellow citizen soldiers to advance over open ground against artillery and machine guns. 'Few of the people concerned have any say in regard to the instructions which they may receive; instructions which may be a matter of life or death to the recipients', he wrote in his diary. 'Life in the army is full of strange puzzles. What man is there alive who will not exert every effort of body and mind to prevent himself being killed by force, and yet nearly every one of these men will obediently and deliberately walk forward into what, in some cases, seems almost certain death or mutilation.'[7] Case had no answer to this rhetorical query.

As Johnny Turk fell back to Beersheba, the infantry did not pursue him, although the official British history claims that the XX Corps could have 'without doubt' captured the town if that had been its assignment.[8] The honour and the glory of securing the town went to the 4th Australian Light Horse in a cavalry charge that in notoriety ranks with the charge of the Light Brigade at Balaklava in 1854.[9] This gallant Australian charge provokes almost as many questions as it had participants. Two points of contention concern the orders for the attack and the decision to deploy mounted troops.

Beginning on October 30, the Desert Mounted Corps had swung wide to the east of Beersheba to position itself at the rear of that town's defences. Its approach to the town had been held up by a stout Turkish defence from a large flat-topped mound called Tell es Sabe. This position finally fell around three o'clock in the afternoon. But the precious wells of Beersheba still remained in Turkish hands, and time was running out because the sun would soon set.

Allenby, who had joined Chetwode at the headquarters of the XX Corps, stayed in touch by telegram with Chauvel, the commander of the Desert Mounted Corps. He feared a repeat of the first battle to take Gaza when the British had withdrawn with victory in their grasp, so he firmly reminded Chauvel of the obvious: 'The Chief orders you to capture Beersheba today, in order to secure water and prisoners.' H.S. Gullett, the author of the Australian official history, argues that this order was quite unnecessary and resulted from a misunderstanding. In reply to a question from Allenby's headquarters concerning the watering of his horses if the wells of Beersheba were unavailable, Chauvel had suggested that he would withdraw his horses to Bir Arara and Wadi el Imshash if Beersheba was not in his hands by nightfall.[10] Allenby, not surprisingly, interpreted this to mean that Chauvel was considering withdrawing, and his peremptory order may have been both necessary and responsible for the cavalry charge.

There are several versions of what happened next. Two mounted brigades in reserve were in position to attack, a Yeomanry brigade, the 5th Mounted, commanded by Brigadier General P.D. Fitzgerald, and an Australian brigade, the 4th Light Horse Brigade, commanded by Brigadier General W. Grant. Although both Grant and Fitzgerald vigorously argued their case in a 'brief but tense discussion', Chauvel chose the Australians, with the Yeomanry relegated to a supporting role. 'If I did ever favour the light horse', Chauvel later admitted, 'it was at Beersheba.'[11]

The Australian official history says that Chauvel told Major General H.W. Hodgson, the British commander of the Australian Mounted Division, which included the Yeomanry 5th Mounted and the 4th Australian Light Horse, to secure Beersheba immediately. His exact words to Hodgson are alleged to have been, 'Put Grant straight at it.' The official record, however, includes only a message from Chauvel to Hodgson ordering him to attack with Grant's brigade, leaving unsaid whether the assault was to be mounted or dismounted. Chauvel himself insists that he gave no personal orders to Brigadier General Grant, the commander of the 4th Light Horse Brigade. Grant, however, claims that Hodgson took him to Chauvel, who personally ordered him to 'take the town before dark'. According to Grant, he alone decided on a cavalry charge.[12]

None of the existing versions of the order to gallop the Turkish defences of Gaza has used Hodgson's account. In planning the

Beersheba operation, Hodgson had anticipated that mounted action in certain circumstances might be justified. His British formations were armed with swords, but the Australian mounted brigades, really mounted infantry, had only bayonets. Hodgson ordered the points of these long-bladed 1907 pattern bayonets sharpened, believing that when held aloft, the glint of the sun on them would be as menacing as any sword.[13] When he received Allenby's order through Chauvel, Hodgson says that:

> ...it was late in the day, and the C in C had ordered the place to be taken at all costs that evening, and I was given the job. A dismounted attack on the place would have been a long job, the light was going, so I decided to gallop it – and sent the leading bde at it in four lines, with a second bde to support them – it was a bit of a risk and I was anxious about it. I could see the trenches full of Turks all round the town at 1000 yards or so from it, but there was no wire that we knew of, aeroplane photos had shown none – it was a splendid sight to see the first bde move out from the hills in column, cross a wadi, deploy the other side and gallop across the plain straight on the town.[14]

This suggests that Hodgson – rather than Chauvel or Grant – was responsible for the audacious decision to mount a cavalry charge against entrenched forces equipped with artillery and machine guns. Of course, it almost goes without saying that if the cavalry charge had been a bloody disaster, there would be few, if any, claimants for the decision to use mounted troops.

A vivid picture of the charge is given by Lieutenant Colonel R.M.P. Preston:

> It was growing dark, and the enemy trenches were outlined in fire by the flashes of their rifles. Beyond, and a little above them, blazed the bigger, deeper flashes of their field guns, and our own shells burst like a row of red stars over the Turkish positions. In front the long lines of cavalry swept forward at racing speed, half obscured in clouds of reddish dust. Amid the deafening noise all around, they seemed to move silently, like some splendid, swift machine. Over the Turks they

went, leaping the two lines of deep trenches, and, dismounting on the farther side, flung themselves into the trenches with the bayonet.[15]

With some 800 men involved directly in this charge, the casualties were amazingly light – thirty-one killed and thirty-six wounded. Savage hand-to-hand combat in the trenches accounted for most of the dead.

The elation that some felt after the capture of Beersheba did not last long. A diet of iron rations and a shortage of water, made worse when a strong Khamsin developed, inflicted intense suffering on the troops. 'Violent wind blowing clouds of dust. Every body *is pretty irritable*', Calcutt grumbled. 'The Fatigues keep pin pricking the troops. There was no delirious joy over the capture of Beersheba as one might expect over something achieved for which one was prepared to die, but just thankfulness that they at any rate are still alive.'[16] Blunt's entry in his diary for the same day mirrored Calcutt's misery: 'All feeling very fed up. Water still very scarce – we were almost "dying" from thirst. Had no hot tea today.'[17]

Beersheba itself proved to be a disappointment to the troops. From a distance, they saw white buildings and minarets shimmering in the sun. Up close, the reality was quite different. 'We had expected to see some sort of town', Private E.C. Powell, 179th Light Trench Mortar Battery, 60th Division, remembered, 'but apart from a few stone buildings which had been occupied by Turkish officials, it consisted merely of a miserable collection of hovels – no vegetation, just brown earth and choking heat.'[18]

Beersheba and the surrounding area became a beehive of activity as the high command consolidated its position and realigned its units to make a move to the north and north-west. 'All bustle and hustle with the Military', Calcutt observed. 'Natives rounded up with their donkeys and camels, all bedraggled (their usual appearance). Camels unshaved and carrying stone jars of water in slings. Military Police on horseback at work on the populace. Red Cross cars parked after their activity with the human scraps. Armoured cars cleaning their guns. Transport dashing about over the heaps and mounds of fodder. Camels with fanatis, aeroplanes flying low over the place. Wrecked pumping station at work… Cavalry details passing and repassing.'[19]

Allenby now had his eye on Sheria. To keep the Turks from reinforcing this centrally fortified position on the Gaza-Beersheba front, he had scheduled an infantry assault on Gaza supported by a tremendous bombardment. Ali Muntar received special attention. Captain N.E. Drury, 6th Royal Dublin Fusiliers, 30th Brigade, 10th (Irish) Division, who inspected this Turk stronghold after the fall of Gaza, described it thus: 'the whole place looked as if a volcano had tried to burst it up. Huge naval shells had burrowed yards deep in the sandy soil, and, on bursting had made holes big enough to put a horse into.'[20]

To reduce casualties in a frontal assault against fortress Gaza, the high command planned a night attack on a narrow front across the heavy sand of the coastal region. The offensive proceeded in two stages. The first assault came at 11p.m. on November 1, the second at 3a.m. on November 2. Lance-Corporal R. Loudon, a signaller with the 1/4th Royal Scots, 156th Brigade, 52nd Division, was in the second attack, the objective being the El Arish Redoubt. The usual tot of rum was issued before the assault. 'I didn't take any', Loudon remembered:

A man who obviously had been able to get more than his allowance started singing loudly, and was removed. We then set off in a long line, and passed through our front line trenches into 'No-Man's-Land.' I saw a man breaking the ranks, and dodging back towards our lines, obviously his nerves having given way. An N.C.O. dashed out, got hold of him, and took him away. I was with Hq. sigs. in the 'fourth wave.' Four parallel lines of white tape had been laid out, and I and the others spaced ourselves out along the fourth tape, and lay down, facing the enemy lines, to await the signal to advance. Two tanks came rumbling up from behind, and a few of us had to jump up and get out of the way to let them pass… Our shelling increased in volume, and at 3a.m. the 4th R.S. advanced in four lines on a front of 300 yards towards the El Arish Redoubt. Two Turkish contact mines exploded as our 'first wave' approached the redoubt, blowing many of the men to pieces. We were not, of course, aware of this at the time. As I got near the Turkish trenches the enemy shell and machine-gun fire became so intense, with shells bursting all around, that I and several others decided to stop in a large shell or mine crater for a few minutes till the shelling eased somewhat. When the barrage moved forward we resumed our advance.[21]

This skilfully executed operation by XXI Corps achieved its objectives with a loss of about 350 killed, 350 missing, and 2,000 wounded. The objectives had been intentionally limited. 'This did not carry us right through the enemy's line—we could not have done that in one rush with what we had available in front of Gaza', Brigadier General Dawnay contended at the time. 'But it gave us all the enemy's front line defensive system on the south-west side of Gaza, and threatened Ali Muntar and the rest of the defences in front of the town.'[22]

After the XXI Corps's attack at Gaza, the focus of the offensive returned to the right flank, where the high command waged war with the boots of its infantry, realigning divisions for an attack against the Sheria position. While on the march, Major Vivian Gilbert's 180th Brigade, 60th Division, lost touch with its camel water convoy. 'Our heads ached and our eyes became bloodshot and dim in the blinding glare reflected from the sand', he recalled. 'After a time our tongues began to swell so that they seemed to fill the insides of our mouths, which had gone dry. It was with difficulty that we could speak. Then our lips commenced to swell; they turned a purplish black and burst; sand blew in the open cuts and flies persistently settled on the wounds, driving us almost mad.' To drop out of the march might mean death. 'Some of the men went temporarily blind from the glare of the sun, the sand, and the lack of water; a few fell out by the wayside, and these we never saw again', Gilbert continued. 'I had previously warned my company that it would be impossible to leave anyone behind to look after stragglers, and so the blinded men linked arms with others not as badly affected as themselves, and by this means managed to keep up with the column.'[23]

Dust rather than sand dogged Calcutt's every step. 'Spend a day of thirst. The most depressing country conceivable. In formation not unlike the downs round Winchester but *unrelieved dust colour,* not a speck of green or a sign of habitation. Perfectly barren. Up hill and down dale and across Waddies we go. Clouds of dust inconceivable. So dense that you instinctively close on the man in front of you in order not to lose sight of him. Could not see your own feet, or where you were putting them down. That was the worst', he muttered. 'In the main, a man was just discernable at ten paces by peering. In the dust go camels, pack mules, limbers, wagons, artillery, and all the rattling paraphernalia of War.'[24]

Calcutt's 60th Division marched from the south-east to the north-west in an attempt to overcome the Turkish defenders of Sheria in enfilade. On November 5, Chetwode issued the following order to his division commanders: 'The attack must be pressed with the utmost rapidity and determination, as the enemy must be given no respite until his resistance is broken down, and it is essential to secure the water at Sheria before nightfall.'[25] On this day, the 60th Division took its place in the line between the 74th on its right and the 10th on its left. Its assignment was to capture the Qawuqa system of trenches and then join the 74th in securing the higher ground to the north to protect the water supply of Sheria.

Two participants, Calcutt and E.C. Powell, who served in a light trench mortar company, provided an intimate glimpse of the 60th Division's assault on November 6. Calcutt awoke at 1a.m. on November 6. 'Tea. Parade as usual. Right dress, etc. You note all these little things when they may be for the last time... There is a bombardment on all around about two miles away. We are to march two miles, but it seems a very doubtful two miles as it is dawn by the time we arrive. Hope the 1000 yards we have to do under machine gun and rifle fire bears a better resemblance to 1000 yards than this march does to two miles.' At the assembly point, he ate biscuits and dates but was not allowed to drink anything:

> No drinking allowed except by order of an Officer. We have a cool young Officer, very capable. Sit in artillery formation listening to the other attacks proceeding at other parts of the line and wait our time... Eventually it comes (at 8.30 about) and we advance over more open ground (undulating) to the place of deployment. The surroundings are

filled in by our guns, all placed and ready, mules, horses and camels relieved of their stuff and picqueted... Troops advancing in artillery formation on either side and we keep in touch with them.[26]

Calcutt and Powell had been given the most current British training in tactics, as his mention of 'artillery formation' suggests. Because of lessons learned in previous frontal attacks against a dug-in and wired enemy, soldiers were trained to advance single file in platoons and sections as they closed with the enemy, the so-called artillery formation. In some circumstances, men were organized into 'blobs' (informal section groups or platoons) rather than in line. Blobs could change direction with greater facility than either the line or column. At close range, they changed to an extended order of waves, with precise distances between each man in line and each wave.[27]

Gunner E.C. Powell, who had been made a temporary corporal because he headed a gun team, provided an eyewitness account of these tactics at Sheria:

We now advanced in 'artillery formation'; that is, in blobs of 30 to 40 men marching in close order[,] each blob (a platoon) about a hundred yards from the others, the object being that the men can be kept under control as long as possible (one shell could wipe out only one platoon). Our party formed one blob. When they came under small arms fire the men got into extended order in a succession of waves, each man about three yards from his neighbour, and following waves at about 50 yards distance. This dispersal minimises casualties and as the leading waves get shot to pieces the gaps are filled by succeeding waves. For the final bayonet assault the front line is built up fairly densely.[28]

'Can see other platoons well in the smoke and dust', Calcutt continued in his account of the assault:

Our artillery is barking and snapping in our ears all the time and shells screeching in both directions. We crouch down as near the ground as possible (our platoon commander quite serene). I shield my head with my water bottle. My telescope sight is on, but covered up. It is getting, together with my rifle, very dirty. Mind working on all sorts of things. With a boom, whiss, snap (which you never hear when it is for *you*) one is on us and Feakes is hit in the neck. Call for Stretcher Bearers, etc. etc. Machine guns and Stokes and artillery and all going we crouch on knowing nothing of how things are going or what is over the hill. 'A' and 'C' Companies are to attack in the first wave.

From his position, Calcutt observed the gallantry of the cavalry gunners of the Royal Horse Artillery as they galloped into action. 'Unlimber and in position in a snap, but not before the shrapnel are bang, bang, bang in amongst them. Not the slightest heed did they take. Carried on as if at drill. Unharnessed horses and take them back (one loose, wounded in the leg, quite calm the horses). I am still expecting them to seek a fresh spot, when they are barking back in their turn, and eventually the Turks guns cease to fire! Magnificent.'

At around 2p.m., Calcutt's company began its assault with fixed bayonets:

We extend into open order in the shelter of the brow of the hill amid shouted orders and over we go. The sight disclosed is our front. A line of trenches on the top of a ridge and the whole line punctuated with clouds of flying earth. The barrage. Then we commence. We have ears for nothing else but the bullets and the machine guns. Our extension is 14 paces and we have to keep in line. This occupies our time. Whiss. Whiss. Whiss the bullets are flying past our heads. Shouts of 'ease off to the left' 'Ease off to the right' Do not bunch' 'Left shoulders up' and so on. A man is hit and the bullets are Zip Zip Zipping on the ground all around (no shells thank the Lord). The man is groaning. I am not excited, merely apprehensive.

Calcutt raced across a small ridge, flopped down on the other side, and was directed to shoot: 'Look through my sights, see only smoke and dust. Fire one round and decide to save the ammunition. Up and on again. Still unhit. Dash over [another small ridge]. Very puffed and hide under shelter of bank at [railway with an embankment on either side]… The other waves and lines have by this time come up and formed on line.'[29]

Powell had been assigned to Calcutt's brigade to provide a mortar barrage to destroy wire and suppress enemy machine gun fire for the final stage of the assault. After 2nd Gaza, every division had been equipped with stokes mortars. Powell and the other members of his gun team were heavily laden with a rifle and parts of the mortar. In addition, each man wore a canvas jacket with four pockets, two in front and two behind, with a shell in each. As he went over the crest of a ridge, Powell experienced a firestorm that he would never forget:

> Our own field guns and machine-guns were firing close above our heads. The noise was unbearable, beyond description; I was literally stunned by the cacophony, unable even to think clearly. In front of us was a long downward slope and then a rise towards the Turkish trenches, but these were quite blanketed in a fog of smoke and dust. The sand all over this slope was spurting up where bullets were striking it as [if] it were a hailstorm. The ground was soon dotted with prostrate figures. Everywhere men were throwing up their arms and falling, headlong, some to lie still, others to writhe and scream in agony.

Powell saw Calcutt's company pause. 'What's holding them up? I ran forward to see. Uncut wire! This is where we do our stuff. I told the fellows to set the gun up, but what was the range. How to even guess in that murk? God forbid that I should lob shells into our own men.'[30]

Calcutt described what happened next:

> The barrage still bursting on the wire and trenches 50 yards ahead. Dash over railway embankment led by Mr. Alexander, and halt in front of wire on account of barrage. High explosive and shrapnel throwing clouds of earth. Cries from the right of 'Come on it's only our barrage' (as if that made any difference). Cries from the left 'Wait till the barrage lifts.'… A minute or so after it lifted, and our Captain BRUCE was first man through the wire. I made for his gap and we

were soon in the trenches 8 feet deep and feeling quite secure. They proved to be a maze which we were ordered to scour, proceeding in various directions. I had the bayonet held out in front, loaded and finger on trigger. Dodged along, saw somebody. I started, he started, then we both smiled. It was Humphreys with bomb with the pin out working in my direction. He seemed more anxious to get rid of the bomb than anything. Round and round this Hampton Court maze of 8 foot deep trenches we went… We followed the maze till it finally sloped up and out. Company completely disorganised now. The Turks running off at the back as hard as they could… everybody very excited and all talking at once. Our shells still banging away very near. Firing with rifles and machine guns on fleeing Turks. Prisoners coming in at the point of the bayonet… lot more dugout places in a dip of the ground and every now and then the Turks dash out.

As the fighting died down, Calcutt took in his surroundings. 'Souvenir hunters at work: nasty sights. Turks with legs blown off. Just the legs and the half body and nothing else. Horrible wounds, and dead, etc. Shell holes all over the place.' After officers restored order, the troops paused to eat:

> We are eating biscuit and jam on their side of the trenches thinking the War won, when we are restored to our senses by being fallen in and marched in artillery formation forward to the afore mentioned dip. The shells are flying over at us again on this piece of ground, and we get into some of Johnnies deep trenches and lie there. Full of flies and smells. It clears off eventually and by four we are out and walking round looking at nasty things… Flies. Flies. Flies. Turkish equipment, dead horse, and muck lying in various dugouts.[31]

It had been another good day for the Territorials and reflected well on their tenacity, training and discipline. In hard fighting, the primary defences of Sheria had been overrun in a single day. Losses had been light, about 1,300, with Calcutt's 60th Division suffering only 300 casualties. The 74th, which had begun its attack in the early morning without any preliminary bombardment or barrage, had suffered more than three times as many casualties. But it too had gained its objectives. The 74th, formed from dismounted yeomanry units and whose divisional sign was a broken spur, had demonstrated its cavalry spirit with its rapid advance. The gap torn in the centre of the Turkish front on November 6 was widened the next morning when the Turkish positions at Tel esh Sheria and the Hareira Redoubt were overrun.[32]

The fight for Tel esh Sheria, an imposing 250-foot hill, proved to be especially fierce. A young lieutenant, S.J.G. Chipperfield, had led his machine gun section, 180th Machine Gun Company, 60th Division, into battle at a little after 4a.m. on November 7. While reconnoitring the Turkish position, he came under heavy fire. 'Walk across the open under shell, m.g. and rifle fire feeling so sacred that eventually begin to feel quite brave',[33] he noted in his diary. As the battle developed, Chipperfield displayed even greater valor. When the infantry was held up by intense fire, Chipperfield led his section through and took on the Turks at close range with his machine guns.

It quickly became 'a battle of Machine Guns v. Machine Guns', Major E.H. Impey, who had assumed command of the 180th Machine Gun Company after it lost its commanding officer, wrote to his father. Chipperfield and his men had no cover other than some mud brick walls, and the outcome of this duel, according to Impey, 'depended entirely on the coolness of each individual gunner'.[34] Two of Chipperfield's men were killed, another two wounded.

As the British machine guns began to prevail, ANZAC cavalrymen arrived and volunteered to gallop the enemy's trenches. Chipperfield's diary described the action:

Most of them mown down before they get near objective but about ten of them actually charge the trenches and are all scuppered except one who lies wounded just under the parapet and a sergeant and two men who manage to escape to us. Their riderless horses start grazing and gradually move towards enemy line. Turks think this is a grand chance to collect some Australian re-mounts. We think otherwise. I organize a competition between the two right-hand guns (prize 50 piastres) to see who can knock off most Turks without hitting horses.

The Turks don't get any remounts. Our artillery start shelling them and make it unpleasant for the wounded Australian. Finally it gets too hot and he makes a run for it. Turks get him with m.g. fire when is about half-way back to our lines. Padre and another fellow dash out to bring him in but are shot down.[35]

After the Turks retreated, an ANZAC officer sought out Impey to inquire about Chipperfield's name. On being told, he exclaimed: 'Well he's one of the coolest beggars I've seen yet. I'll pay for his drink. He saved all you boys (this last to the infantry). The enemy had concentrated a counter attack when Chipperfield caught them coming out of the trench.'[36]

Meanwhile, other Territorials were in action north of Beersheba in a battle that Allenby had not anticipated. The Turks drew on their reserves, which included the crack 19th Division, and threatened Beersheba from the north. Fierce fighting erupted over control of the heights of Khuweilfe, which commanded the surrounding countryside and included the best source of local water. After British aeroplanes observed the advance of these Turkish columns, the 53rd Division was ordered to link up with mounted troops operating in the direction of Khuweilfe. The 53rd advanced in three columns with M.R.L. Fleming's 160th Brigade marching across the rugged countryside of the Judean foothills. 'We wore "tin hats," and the intense heat of the sun on them made our heads feel like poached eggs', he lamented. 'The battle of Khuweilfe has been described in many narratives and dispatches, but I have never seen mentioned the appalling shortage of water from which we suffered. We had about three pints for forty-eight hours, which included a long march up the stifling, winding ravines of the Judean foothills... It was real hell.'[37]

According to Private Castle, 'D' Company, 160th Brigade, many of the marchers were 'so exhausted that they could carry on no longer'. Yet the 53rd Division immediately went into action on November 3 upon reaching Khuweilfle. 'Bullets whizzed everywhere, machine-gun clatter was deafening, while the constant roar of artillery caused an everlasting din', Castle continued in his account.

The next day [November 4] found us in still worse condition, for we were without rations or water… Despite the conditions, the general fatigue and burning thirst, our troops stormed the hills and held them, while one counter-attack after another was beaten off with grim determination. Midday arrived with its intense heat, and still we were without water, and many of our brave fellows were crying like children in their agony… After long hours with the treacherous tropical sun beating down upon us, hours that seemed interminable, slowly the sun began to set, and by this time the majority who were not unconscious were delirious.[38]

In desperation, some men sucked buttons, pebbles and even rubber bands from their helmets. Many of the wounded could not be brought in. Some of the wounded died after 'acute suffering on account of the lack of water'.[39] Water finally reached the men around 5p.m.

As the 53rd engaged the enemy during the afternoon of November 3, a Yeomanry brigade, the 5th Mounted Brigade, relieved the Australian Light Horsemen who had occupied Ras en Naqb, the high ground that protected the right flank of the infantry assaulting Khuweilfe. To reach the Australian position, the Yeomen had to advance up a valley within 800 yards of the Turks and then bear right up another valley to reach their objective. 'I shall never forget the sight as line after line of Yeomen swept up the valley at a steady canter under a hail of machine gun and rifle bullets. Whether it was our pace which put the Turkish marksmen off their aim or not I cannot say, but we managed to reach the comparative safety of the second valley with little loss',[40] Major Lord Hampton, a squadron commander in the Worcestershire Yeomanry, recalled.

The Yeomen spent the rest of the day and a restless night expecting a Turkish attack that never came. The next day, the sun proved to be their greatest enemy. 'Few of us will forget that day', Hampton continued:

We had been promised relief in the early morning, but the sun rose higher and became hotter, and no relief came. The horses had now been without water since 8 o'clock on the previous morning and the men were not much better off. The sun beat down with relentless power upon the bare mountains slopes. Shade there was none, and we had soon exhausted our meagre supply of water. We could only lie still and be slowly roasted until it pleased the author of our misery to go down again. It was practically impossible to eat anything… Those who have attempted to assimilate bully beef and ration biscuit with a parched throat will understand. Bully becomes a sticky mass which provokes thirst, while the biscuit effectually dries up all traces of moisture which one may have succeeded in retaining in the mouth… The 4th November was the longest day I for one have ever spent, and the long delayed counter-attack in the late afternoon came almost as a relief.

The Turks came on strong, according to Hampton:

Advancing with great rapidity and dash amongst the rocks, it was not until their rush had carried them within 80 yards of our position that they were broken, scattered and hurled back whence they had come. D Squadron, which had been back in support during the day, were sent at the gallop to the succour of our right flank which had been temporarily driven in. If anybody in cold blood had suggested to me galloping up those mountains and over those rocks I should have been inclined to doubt his sanity. As it was, if the pace was not quite of a flat race, the Yeomen managed to cover the ground at an amazing speed with only one fall.[41]

The 5th Mounted Brigade withdrew that evening from Ras en Naqb and was relieved by New Zealanders, who subsequently put up a dogged defence against another Turkish assault.

The indecisive and ragged struggle that raged in the steep hills and jagged outcrops resulted in a tragedy: the shelling of British soldiers by their own artillery. On November 6, the 1/6th Royal Welch Fusiliers, 158th Brigade, participated in an attack before dawn with the 1/7th Royal Welch Fusiliers, commanded by Lieutenant Colonel T.H. Harker, on their left. According to the official history, the 1/6th was late in starting. The reason for this, according to the future commander of the 1/6th, E.H. Evans, was that Colonel Harker's 1/7th 'went wrong at start'.[42] Nonetheless, the attack went well for the 1/6th, and the Turkish defences were carried by bayonet. But a heavy mist now settled over the battlefield, and 'a certain amount of mixing of units and general confusion ensued'.[43] Evans described the tragedy that followed. 'Were doing splendidly & had just beaten off counter attack when Harker turned our artillery on us... Ran back to Bde & explained situation to BGC [Brigadier General Commanding]. Guns then off.'[44]

Evans watched with horrified fascination as British shells blew his comrades to bits. As he later wrote to his wife:

I wont propose writing you an account of what happened. It's ill dwelling on horrors & would do neither of us any good. But oh darling the wicked waste of it & worst of all to see ones own men & ones brother officers & decent friends blown literally to pieces by ones own artillery within a few yards of one. And yet it is funny how one is made – in the very middle of it one could not help admiring & being proud of the accuracy & destructiveness of their fire... Of our 16 officers who went in (I do not count H.Q. who were behind) 6 men killed, 5 wounded, 1 wounded & captured by the Turks & escaped.

Two days later, after their bodies had been recovered, Evans helped bury his brothers in arms in the rocky soil. 'It was only when one saw them lying there side by side, the pick of the Battalion, grown men & boys with all their lives before them – but such splendid fellows all – that one realised the awfulness & wickedness of it all.'[45]

The fighting around Khuweilfe, which drew in Turkish reserves that could have been deployed elsewhere, was an important sideshow to the collapse of the entire Turkish front from Gaza to Beersheba. On November 7, the XXI Corps completed its conquest of Gaza. Meanwhile, the gap at Sheria was widened. Turkish forces fell back all along the front that they had held for nine months.

On the western front, where trench warfare dominated, the cavalry had never enjoyed such opportunities. 'I simply must write', Buxton (who now held a staff position with the 20th Brigade, Royal Horse Artillery, Yeomanry Mounted Division) penned to his mother:

> …though I ought to go to sleep. But thanks to being still alive and having seen such cavalry fighting as will make the Cavalry in France green with envy, I must just finish this off. I can now get it posted, and want to let you know how wonderful it all is, and how glad I am to be fighting here, instead of France. Not that I am not nauseated, and also often in a funk, but if one has got to fight, I am glad it is this big open fighting. Some of the charges have been wonderful.[46]

Infantry officers were equally pleased to escape the trench warfare of the previous months. Lieutenant Colonel V.M. Ferguson, a general staff officer with the Lowlanders of the 52nd Division, could not contain his enthusiasm in a letter home. 'Altogether it has been a great show and the open fighting such a treat after the trench warfare in France. It has been just what one has always thought war would be except when trenches first made their appearance and spoiled the whole thing.'[47] Both Buxton and Ferguson had been thrilled by the exploits of the Warwicks and Worcesters in their heroic charge at Huj.

One can easily gain the impression that once the stalemate at Gaza had been broken, the Egyptian Expeditionary Force had an easy time advancing on Jerusalem. Nothing could be further from the truth, as the next chapter illustrates. A fluid war had its own privations and difficulties for the common soldier. Ferguson's division, for example, fought four battles and marched sixty-nine miles during a nine-day period. Buxton's comrades in the mounted forces also quickly discovered that the pursuit was no picnic. Many troopers rode 170 miles from October 29 to November 14. New obstacles replaced the old ones that the Egyptian Expeditionary Force had overcome in its clearing of the Sinai and its capture of Gaza and Beersheba.

7

Relentless Pursuit

The Turks were driven into the open and on the run, with columns of Turkish infantry and transport streaming northward to escape capture. The decisive moment had arrived for Allenby's enormous mounted force, considering the strength of his army. Never before, in fact, had a British general had cavalry in such strength at his disposal. If the Desert Mounted Corps acted aggressively, the retreating Turkish infantry might be cut off while the British infantry came on to finish them off.

Allenby had the highest expectations for his cavalry, arms glittering and hoofs thundering, as it swept forward through the gap at Sheria on November 8. When Dawnay had submitted a draft of orders for the pursuit, Allenby scratched out the line that he had drawn for the limit of the advance, substituting a line further north. Dawnay, believing such a distant objective was unrealistic because of inevitable delays and mishaps, demurred. Asked by Allenby whether he thought the new objectives were 'impossible' to reach, Dawnay responded, 'not necessarily impossible, but ———'. 'No but', Allenby shot back. '*In pursuit you* must always stretch possibilities to the limit. Troops having beaten the enemy will want to rest. They must be given objectives, not those you think they will reach, but the furtherest they could possibly reach.'[1] These words could have served as the watchword for his forces during the next few weeks.

The cavalry's initial advance was hampered by a strong Turkish presence on the British right at Khuweilfe, which forced the cavalry through a gap rather than across an open flank. Moreover, the gap at Sheria was not widened until after the remaining Turkish positions at Tell esh Sheria and Hareira had been taken on November 7. Although the Turks had been beaten, they conducted a fighting withdrawal with a series of rearguard actions. Operating on the flanks of the retiring army, the enemy's field batteries went into action against the advancing 60th Division, selected by Chetwode to support the Desert Mounted Corps in its drive through the gap at Sheria. The enemy's guns lobbed shells into the advancing infantry, withdrew a short distance, and then repeated their deadly harassment.

Reveille was before dawn on November 8 for Captain A.C. Alan-Williams of 'B' Company, 1/1st Warwick Yeomanry, 5th Mounted Brigade, Australian Mounted Division. He had been able to snatch five and a half hours' sleep. This had been the norm for the last week as the men of 'B' Company had been constantly on the move, eating and sleeping when the opportunity arose. His regiment's orders were to advance alongside the 60th Division, eliminating hostile rearguards, in an effort to outflank the fleeing Turks and block their retreat.

The 1/1st Worcester Yeomanry, also of the 5th Mounted Brigade, joined the Warwicks in line of troop column; the two regiments covered a frontage of some two miles. The undulating ground, broken by the occasional wadi, was burned, dusty, and generally easy-going. The troopers' horses were in good condition because they had been fed and watered twice the previous day. 'The fun began almost at once', Alan-Williams wrote in his account of the day's actions, 'for "B" was sent as connecting squadron with a Bde [brigade] of infantry, part of the 60th Division which were moving up on our left. We soon came up to the spot the Turks had bivouaced over night & found all manner of stuff. Kit, blankets, cooking utensils, pots with the remains of last night's meal in, limbers full of ammunition, officers' mess stores, horse fodder, shovels, forks, & a hundred & one other things just scattered about anyhow, showing the hurried way in which they had evidently departed.'[2] As they rode across the far-flung battlefield, a lasting memory for many of the Yeomen was the sickening smell. The stench of the swollen and rotting flesh of dead Turks, horses, and camels filled the air.

1 Middlesex Yeomanry disembarking from the *Nile* at Alexandria, April 1915.

2 1/4th Northamptonshire Regiment, 162nd Brigade, 54th Division, at Mena Camp, 1916.

3 Defending the Suez Canal: Round House Post on Christmas Day, 1916.

4 Men of the Camel Transport Corps.

Above: 5 Camels used as a desert ambulance.

Left: 6 The advance across the Sinai.

7 Desert dining: stacked dixies in a field kitchen.

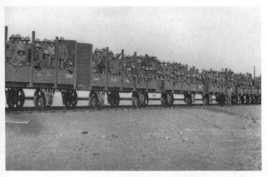

8 Travel on the Kantara Military Railway.

9 Desert Column on the march, accompanied by its camel transport in the distance.

10 Burying the dead after First Gaza.

Above: 11 Digging in on the Gaza Front.

Right: 12 Private Doug H. Calcutt, Queen's Westminster Rifles, 60th Division.

13 Soldiers at play.

14 Scrubbing camels in
the Mediterranean.

15 Rest camp at
El Arish.

16 Yeomanry bathing at a well.

17 Surrendering Jerusalem: Sergeants Hurcombe (right) and Sedgewick (left).

18 Elements of the 60th Division entering Jerusalem.

Right: 19 Front line bivouacs in the Judean Hills.

Below: 20 El Arish Military Cemetery.

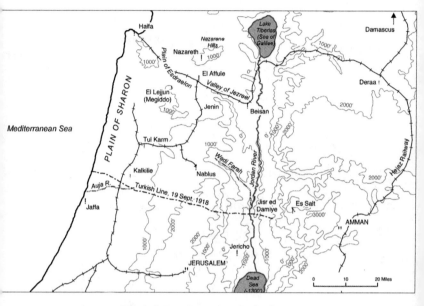

21 Allenby's Last Campaign, September 1918

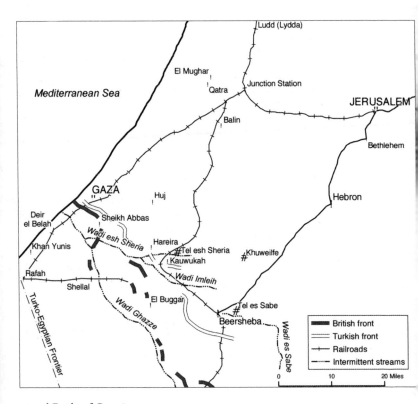

22 3rd Battle of Gaza

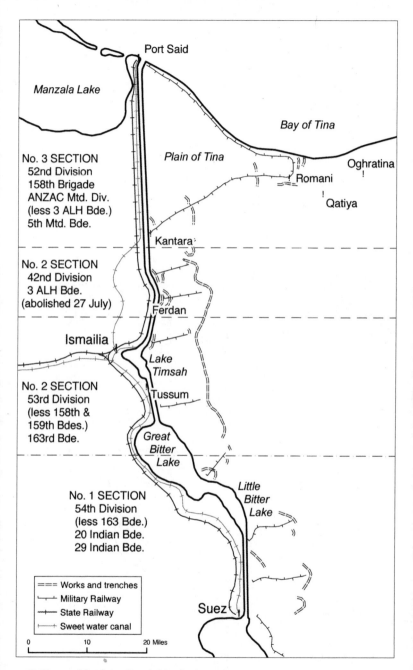

23 Defence of the Suez Canal, March–August 1916

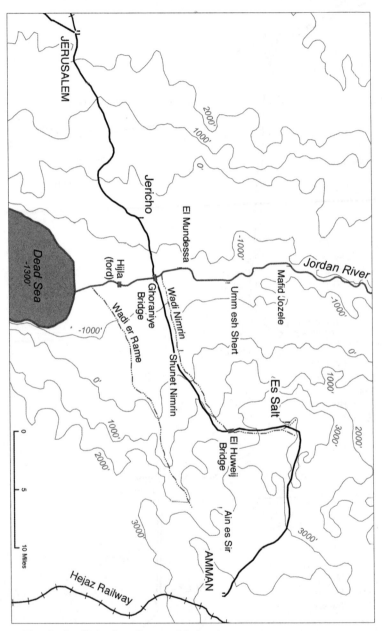

24 Transjordan Operations, January–May 1918

The going had not been as easy for the infantry. Calcutt's brigade marched out at 7a.m. in full pack, soon coming under artillery fire. 'Shells very near', he wrote:

> Trying. Split up into platoons, artillery formation. Continue like that. Then we have to open out still further into extended order and load our rifles (wind up here) to go over a brow of a hill, but it proves all right so far...Very trying, this "over the top any minute" atmosphere, and death, like a brush and comb on a lady's dressing table, always to hand in the shape of a shell. We were in for an attack *it appears* last time we extended, but he retired... The 'War' is always just over the next ridge of hills...We march, march, march, march, instead for what seems hours.

As some soldiers approached their breaking point, Calcutt kept his sanity by jotting down his thoughts in his diary throughout the day during halts in the march. 'Rumsey is frantic', Calcutt scribbled, 'and I am alternately Happy (stupidly) and depressed, and my brain is working with that insane clarity that is usually associated with the sleepless hours of night. I want to write a book setting forth the candid cowardly feelings of the average man, a virulent book, as an antidote to the Lord Northcliffe "heroic Tommy."... I have got a septic sore on my heel which is running and very painful, and together with my sciatica, making things up hill. Cheer up! Keep smiling.'[3]

Captain Alan-Williams was struck by what appeared to be the infantrymen's extraordinary composure as they were being shelled by Turkish guns. From his vantage point on the 60th Division's right flank, he noted:

> The infantry were in open order & coming along steadily when two batteries of field guns opened fire at about 3000 yds range. Shells burst amongst them & around them & above them & still they came steadily on. Not a man turned back, not a man slackened his pace. Now and then a shell would land in the middle of a little clump & one or two would be thrown in the air & others jump to one side wounded, to await the stretcher bearers when they came up.[4]

Little did Alan-Williams realize that his own willingness to advance into the teeth of enemy fire was about to be put to an even greater test. At about 2:30p.m., the enemy's artillery, which had been intermittently harassing the infantry all day, opened up once again. Shells burst in salvoes of six and eight among the infantry, inflicting considerable casualties. As Alan-Williams' squadron began to close with these retreating field batteries, which had once again paused to open fire, Major General Shea, the commander of the 60th Division, abruptly drove up in an armoured Ford car. As Shea later explained, he had gone forward to reconnoitre. He observed some three miles away 'a long and straggling column of Turks crossing my front from right to left.' He then saw an enemy battery getting into position on his right front. 'My whole idea was to push for all I was worth which we had always done ever since Beersheba and I knew perfectly well that my infantry could never catch the long column of Turks.'[5] He ordered the commander of the Warwicks, Lieutenant Colonel H.A. Gray-Cheape, to capture the guns, thereby opening the way for a cavalry pursuit.

Gray-Cheape, a world-renowned polo player, immediately collected as many men as he could from his regiment and the Worcester Yeomanry, a squadron and a half from each, perhaps as many as 165 men, of which some 120 participated in the charge. Opposing this small force was an Austrian field battery of 75mm guns protected by machine guns. To its left there was a body of about 200 Turkish troops with a 150mm battery to its rear. Further along the ridge to the west was yet another body of Turkish infantry. The plan was for the Warwicks to charge the 75mm battery directly and the Worcesters to take the infantry on the enemy's left flank, both bodies of cavalrymen making use of the undulating ground to approach without being observed before they charged.

Alan-Williams, writing in 1920, recalled what happened next:

A hasty reconnaissance by the Squadron Leader and myself, which, incidentally for the first time, gave us a view of the actual guns, but also brought us under point blank Machine Gun and Shrapnel fire at about 800 yards, was made. This reconnaissance determined Captain

[R.] Valentine to take advantage of the cover afforded by the folds in the ground, for, by swinging to the right, we could advance under cover to within about 300 yards of the enemy Gun position. This we did, and five minutes later, with a slight check to change formation and with swords at the engage, we galloped across those 300 yards in Column of Half-Squadrons, with an interval of about 6 feet between ranks and 80 yards distance between front and rear ranks.[6]

In an earlier account of the affair of Huj, written from a hospital bed several weeks after the charge, Alan-Williams' emotionally described what happened when the Warwicks topped a ridge and came within sight of the Austrian gunners. 'Every second counted', he wrote:

The Colonel gave Val the order to form 'column of half squadrons, draw swords & charge.' Before we had time to actually move off, the Turks who had of course seen us, shortened their fuses & burst a salvo of shrapnel six feet from the ground & right among us. Over the top we went & in a cloud of dust & a shout went straight for them. Never do I want to experience another cavalry charge of a similar nature. The reception they gave us was like riding into hell. Men & horses going the most awful losses I have ever seen anybody go. Some killed outright others wounded. I was just conscious of having been hit, but could hold on to reins alright. The shells tore through the air so close one could almost feel them. The crack of machine guns bullets was terrific. I won't describe in too much detail what happened when the guns were reached but suffice to say that the gun teams were killed or captured to a man. Sgt. Lambert got the Austrian commander clean through his Iron Cross ribbon, but unfortunately was killed a second or two afterwards. Val got a nasty shell wound in the leg & was being led away by Gilman, when he was hit in the head & never stood on his legs again, while Gilman was hit in the back slightly.

Elsewhere, according to Alan-Williams, 'the Worcesters consisting of a squadron & a half had charged round behind the guns & found themselves amongst the gun escort, consisting of six M.G.'s & 300 infantry. Unfortunately we were both so reduced by casualties that we couldn't hold the guns or capture all the infantry & so retired some 400 yds. But the Turk expecting another wave to come over, bayoneted our wounded & then retired himself leaving everything behind.'[7]

The clash had been short but extravagantly bloody. The gunners had fired point-blank into the charging Yeomen. 'The mixed Austrian and Turkish gun detachments served their guns till our advanced line was within 20 yards and them threw themselves under their guns', Alan-Williams recalled. 'Few remained standing and, where they did, were instantly sabred. Others running away from the guns, threw themselves on the ground on being overtaken and thus saved themselves, for it was found almost impossible to sabre a man lying down at the pace we were travelling.'[8]

When Yeomen reinforcements arrived within minutes to consolidate the position, they were greeted by an horrific scene. A young lieutenant, Robert Henry Wilson, 1/1st Gloucester Yeomanry, 5th Mounted Brigade, whose regiment had been in reserve, wrote:

Eventually we found ourselves doing a good gallop, and as we crossed a ridge, there was a scene revealed that few can have seen. There were eleven heavy guns, surrounded, in many cases, by their crews, dead or wounded; many gallant yeomen, and many gallant horses that had carried them over their farms at home, as hunters. I am not particularly emotional, but this was the most distressing situation I had ever experienced. The first man I saw was a friend of mine in the Worcester Yeomanry, who had been killed by a bayonet, and whose horse had been killed under him. The next sad, but noble, sight was a Sergeant of the Warwicks, who I also knew. His horse was dead, on his knees, wedged between the wheel and the barrel of the gun. The Sergeant was dead in the saddle, and an Austrian gunner was dead with the Sergeant's sword through his chest, and his own rifle still in his hands. The only elements of the enemy force who really stood their ground were the gunners, mostly Austrians.[9]

It had been a near thing for the Warwicks and Worcesters who reached the guns. If the Turkish infantry had held their ground, the survivors who got to the guns would have had no chance. Even then, the losses had been catastrophic. Of the some 120 men involved in the charge, seventy were killed or wounded, and about a hundred horses had been lost. All three squadron leaders lost their lives. Lieutenant W.B. Mercer was in the first line with Valentine. He saw so many men and horses go down that he 'had the impression' that he 'was the only man left alive. I was amazed to discover we were the victors.'[10] This was the first charge with drawn sword in the Palestine fight. It was also the first and last time in the campaign that the Yeomen went into action without covering fire. All Yeomanry regiments had machine gun sections, but for reasons that remain obscure, they were not used at Huj.

In the end, this charge hastened the fall of Huj by perhaps a few hours and protected the advancing infantry from artillery fire, but it did not open the way for the cavalry to intercept the retreating Turks that Shea had observed crossing his front. Shea blamed Chauvel, the commander of the Desert Mounted Corps, for this lost opportunity. 'There is nothing to stop you', Shea told him. 'This flank guard has been completely smashed. You have only to send a brigade on to get the Turks as they are demoralised.' But Chauvel refused to act. 'I utterly failed to get him to move a yard and so the opportunity was lost',[11] Shea later wrote the editor of the official history.

If Shea is correct, the sacrifice of many brave men had a negligible impact on the course of the pursuit. Many soldiers, however, perceived glory in this cavalry charge when compared with the monster battles on the western front, where men seemed mere cogs in a great killing machine. 'The charge itself must ever remain a monument to extreme resolution and to that spirit of self-sacrifice which is the only beauty redeeming ugly war'[12] is the way that soldier/historian Captain Cyril Falls expressed this sentiment. That this view was not an isolated one is reflected in the letters and diaries of other members of the Egyptian Expeditionary Force. Rather than being seen as a tragic and senseless affair, Huj was viewed in heroic and romantic terms. But some soldiers had mixed feelings. 'A lot of old familiar faces have gone amongst the men & ten guns are not worth men like Valentine', Alan-Williams wrote his father, 'but the job had to be done.'[13] Wilson, of the Gloucester Hussars, who attended the burial of the fallen Yeomen 'whose names were household words' in 'the hunting fields' of their counties, 'found it difficult to resist a feeling of the wicked waste of war'.[14]

Despite the true grit displayed by the Desert Mounted Corps at Huj and elsewhere, the Turkish army escaped envelopment. Scarcity of water proved to be an insurmountable obstacle for the Desert Mounted Corps, especially for its thirsty and tired horses. 'Nearly every fight was a fight for water', Chetwode later explained to the army historian, Lieutenant General Sir George MacMunn, 'and if you did not drive the enemy off the water you had to go back to where you started from and begin all over again.'[15]

Even if the local water supply was captured, it took a long time to water man and beast. Before abandoning Huj, for example, the Turks destroyed all but two of the town's wells. The two deep wells that survived had had their lifting gear demolished. 'My Brigade, the 5th Mounted, were pursuing the retreating enemy but, owing to the difficulty of watering the horses, we could never catch up with them', Robert Henry Wilson explains:

> What water there was in the area was chiefly in deep wells and, after the Turks had helped himself, he smashed what lifting gear there was and did his utmost to ruin the wells. As a result he could travel as fast on his flat feet during one night as we could in twenty-four hours on horseback. I have, on more than one occasion, queued up with my Squadron from dark to dawn waiting our turn to water, and then had to resume the march next day without having had any.[16]

To conserve water, the men were not allowed to shave. 'Everyone has a beard about an inch long, and a conference of respectable field-officers looks like an anarchist meeting',[17] Captain R.E.C. Adams of the 231st Brigade, 74th Division, lamented.

Many troopers, hollow-eyed with exhaustion, had not had a night's rest for days. 'At every halt the men automatically fell asleep, as we had now had no sleep for five nights. In fact, we rocked in the saddles as we rode, and we were heavily laden with equipment, one of the irksome articles of which was the gas respirator, which with the bandolier, haversack, water-bottle, etc., fitted tightly round the neck and nearly choked one', S.F. Hatton, a sergeant with the 1/1st County of London Yeomanry, 8th Mounted Brigade, Yeomanry Mounted Division, wrote about his trek across the Maritime Plain looking for water. 'I heard this conversation in my troop behind me', he continued:

> 'There won't be no b——y gas – I can't stick this bastard thing any longer.' A faint thud on the sand.
> 'Same as you, chum' – another thud.
> 'Old So-and So's dumped his' – another one.
> In a few moments, looking around, I found I was the only one carrying the respirator, and so mine went too.

When Hatton and his men finally found water, it was in short supply. One thirsty and disgruntled trooper summed up the day: 'One whole b——y day spent in getting half a b——y drink.'[18]

The Royal Engineers did their best to water the thirsty men and horses. A letter home by Captain R.C. Case of the 60th Division provided a revealing glimpse of the superhuman efforts of the engineers to resolve the watering crisis:

> The following 2 days were raced thro' in supplying thousands upon thousands of men and horse with water. A really pathetic task at times, when one had to refuse units and men with a drink. I have seen men eagerly down on their hands and knees lapping up the overflow from horse troughs... 2.30a.m. saw my section and self off to the wadi to take on the water development which had been partially completed by 2 other sections. The outlook at this time in the morning was very rosy, for there were continuous pools of water lying in the wadi, and we rapidly filled all our troughs, and by daylight everything was ready. No sooner was it light when we discovered that we were indeed in a filthy spot. All the open pools which had looked so nice were fouled with blood, wine, and dead animals, and in about 1½ hours the pools were sucked dry and the stenches became overpowering. Sumps were

hastily dug, and fortunately provided an ample supply of water, in as much that during the day we watered a whole Cavalry Division, besides many other units...The morning was about the most frenzied performance that I have ever experienced, owing to the huge numbers of animals watered.[19]

Captain Teichman, a Yeomanry medical officer, took note of the effect of thirst and little or no rest on the cavalry in an entry in his diary on November 11:

During the morning a large number of sick men and horses were evacuated. The strain was beginning to tell; We had now been on the move for fourteen days, and the horses had on more than one occasion been forty-eight hours without water and often twenty-four; on many occasions the latter had been equally long without having their saddles off – the men were badly in want of sleep, and many had broken out again with septic sores, chiefly on account of their inability to wash or take off their clothes for the past two weeks... However, the advance had to go on, however great the wastage in men and horseflesh might be.[20]

The infantry was nearing the end of its tether as well. After the affair of Huj, the 60th Division advanced to within sight of the sea north of Gaza. But the Turks had escaped envelopment, and the campaign entered another phase, which emphasized keeping constant pressure on the Turks rather than envelopment. On November 9–10, when the 60th Division finally got several days' rest, Private Blunt of the Civil Service Rifles reflected on the past ten days:

Rations nothing but bully beef, biscuits and jam. No cigarettes. No one night's proper rest and continually on the march. We had marched and fought from Beersheba to the sea. Owing to casualties the battalion is now only just over half strength.

Everyone seems just beat and worn out. I am as weak as a kitten, feeling done up all over. My face is covered with septic sores and my feet are all blistered... I hope I shall never have to go through such

a period again. What with no water, fighting, marching, and short
rations. I thank God I am alive and well.[21]

Unable to intercept the routed Turks, the 60th Division after the
affair of Huj had its transport (which included its camels) transferred
to the XXI Corps, which was advancing along the coast from Gaza.
Nonetheless, the 60th Division kept on the move. Weary soldiers
grumbled that they were being marched in circles by the 'brass hats'.
After advancing to within sight of the sea near Gaza and given a
couple of days' rest, the high command marched them from one end
of southern Palestine to the other. Their march routes were often
determined by the availability of water. First they were realigned to
block a possible Turkish counterattack from the Judean Hills. When
this threat evaporated, they pulled back to their former battlefield of
Sheria, and from there they marched to a spot north of Gaza, only
to be sent to relieve the XXI Corps in the Judean Hills.

Excerpts from Blunt's diary suggest that a war of movement
imposed perhaps even greater hardships on the infantry than did
trench warfare:

On November 11: We marched all the morning a distance of 9 miles to
a village where there are wells. The march was absolute cruelty; nearly
killed me. The fellows rushed the wells for water and drank any old dirty
stuff they could get. Very high wind and dust storm this afternoon.

On November 13: No peace for the wicked. Marched to another place
this morning five miles further east.

On November 15: Army 'Buggery' [nonsense] commenced again today.
We had 3 hours parade during the day for drill, extended order and
other muck… Still feeling very run down in strength and nerves.

On November 16: Marched 9 miles this morning to Sheria. Quite
a good march.

On November 17: Marched 4 miles to wash; making everyone rather
fed up. This afternoon everyone happy. Parcel post of many weeks
accumulation arrived… Everyone was eating luxuries… Buck-shee
[free] rations and cigarettes were also going. Never seen such a jolly
day as this for ages.

On November 18: Handed in our light drill tunics that we have been wearing ever since we landed in Egypt. Issued with serge khaki tunics – as worn in England – for the Winter Season. Brigade moved 4 miles westward. Had fresh meat gippo [stew] for dinner, quite a nice change.[22]

The arrival of mail was always a high point in the daily routine for members of the EEF. With home leave virtually unobtainable, it represented the only means to keep in touch with home. 'I enjoyed writing letters', Blunt remembered. 'It kept me in touch with home and friends and it invited return letters. Letters from Blighty just kept one sane. The greatest thrill in service life is when the mail arrives.'[23] When letters failed to materialize in the mail call, the reverse was true. 'I have known men not to receive a letter for months on end, owing to the continual loss of mails at sea or other causes, and they have become so depressed and miserable that they were entirely indifferent as to whether they survived the war or not. They felt absolutely forgotten', Blaser, a scout in the 2/14 Battalion, 179th Brigade, 60th Division, claimed.[24]

As Blaser noted, many letters never found their way either to or from the Palestine theatre. 'This is an awful place for mails – one only gets a mail from England one a fortnight... I think a great many more mails are submarined than we ever know about', Brigadier General Sir Hugh Archie Dundas Simpson-Baikie, the GOC Royal Artillery, 60th Division, wrote to his wife. 'It is submarines for a certainty – numbers & numbers of my letters go astray – you see the Army letters are sent by any old ship & if one old tramp is sunk probably many mail bags go down with it.'[25]

The brief respite for the men, which included mail from home, better food, warmer clothing and free cigarettes, portended difficult days ahead for the 60th Division. To relieve the XXI Corps, which had borne the brunt of fighting the Turks in the Judean Hills, Allenby moved forward the XX Corps that included Blunt's division.

Blunt's diary entries depict the difficult march from Gaza to the Judean Hills:

On November 20: A Brigade trek of 12 miles. Just before the march ended a terrific rainstorm came on and continued well into the night. Never had such a night before. We were all absolutely tired out by the march and then we had to put up 'bivies' [bivouac] and sleep in all the slush and wet… I had no sleep, wet through to the skin.

On November 21: Brigade trek continued. We marched another eight miles… This continued marching is now telling on the battalion. Almost everyone seems just about 'done in' [exhausted]. Ten men from our Company went to the Ambulance with bad feet.

On November 22: Continuing the trek, went another nine miles today. On November 23: Still on trek – did a further ten miles today. The marching is getting regular torture; my feet and everyone else's are covered with blisters. Today we passed through much wilder country and camped right among the hills which are covered with boulders and very rocky.

On November 24: Had a stiff uphill march of six miles right up into the hills. For the past ten days we have seen nothing of the war and fighting. We have been trekking to catch up with the retreating Turks.[26]

Surely the most extraordinary march of this phase of the campaign was conducted by another division in the XX Corps, the 74th Division. A sense of urgency characterized its trek because of a desperate Turkish counterattack launched on the morning of November 27. The 74th Division departed Junction Station on November 28 at 7a.m. and began to climb the Judean Hills. They got into bivouac near the village of Latron, only to break camp and march in darkness. They reached Beit Anan just before dawn the next day after marching twelve of the last eighteen hours. According to Captain R.E.C. Adams, the brigade major to the 231st Brigade, they 'had marched twenty-six miles since the morning, up-hill all the way and finishing up over eight miles of the most poisonous going imaginable'.[27]

Soldiers became like zombies during these long treks. 'Usually during such marches the mind is apt to allow itself to lie dormant, making no response to appeals made to it through the senses', H.J. Earney, a signaller with the 9th Mountain Brigade, RGA, XX Corps, wrote at the time. 'Such is the effect of over-fatigue. After a while the mind and body develop mechanical properties the sole business of which is to continue the plodding and tramp, tramp, tramp is all that matters.'[28] The Judean hills proved treacherous and brutal. 'The usual grunts in chorus, and old stock jokes when troops march uphill had run down the ranks and been forgotten',[29] Rowlands Coldicott, a captain in the 60th Division, remembered. Marching in the rain on the Maritime Plain was just as difficult, as Coldicott's account shows:

> We had now done about twelve miles and the time was half-past six in the evening. No one had fallen but the pace had become slower and slower, until the men hardly seemed to move... No one took any interest in the landscape, a sodden, featureless plain. There were no sounds but the sploshing of boots in mud and the irritating clank here and there of a man's badly swung mess-tin. No one spoke, and I had failed so utterly to get the men to put a brighter face on the affair... There was no doubt that everyone was getting to the end of his tether, and I hoped and prayed continually that the bivouac ground was not far off. We were cursed and exhorted by everybody.[30]

Under normal circumstances, the column marched fifty minutes and rested ten. The brigade commander's three-cornered flag, called by some the 'triangle of error', drew particular attention from the infantry. They followed its every move, with anxiety growing as the afternoon grew late and the march continued. If the flag strayed into a field alongside the route, it might mean that the brigadier was about to choose their bivouac. Once the bamboo lance bearing the flag was planted in the ground, the men's blistered feet and weary legs would get a well-earned, although temporary, respite.

The day was not yet over, however, for camel drivers, especially if they were under the authority of regular soldiers rather than Camel Transport Corps (CTC) personnel. Although the army largely depended on the CTC for water in its advance on Jerusalem, the camel drivers were frequently treated as less than human. The infantry expected its water ration as soon as it made camp. The four-legged beast, however, had difficulty matching the pace of the infantry, so the Egyptians leading him often did not get a break. After keeping up with the column all day, the driver then had to make two or three trips to the nearest source of water to fill his fanatis in order to add to the mobile water allowance. It was not uncommon for camel drivers to walk from twelve to sixteen hours a day.[31]

Despite the physical pain endured, the advance across the Maritime plain and into the Judean Hills was marked by several important British successes: the action of El Mughar and the occupation of Junction Station, November 13–14, which severed Turkish rail communications with Jerusalem and which opened the way for an advance into the Judean Hills. By November 11, Bulfin's XXI Corps had advanced thirty-five miles from Gaza, and the British forces on the right, which included Chetwode's XX Corps and the Desert Mounted Corps, had advanced further than that. When Turkish resistance began to stiffen, Allenby directed his attention to Junction Station, where the Beersheba railway joined the Jaffa–Jerusalem line. Its capture would disrupt Turkish communications and drive a wedge between the Turkish 7th and 8th armies.

After concentrating his forces on the plain, Allenby launched a broad front attack on November 13. 'The advance on the 13th was a great sight', Dawnay wrote:

> Our troops advanced all day across a great open plain—on a 12 mile front exclusive of the mounted troops on the right—pressing the enemy back everywhere towards the Judean hills. Dawnay himself observed the most famous action of that day, the affair of El Mughar, that took place on the British left. The Turks had taken advantage of the rocky knolls, cactus hedges, orchards and groves, establishing a strong position in the hill towns of Qatra and El Mughar.

In Dawnay's words, this Turkish position dominated 'an absolutely level plain on which a mouse would hardly find cover'.[32] Although the Lowlanders of the 52nd Division captured Qatra in a bayonet charge, they were held up by heavy enemy fire when they advanced on El Mughar. The 6th Mounted Division was close at hand, so the 52nd Division asked for its help. Lieutenant Cyrus H. Perkins of the 1/1st Bucks, 6th Mounted Brigade, Yeomanry Mounted Division, played a key role in the subsequent cavalry charge. His account noted:

> General [C.A.C.] Godwin, our much admired Brigadier, ex Indian Cavalry, who had recently taken over the command of our 6th Mounted Brigade was up among us looking over the situation with my Colonel Fred Cripps and when a request for assistance was received it was offered at once. The Colonel then asked me to recce the ground between us and the ridge about two miles away. Having learned in my days with the 7th Reserve cavalry at Tidworth that Cavalry charges should not exceed about 300 yds, I had in mind looking for cover for led horses, whence a shortish dismounted attack could be made and although the map indicated what seemed a depression about a mile away between us and the ridge, it wasn't obvious whether it would serve as sufficient cover for the led horses after dismounting.[33]

Perkins's harrowing few minutes as he scouted the enemy's position won him the Military Cross. In the words of Captain Cyril Falls, 'he cantered up and down under a hail of machine-gun fire which, in the words of an eye witness, "following him as the spotlight follows a dancer on the stage," seeming to bear a charmed life'.[34] After he returned, he reported that there was no cover for the led horses. 'During the somewhat anxious pause' that followed his report, he wondered whether the dismounted action would in fact be attempted, when quite suddenly and unexpectedly, General Goodwin exclaimed, '"We'll gallop it."' Godwin placed the Berkshire Yeomanry in reserve and sent the Bucks and Dorset Yeomanry forward under the cover of the Wadi Jamus. At 3p.m., the two regiments emerged from the wadi and launched what many consider the last major cavalry charge in the British Army.

'As our B Squadron, to be following at intervals by the C and A squadrons got out of the wadi, we extended into line and open order', Perkins continued:

My troop was on the left and away to my right I could see Crocker Bulteel, my squadron leader, out in front keeping us at the trot to save the horses for the two miles to the ridge. As the enemy's fire hotted up it became harder to hold the horses to the trot, so gradually the pace quickened while we still tried to keep the galloping squadron in line. As we neared the ridge swords were drawn and very soon we were breasting the rise with their gun blasts feeling like pillows hitting one's face. Then in seconds there they were all around us, some shooting, some scrambling out of slit trenches and some sensibly falling flat on their faces. It had taken us, I suppose, a bit over five minutes.

Blown and galloping horses are hard to handle one-handed while you have a sword in the other – so hindered by the clutter of rifle butt and other equipment troopers found it nearly impossible to get at a low dodging Turk. One missed and missed again until the odd Turk wasn't quite quick enough. In just such a case, the hours spent in arms drill paid off for one instinctively leaned well forward and remained so to offset the jerk as the sword comes out – in fact, precisely as one has so often been told.

By then, those of us who had got there still mounted were among a seething mob – literally like mounted policemen in a football crowd – shouting at them to surrender in the only words we were supposed to know, sounding like 'Tesleem Olinuz.' Years later in Cyprus I learned the proper translation – said to be 'Handsup the lot of you.'

All this shouting however didn't seem much good – probably because on our bit of the front only about nine blokes had arrived on the ridge until the next squadron reached us. The Turks were milling about and heading down the far side of the ridge where a few hundred got into what I found later to be a quarry.[35]

Perkins had shown no fear as he galloped the ridge. 'In all honesty', he wrote later, 'I think it was the only occasion I was not frightened – probably one was too occupied and the final excitement was pretty intense. Altogether like champagne on an empty stomach.'

Unlike the earlier charge at Huj, the Yeomen had support from its machine guns and artillery. This suppressing fire was obviously important, but Perkins provided another reason for the success of this classic cavalry charge. Austrian gunners at Huj held their ground, the Turks at El Mughar panicked:

> One may well ask why Johnny Turk, acknowledged to be a tough customer, was overcome in perhaps 10 to 15 minutes by galloping cavalry? Imagine, however, his reactions. A line of horsemen appear out of a wadi two miles away, but too far to shoot at. Soon they are in range, but by then another line of horsemen emerge and apparently your rifle fire and the machine guns show no dramatic result. In your growing anxiety your aim is dodgy to say the least, and again a third lot of horsemen appear. It is all very quick and even in those days when most men were used to horses the galloping onrush is frightening – so, do you stand pat, or run? Foolishly, in their indecision many got out of their slit trenches – shooting or running. Had they sat tight they would have been an almost impossible target for troopers' swords on galloping horses, and our success could not have been so sudden.[36]

And the Yeomen's losses would have been much higher. In Perkins's troop, nine reached the ridge mounted and two were killed. The 6th Mounted Brigade suffered 130 casualties, with only one officer and fifteen other ranks being killed. These casualties represented about sixteen per cent of the attacking force. Twice as many horses were put out of action. The infantry in the 155th Brigade, 52nd Division, suffered considerably higher casualties (486) in the capture of the village.[37] Over 1,000 prisoners were taken, with many Turkish dead scattered around the village. Elsewhere the Turkish front crumbled. On November 14, Junction Station was secured. Two days later, the New Zealand Brigade occupied Jaffa.

Captain Case attempted to summarize for his family what the EEF had accomplished in some two weeks of fighting and marching: 'I am sure you would be astonished if only I could tell you of the marching and fighting of this period. This would have been magnificent even with a decent climate, good food, water and roads, but considering the wild country, the heat, and the shortage of water, I think the achievement must be one of the foremost that the war has produced.' Case admitted that his version of events glossed over much of the 'blood and beastliness' of the advance. Nor had he witnessed anything 'beautiful and romantic'. In his view, 'one thing only stands out alone, and that is the truly magnificent heroism and endurance of our splendid infantry; men who before the war were mostly weaklings and townsmen, and who are now stamped with a hall mark of quality equal to anything the nation has ever produced'. Case concluded his letter with a question that was much on the minds of many other members of the EEF. 'So ends the first phase. What will the second bring forth?'[38]

8

Sacred Soil

With Junction Station in the hands of the British, the Turks lost their railway connection to Jerusalem. The Turkish 7th Army retired into the hills around Jerusalem, and the Turkish 8th Army retreated northward along the coastal plain towards Jaffa. Faced with mounting logistical problems because of his rapid advance and the approach of the wet season, a prudent policy would have been for Allenby to avoid the treacherous Judean Hills, halting his advance once Jaffa had been secured. Allenby's daily reading of the Bible and Adam Smith's *Historical Geography of the Holy Land* had certainly impressed upon him the difficulty of campaigning in the rocky, trackless wastes of these hills. But Allenby had a mandate from Lloyd George, 'Jerusalem before Christmas', and he had the necessary flexibility from Robertson to exploit the breaking of the Gaza-Beersheba front. The Judean Hills it would be, despite the inevitable hardships on his troops. As one soldier who knew him well wrote: 'He applied to his soldiers the old hunting maxim, "Care for your horse in the stable as if he were worth five hundred pounds; ride him in the field as if he were not worth half a crown."'[1]

In his advance on Jerusalem, Allenby firmly rejected the notion that he was a modern-day Richard Coeur de Lion. In this he was being pragmatic. As commander in chief in the Holy Land, he had a political as well as a military role to play. He especially understood the delicate situation in the Holy City, which was sacred to three world religions, and was acutely aware that many of his soldiers and labourers were Muslim. The idea of a crusade, however, resonated with many of his men. In an effort to boost morale, some officers impressed upon the ranks that they were fighting on sacred soil. 'The Crusader idea was worked for all it was worth', General Shea asserted in a postwar lecture at the Staff College, 'and the men were systematically taught the story of the country as they passed through it, to increase their interest. Clergymen were mostly used for this, and I would here lay stress on the great value of clergymen to reach the actual psychology of the men from a different stand point to that of the Company or Platoon Commander.'[2]

Many soldiers, far more instinctively Christian than their present-day countrymen, apparently needed little prodding from their chaplain to be deeply affected by their surroundings. Brigadier General A.C. Fermperley, a staff officer in the 60th Division, believed that the advance on Jerusalem was the 'only campaign in the Great War that was tinged with Romance. Speaking for my own Division at any rate, I know from constant conversations with all ranks, that they were deeply imbued with the significance of the campaign and with its historical background, in a way that I have never found in British soldiers in any campaign or in any other war.'[3]

The reminiscences of many soldiers who fought in the Holy Land support the view that most soldiers were conscious of their historical and religious surroundings. A soldier, dying in the hospital at Kantara, confessed to army chaplain J.P.Wilson: 'As I went through Palestine, I used to wonder whether Christ had been there; perhaps He walked along this road; perhaps He climbed that hill; perhaps He drank from this well.'[4] Captain A. Douglas Thorburn, an artillery officer with 2/22nd Country of London Howitzer Battery, 60th Division, reacted similarly: 'Our battery came into action on the slope in front of Bethel, famous for Jacob's ladder, and now called Beitin. Behind the village was a kite-balloon for observation, to the east of it the ruins of Ai which Joshua captured by a strategem.'[5] But Thornburn also could not help but notice the incongruous contrasts caused by the presence of a modern fighting force in Palestine: 'Ford's Tin Lizzies ploughed through the sandhills and raced along the coast tracks where Pharaoh's war-chariots had traveled, a derelict tank lay in No Man's Land within rifle-shot of where Samson's primitive weapon of the jawbone of an ass had proved more deadly.'[6]

Some Egyptian Expeditionary Force members openly embraced the 'crusader' image. 'Great things are about to happen & I hope the Turk will be justly punished for all the atrocities he has committed in the Holy Land', Captain Alan-Williams wrote to his father, who was a minister.[7] It seemed to Brigadier General A.B. Robertson, who was in charge of troop training at General Headquarters, 'as if each man, including officers, was inspired by an intense fervour which had its origin in a deepseated religious impulse to wrest the Holy City from the grip of a sacrilegious interloper. I have not the slightest doubt, and many officers who took part in that fighting were and are of the same opinion', he later wrote to the compilers of the official history, 'that but for that inarticulate emotion the troops would never have overcome the almost unsurmountable obstacles in the time and in the manner they did. The spirit of the Crusaders was present. After the capture of the City never again during the campaign did that amazing dogged selfless determination to overcome all resistance shew itself in such intensity.'[8] Private Blunt agreed, writing in his diary, 'to me the fact that we were near Jerusalem probably camped on the very ground where Richard 1st of England and many English Crusaders camped was often uppermost in my thoughts. I read a great deal of the Bible trying to recognize the land and environment.'[9]

Buxton turned philosophical about fighting in what he called the 'promised land' in a letter to his mother. 'I do not feel very thrilled about the conquest of it. I want to be at the Turk, but I don't feel the Crusader's desire to possess the land. However, it does make one feel excited to be entering it – the cradle of our civilization… I hope, perhaps, entering Holy ground will be a difference for me too – up to now I can see I have been a pagan, never worshipping beyond the end of my nose; all selfish revelling in what was beautiful in nature in mind, but very little faith in what was beyond my senses.'[10] In another letter, Buxton talked about the prospect of being killed on sacred soil: 'I have been trekking up and down the country, and been within

20 miles of Jerusalem on two sides. I have seen real war, and I have seen the Holy Land. So that now it would not be so bad, as if I had rolled from some putrid, sniping incident down in the desert.'[11]

Not every soldier, of course, was moved by the experience of walking in the footsteps of biblical and historical figures. The prospect of being killed in taking Jerusalem overshadowed any romantic notions for Calcutt. On the eve of the final push to take Jerusalem, he wrote in his diary: 'Persistent rumours of going over the top. *How* romantic a death for a conscientious objector, to die at Christmas time fighting for the Holy City.'[12] Others were cynical about religion in general and had a difficult time, as they marched through the squalid villages, connecting the inhabitants with biblical characters. 'As regards the Bible Stories', Captain Case wrote to his father, 'one has only to see this place and the occasional native village to have one's perspective pulled roughly into line... Altho' my own opinion of Bible Stories was very low, they had a rude shock and dropped with a bump to a much lower level still when I saw this country. There is one thing, however, which astonishes me, and that is that sentiments such as expressed in the Bible could have emanated from such a low grade of people as must have lived here in those days.'[13] L.J. Matthews, an engineer with the 74th Division, probably spoke for the majority of the soldiers in his recollections of service in Palestine. 'What were our thoughts', he wrote in his memoirs:

> ...as we neared Jerusalem? When we did have time for thought, other than those which concerned our daily routine, we did give some thought to the HOLY LAND – true; we did not feel much like Crusaders, and I doubt if the rank and file of the English and French Armies in the early Crusades felt very much Holy Zeal as they too fought heat, flies, thirst, malaria and dysentery – but our home upbringing had been in a Christian home and we did think that now we could see for ourselves the Ancient Biblical Cities and we, perhaps, would be able to picture what life could have been like in those far off days.[14]

A military consideration for Allenby in advancing into the Judean Hills without a pause was his fear that the Turks, if given the opportunity, would dig in. Fortunately, the Turks initially made their stand on the Maritime Plain. If they had fortified the hills, Dawnay contends, 'it might have taken us months to get Jerusalem, if he could have kept his defending force supplied'.[15] Allenby maintained his position on the coastal plain with the 54th Division and the Anzac Mounted Division, assigning elements of the XXI Corps the job of capturing Jerusalem. Allenby was desperate to avoid any damage to the Holy City: he disallowed any fighting within six miles of the city. He hoped to force the Turks to abandon the city without a fight by cutting their vital supply route, the Nablus-Jerusalem road. The 75th Division was sent up the road from Jaffa to Jerusalem with the 52nd Division advancing on its left. Allenby selected Major General G.D.S. Barrow's Yeomanry Mounted Division to make a lightning strike across the hills to cut off any Turkish troops retreating along the Jerusalem-Nablus road. Although Allenby admitted to Barrow that his infantry was better suited to mountain warfare, he believed that only horse soldiers could get in place in time. He knew his 'fellows could do it',[16] Barrow later recalled.

The cavalry, however, found the going very difficult in fulfilling its mission. Short rations, torrential rain, frigid nights and rugged hills had to be overcome as well as the Turks. According to Barrow, the terrain resembled, 'on a small scale, the Himalayas that compose the north-west frontier of India. It is a waterless wilderness of tumultuous hills broken by steep ravines and stony valleys and marked by the built-up terraces and decayed wine presses of a bygone system of agriculture... Stones are everywhere, ranging in size from pebbles to boulders a couple of feet high. There are no paths or tracks between villages as are usually to be found in mountainous regions that are inhabited.'[17] Horses, which could not be fed or watered properly, proved a serious liability. They had to be led single file rather than ridden, adding to the fatigue of the troopers. Columns stretched for miles. A height of some 1,500 to 1,800 feet took almost three hours to climb. To many troopers, the Judean Hills represented Gallipoli on horseback.

While attempting to block the Nablus road, the troopers became involved in a fierce fight against the strongly defended village of

Beitunia on the eastern end of the prominent Seitun Ridge. The Yeomen, outgunned and outnumbered, failed to capture this Turkish position in repeated attacks. The following excerpts from a report written for the Historical Section, Committee of Imperial Defence, to assist in the writing of the official history, vividly illustrate their plight:

> The ground was rocky, boulder shorn, often precipitous, slippery after rain. The division had suffered heavy casualties in previous fighting and had had few reinforcements... Horses and men were half starved. The Bucks Yeomanry reports that its horses had neither food nor water from the night of the 19th until the morning of the 22nd. The East Riding Yeomanry reports that in 60 hours the men had one half day's rations and some figs, which, with a little tibben [chopped straw], were found in the hamlet of Ain Ariq.[18]

Men in wet desert clothing shivered in torrential rains and freezing wind. They went unshaved and unwashed, and they slept in their boots, which were starting to fall apart. 'The uppers of my boots had been cut and slashed about on the sharp stones. One boot had the sole off and my bruised and aching foot was bound round with a piece of puttee, and two toes protruded from the other as the upper flapped about when I moved',[19] recalled sergeant S.F. Hatton of the 1/1st County of London Yeomanry, 8th Mounted Brigade.

On November 23, Barrow sent back all of his horses except for those belonging to officers and a few delegated for transport. 'I have never seen the endurance of troops tested so greatly as was that of Yeomanry Mounted Division during its ten days in the mountains of Judea. Never have I seen hardships borne more cheerfully and uncomplainingly',[20] Barrow later wrote.

Winter campaigning in the rugged hill above Jerusalem presented similar difficulties for the infantry. The 75th Division, the last British division formed during the war and composed of units that had served in India, which included Ghurkas, soon cleared the ridges of the Turks alongside the Jaffa-Jerusalem road. While standing on the road near Saris, General Bulfin heard the welcoming sounds of a

British success on November 20 – the 'shrill cheers of the Ghurkas and the deep-throated roar of the British troops, following by regimental bugle-calls'.[21]

Frigid rain, however, greeted the troops when they camped that evening. The next day, the 75th Division, abandoning its artillery, left the main road in a north-westerly direction to cut off the Turkish retreat from Jerusalem.

The height of Nebi Samwil dominated Jerusalem and its defences. It was from this site during the Third Crusade that Richard Coeur de Lion supposedly covered his eyes to avoid gazing on the prize beyond his reach. Because of its role in the capture of this 'key' to Jerusalem's defences, the 75th adapted a heraldic 'key' for its divisional badge. It was well deserved: Nebi Samwil was the scene of some of the campaign's most savage fighting as Germans, Austrians, Turks and Syrians repeatedly came to death blows with Scots, Irish, Welsh, English and Ghurkas. Although the 75th captured the famous hill of Nebi Samwil with its picturesque mosque on November 21, the intensity of the fighting around this strategic site intensified as the British continued their advance and the Turks counterattacked. It was an especially tough day for the 75th Division. In close fighting, Turkish soldiers reached the gates of the mosque on Nebi Semwil before being repulsed by Ghurkas.

The ordeal for the wounded retrieved from the battlefield was just beginning. The front was now a great distance from the general hospitals with their clean sheets, British nurses and modern facilities. From the hills above Jerusalem, it usually took a week or more for the wounded to reach the cities of Egypt. One officer compared this journey to the stages of the cross: '(1) Field dressing. (2) Field Dressing Station. (3) No. 1 Casualty Clearing Station. (4) No. 2 Casualty Clearing Station. (5) No. 1 Stationary Hospital. (6) No. 2 Stationary Hospital. (7) General Hospital.' He grimly concluded that 'for a badly wounded man the numerous moves necessary were occasions to be dreaded, and I have known many cases where the soldier has begged in his agony to be left where he is rather than undergo the torture of being shifted'.[22] His means of transportation usually included a combination of the following: camel, mule, sand cart, motor ambulance, cattle truck, and finally a hospital train.

Signaller H.J. Earney of the 9th Mountain Brigade, RGA, who suffered from a fractured skull, a split eardrum, and two knocked-out teeth, describes his relief at finally reaching a British railhead and a proper hospital train that took him to Kantara. 'Here was another short stop and our first sight of nurses in the hospital tent. It *was* good to see an English woman again. Had breakfast of porridge, bacon and bread and butter and dinner of *chicken*. Boarded another hospital train at 4p.m. This was a splendid train too – very comfortable and the attendants were most kind and considerate. Had tea on board. Reached Cairo at 8.30p.m. and soon found myself at the Hospital 70: General.' It had been exactly a week since he had been shelled. 'During that time', he notes, 'there had been no opportunity of getting a wash or any attention beyond having wounds dressed and taking food, so when I was undressed, washed and put into a nice clean bed one can imagine how delightful was the feeling I experienced.'[23]

British wounded were given a field service postcard to inform their loved ones of their condition. It included a stern command: 'Nothing is to be written on this side except the date and signature of the sender. Sentences not required may be erased. *If anything else is added the post card will be destroyed.*' The soldiers' options were as follows:

I am quite well.
I have been admitted into hospital
(sick) and am going on well
(wounded) and hope to be discharged soon
I am being sent down to the base
I have received your letter
telegram
parcel
Letter follows at first opportunity
I have received no letter from you
(lately)
(for a long time)
Signature only
Date

Allenby was nothing if not unrelenting in the pursuit. Since the rolling up of the Gaza-Beersheba front, he had driven his men forward despite their thirst, hunger, inadequate clothing, and exhaustion. He wanted to go as far and as fast as his resources allowed to prevent the routed Turks from recovering. Yet at Nebi Samwil, on November 24, he uncharacteristically suspended his drive to take Jerusalem. The 75th and 52nd Divisions had been marching and fighting since the capture of Gaza, and Allenby realized that continuing the attack with depleted, half-starved and exhausted divisions might lead to their demoralization.

This was the mark of a great soldier. Dawnay wrote of Allenby on the day that he suspended his offensive temporarily, 'More and more I am struck by the Chief's decision, and his flair for estimating how far and at what point it is right to keep up the pressure in spite of difficulties. I think he is wonderful.' Several days earlier, Dawnay had witnessed exhausted troops resting on their march rise to their feet and cheer Allenby 'again and again as he passed'.[24]

The lull in the fighting was brief. Allenby ordered forward the XX Corps to replace the XXI Corps. The 60th Division, which took the place of the 75th and 52nd Divisions in the hills above Jerusalem, was by no means a fresh division. In many ways it was no better off than the divisions it replaced. 'The troops are all well done up. All hobbling about... Country all hills, hills, hills, hills', noted a crippled Calcutt. 'After some bully and raisins, and I have vaselined my feet with Padbury's Vaseline so that they are bearable, we are marched off. I am on guard! Good! Felt absolutely hopeless on these rocks and I fall hopelessly behind',[25] he continued in his diary the next day.

Marshal von Falkenhayn, who had assumed effective control of all Turkish operations on November 6, launched a counterattack on November 27 that continued until December 3. His desperate assault fell first on Barrow's shorthanded Yeomanry Mounted Division and the 60th Division, which had just arrived at the front. Turkish infantry swarmed up the slopes of Nebi Samwil. Vivian Gilbert, the commander of a machine gun company in the 180th Brigade, 60th Division, described the ragged and savage fighting:

One sergeant, whose entire gun team had become casualties, sat at his gun alone surrounded by the corpses of his comrades. His ammunition was getting low, he could not leave the gun, and had no one to send for a fresh supply. Just as his last belt was running through the feed block, a giant Turk appeared over the crest of the hill, his bayonet held out before him, his eyes staring as though mesmerized… but the sergeant, who had kept a few cartridges for the end, with some rapid turns of the wheel, elevated his gun, aimed point blank at his adversary, and pressed the thumb piece… the Turk suddenly crumpled up, his arms shot forward over the gun, and his rifle fell with a clatter on the stones. The centre of the cone of fire had caught him in the throat, severing his head from his body; the blood from the headless trunk poured in a red stream over the sergeant's khaki tunic as he sat on at his gun transfixed.[26]

Reserves that included the Royal Scots Fusiliers, 155th Brigade, 52nd Division, were ordered forward to ease the pressure on the British front. The fusiliers arrived just as the Turks were mounting another attack against the dismounted 3rd Australian Light Horse. As the fusiliers drove the Turks back, one Scotsman spoke for his comrades in arms. Furious with losing yet another night's sleep, he roared as he hurled one Mills grenade after another:

They mairched us a hunnder miles! (Tak' that, ya …!) An' we've been in five fechts! (Anither yin, ya …!) And they said we wur relieved! (Tak' that, ya …!) And we're ott oor beds anither nicht! (Swalla that, ya …!).[27]

Allenby, having beaten off the Turkish counterattack, prepared for the final push (this time by the XX Corps) to take Jerusalem. GHQ established December 8 for the attack. The 60th and 74th Divisions bore the brunt of the fighting. Unlike the first effort to take Jerusalem, a route was chosen that made adequate artillery support possible for the infantry. But the weather turned worse, if that was possible, during the second attempt to take the Holy City. 'Had rations for two days issued, dumped our packs, and moved off at 11a.m.', Blunt wrote in his diary. 'It was an awful day raining all the while. The hills were absolutely wrapped in rain clouds. There was no shelter whatever [and] we simply huddled together in groups wet through. As soon as it was dark we had a rum ration to warm us and then we moved off in single file into the mountains, down gullies and over hills until morning. How I longed for daylight. It was a strength breaking journey, slipping and sliding, in the dense rain and darkness.'[28]

Blunt's company advanced to the front to act as a reserve in the attack against the village of Ain Karim. Calcutt, for his part, remained out of combat because of his bad back and feet. Conditions, however, were no less miserable for him as he collected the packs and blankets left behind by the attacking units. 'Quiet. The lull before the storm', he wrote in his diary:

It proves to be an awful night. The 'naffers' are shuddering with the cold, nothing on their feet and their blue cotton robes no protection. Designed for the desert. The earth runs with water and 'custardy' mud. Trouble in getting camels out to start with. They slip and slide about the whole night, their feet being wonderfully adapted for walking on sand but hopeless in the mud. I am in the rear of the train. Go to Brigade, Brigade to old 'C' Company cook house, from there to new position of the Battalion. It takes us *eight* hours to get there. We should do it in two at the most. Rain and wind all the time and us in shorts and pith helmet and no coat! Wrap myself up in a wet sack. Traffic tremendous, ambulance, camels, tractors, horses, guns, limbers, troops, wagon, all slipping and sliding about. Cursing horses and niggers, 'Kelp' 'Kelp' 'Kelp' 'Ig-gor-ee' 'Ig-gor-ee' 'Ig-gor-ee' 'bastards' flying whips, jerking harness and exasperating immobility of guns and limbers. Get held up by a gun for an hour in one place. Everybody curses camels. Some because they stray, some because they frighten the mules, others because they are not used to them, and others because they curse anything.[29]

The attack by the 60th and 74th Divisions on the 8th thus took place in driving rain and mist. The London Scottish (2/14 London Regiment), 179th Brigade, 60th Division, won the first of its two Victoria Crosses during the campaign on this day. Corporal C.W. Train, who led the No. 10 Platoon rifle grenade section, took on two

German machine guns single-handedly. With 'C' Company stalled by heavy machine gun fire, he moved on his own to the left flank of the enemy's breastworks, which had been constructed of boulders. After crawling to within sixty yards, he fired several rifle grenades. When a German officer returned his fire, he put him out of commission with a bullet in his buttocks. He then finished off with rifle and bomb those who continued to resist. When 'C' Company occupied the enemy position, it found seven Turks dead by the first gun and two by the second. The wounded German officer and two other men were taken prisoner.[30]

After encountering stronger-than-expected resistance, the troops endured another miserable night. They had dumped their packs before the attack, so the troops had only iron rations to eat and rolled waterproof sheets, which they carried on their shoulders, to protect them from the elements. 'My word how the cold and rain blew through my shorts',[31] Blunt recalled. The weather improved on the 9th, as did the spirits of the Tommies when they discovered that the Turkish 7th Army had retreated during the night. By 7a.m., no organized body of the enemy remained in Jerusalem. Four centuries of Turkish rule had abruptly come to an end.

December 9 proved a busy day for the Turkish mayor and other city dignitaries as they sought to hand over the keys to the city to the British. Perhaps no famous city has ever surrendered as many times in a single day and to so diverse a groups of soldiers, who ranged from cooks to sergeants to artillery officers to generals. And then, ironically, none of these capitulations was publicized and GHQ ordered the destruction of all photographs recording the various surrender ceremonies. Why? Because Lloyd George wanted the honour of announcing the fall of Jerusalem in Parliament, which he did on the 10th.

The day after the prime minister spoke in the House of Commons, Allenby, in the most dramatic and photographed event of the campaign, made his official entry into the city. Out of respect for the sacred nature of the city, he walked rather than rode through the Jaffa Gate as the thirty-fourth conqueror of Jerusalem. After a campaign of forty days and approximately 18,000 casualties, Allenby's predominately Territorial forces had given the nation the Christmas present that Lloyd George had demanded.

It is perhaps only just that the Turkish mayor initially tried to hand over the keys to the city to the ranks and lower officers who had borne the brunt of this extraordinary campaign that rivalled in suffering and intensity, although not in duration, such British offensives on the western front as the Somme and Third Ypres. The bizarre chain of events on December 9 had gone as follows. When the Turks abandoned Jerusalem, the mayor and other dignitaries attempted to find someone to accept the keys to the city. The first soldiers they encountered were two mess cooks of the 2/20th London Regiment (Blackheath and Woolwich), 180th Brigade, Privates R.W.J. Andrew and H.E. Church, who had lost their way trying to find water and had wandered near the gates of the city. These two privates, out of their element, beat a hasty retreat. The next soldiers to be approached were two sergeants, F.G. Hurcomb and J. Sedgewick, 2/19th London Regiment (St Pancras), 180th Brigade, who were on outpost duty. They too were reluctant to accept the capitulation of the city. This was also true of two artillery officers from the 60th Divisional Artillery, Majors W. Beck and F.R. Barry, who promised to report to their superiors. At this point, Lieutenant Colonel H. Bayley, the commander of the 303rd Brigade RFA, 60th Division, appeared on the scene. 'Arriving at the top of the road within sight of the Jewish Hospital in Jerusalem and with my 3 battery commanders I was amazed to see a white flag waving and a man coming towards me. I beckoned him on and speaking French he said the Mayor of Jerusalem was at the flag… We sat on chairs on the road outside the Jewish Hospital and he informed me the Turks had left Jerusalem during the night retreating towards Jericho... Much photographing of me and mayor.' Bayley then sent the following message to the 60th Division headquarters: 'Jerusalem has surrendered. Col. Bayley D.S.O., R.F.A. is now with the Mayor awaiting any General Officer to take over the City.'

The first general to appear on the scene was Brigadier General C.F. Watson, the commander of the 180th Brigade, 60th Division. Watson, characterized by Bayley as 'an awful little ass who specially

wanted to be first there', joined Bayley in making their way to the
Jaffa Gate and walking through the gap (made especially for Kaiser
William II's earlier visit) to be greeted by an enthusiastic crowd.
General Shea arrived shortly thereafter. Shea, unhappy that he had
been upstaged by Watson, repeated the surrender ceremony, only to
be informed by Allenby that the honour of receiving the surrender
belonged to him.[32]

Some ordinary soldiers, however, could not be denied their
moment of glory on December 9. Sergeant John Francis Jones, who
had five brothers in the service, four in the army and one in the
navy, and Private Blunt were in the 179th Brigade, 60th Division, as
it marched to within sight of the city. It was a motley-looking group,
and Major Vivian Gilbert took note of their altered appearance since
the beginning of the campaign. Before the XX Corps breached the
defences of Beersheba, initiating a fluid war of movement, the 60th
Division had been 'the last word in smartness, with their new drill
tunics, shining brass buttons, pith helmets and shorts. Now', Gilbert
wrote:

> …their uniforms were tattered, dirty and blood-stained; most of them
> had beards and had not enjoyed a real wash for weeks; many were
> wounded, and practically all had bandages round their bare knees
> where the rocks had cut them and produced septic sores. The tor-
> rential rains had reduced their smart pith helmets to shapeless pulp.
> Tramps would have thrown away as useless the boots my men were
> glad to wear. They were terribly thin and wretched looking; their
> cheek-bones stood out prominently; dark rings under their eyes were
> the legacies left by sleepless nights and countless privations.[33]

Yet they persevered. Venables, a lieutenant in the Egyptian Labour
Corps, observed with amazement how the infantry plunged 'on
through the mud, whistling and singing, or passing humourous
remarks: "Why did I join the Army," "Don't kick up the dust," and
so forth. They grouse, naturally, but not seriously, for a spirit seems
to determine them, whether they are prepared to admit it or not, to
"stick it." The way they do stick it is a miracle past all understanding.'[34]

For a brief moment, the hardships of the campaign were forgotten, and the men of the 179th Brigade had a spring to their step. 'We hadn't seen a town for months', Jones remembers, 'and did not of course expect to march through. But as we drew nearer and nearer, and the column did not turn off, we began to hope. Would they turn? Everybody was watching the front, some betting odds that they would never march in. Yet they did.'

Excitement rippled through the ranks. 'It was a triumphal entry. Thousands of people, most of them of European origins lined the route, cheering, laughing, and welcoming us in all imaginable languages', Jones continued. The presence of European women was thrilling to both Blunt and Jones. 'Girls – real live white girls – threw flowers', Jones wrote. 'It was an exhilarating experience, and we swung our arms and swaggered like guardsmen as we went through.'[35]

But at the moment of its triumph, Allenby's forces faced starvation. 'The line of communications had been, by the lightning advance, suddenly lengthened by about fifty per cent. Across this newly-won area a railway was being pushed with all possible speed, but the engineers' labours were doubled, tripled, by the rain and floods, which washing away banks, bridges and rails like toys, and mercilessly cut communications again and again',[36] Venables, a lieutenant in the Egyptian Labour Corps, reported in a letter home.

When the British had advanced into the hills to Jerusalem, the camels and their long-suffering drivers, assisted by a small number of mules, had literally carried Allenby's forces on their backs. Yet, as Barrow comments, 'one cannot imagine in the whole animal world any creature less suited to mountain warfare than the camel'.[37] Its feet were designed for marching over sand, but they were not suited for traversing a wet and slippery surface. Camels fell from steep rocky paths, breaking their back or legs. Others ruptured themselves by doing splits in the slippery mud and slush of the roads. Their drivers, many of whom were barefoot and wore only thin cotton robes, fared little better. 'Poor beggars, they come from a dry sunny climate, where rain is never seen. Their bodies therefore cannot stand these drenching, chilly torrents, and their simple minds, unfortified by any spirit of determination, utterly fail to understand the meaning of "sticking it", a concerned Venables wrote home. 'At the first shower they are down, done, dejected, dispirited, demoralized.' With little success, Venables showed them how to improvise shelters in the constant and driving rain. 'Rather than make any attempt at shelter, they preferred to lie down as they were, or sit crouching in the mud, mourning helplessly, "It is better to die." In vain we would rouse them and urge them to make a fight of it against the weather, and assist them in the fashioning of a shelter. As soon as we moved from one spot to another, they would lapse into their fatalistic help-lessness, 'It is better to die, It is better to die!"[38] And many did die, literally sobbing themselves to death.

Truck drivers, along with the fellahin, were some of the unsung heroes in the EEF. They brought supplies from the closest British railheads to forward depots such as Latron, where it could be trans-ferred to camel convoys. 'The state of this road [to Latron]', according to Venables, 'under the continuous traffic of convoys of three-ton lorries can be better imagined than described. In many places the thin stone covering was worn right through, leaving gaps of earth beneath. At best the road was only wide enough for one vehicle at a time, and when one convoy met another, the empty lorries return-ing south, having to give place to those loaded going north, would have to leave the road, and pull on to the earth at the side. Here, in the wet weather, they would at once stick fast in the oozing mud, from which it might take hours to drag them on to the road again.' There was little time for sleep or rest for the drivers. One driver told Venables that 'he had been sixteen hours coming as many miles, he still had nine miles to go, and that he was under orders to return immediately, for another journey'.[39]

A combination of untoward events brought the EEF's make-shift services of supply to a standstill as Christmas Day approached. Railways were either cut or under water at many points, stormy seas prevented supplies from being landed, and camel and truck convoys were stymied by water and mud. The miserable weather and the unavailability of promised special rations, such as tinned chicken and plum pudding, made the EEF's Christmas of 1917 one of the worst ever experienced by a British force in modern times.

The experiences of Blunt and Calcutt in the 179th Brigade, 60th Division, were typical of many soldiers in the hills surrounding Jerusalem. On Christmas Eve, Blunt discovered that his camp was under water. 'I don't think I have ever felt so despondent. After a ration of rum Hewer & I got out of the quarry on to a high slab of stone where we felt safe from being drowned and huddled together to keep as warm as possible. Both of us felt we were bound to die of exposure. What a Xmas Eve.' Christmas Day was little better. 'Rations were almost non existent. We only had one cup of tea all day', he continued in his diary. 'Another awful night. Rained continuously. Mud stuck half way up our puttees. When you sat down you could not get up without assistance. What a Xmas Day? How we shall all remember it.'[40] Conditions were no better in Calcutt's unit. Shivering, with the rain 'beating and swirling' against his 'frail bivvy', Calcutt used the dim light of a flickering candle to record the day's events:

> Blankets all soaking and covered in mud. The place is a quagmire. Blanket wet throughout, but my sack has protected me a bit. The bivvy fell in or was blown down or something in the night and had to be propped up with rifles and sticks. It is all wet and floppy and muddy and pegs coming out. It rains all day. We get out in the rain and make effort at setting it right, and at draining the water off. But the mud is eight inches deep and you cannot dig as you simply get a daub of heavy stuff on the shovel and cannot get it off!! Rations bad: we have two cups of cocoa all day and lucky to get that. Bit of cheese and a few biscuits: about 10 small square ones, and a few dates. So we sit huddled up in our overcoats all day. Lousey. Sopping wet. Boots letting water and with three inches of mud on them that sticks and clings to everything.[41]

Although Calcutt hated army life, he was prepared to 'stick it'. He spoke for many British soldiers who accepted their fate, either through sheer bloody-mindedness or a fatalistic pragmatism, when he concluded his diary entry on Christmas Day. 'But one bears hardships when one sees the reasons. Rain! Well that can't be helped, grin and bear it. Mud! Well that is the result of the rain, nobody's fault that, and so on. I think I have been infinitely more perturbed by some irritation I could not see the reason for.'[42]

Although the weather improved on December 26, the situation remained grim. The members of the 179th Brigade began to dig in, in anticipation of a Turkish counterattack to retake Jerusalem. Sergeant Jones, who had a teacher's certificate and was working on a degree as a student at London University when he joined the Territorials, was apprehensive. 'I had lost confidence in my capacity to avoid being hit. A premonition, perhaps; perhaps only the result of over-strain; for that Christmas Day, coming on top of months of hardship, was taking its toll of all of us.'[43]

On December 27 at about 1.30a.m., the Turks struck, with the weight of their attack falling on the 179th Brigade, which was positioned north of Jerusalem on the Nablus Road. The fighting focused on control of the dominating heights of Tell el Ful and the Khadase Ridge, which were just east of the Nablus Road and some three miles north of Jerusalem. Jones's Company 'D' of the Civil Service Rifles was sent forward, platoon by platoon, to attack the Turkish flank and sweep them off the hill. The company commander, according to Jones, 'decided which platoon was to go first by counting heads; the other platoon had one more than we – their officer – so they led the way, and we followed'.

Jones was all too aware of the heavy losses suffered by 'D' Company since the breaking of the Turkish front. 'It is a striking commentary on the depletion of our forces at this time that of these two platoons of D Company, mine was made up of the remnants of 14 and 16 platoons, 14 platoon having temporarily ceased to have any official existence; while the other one was a borrowed one, not a man in it belonging to D Company. If my memory serves, there were twenty-three of them and twenty-two of us.'

Initially the attack went well, with the surprised Turks ejected from their position with the bayonet. But Jones and his comrades now came under heavy enemy machine gun fire. There were no trenches on this mass of rock, only boulders to offer some cover. 'I found myself behind one such rock with about half a dozen men, including my bivouac-mate Murphovitch, who was wounded in the leg', Jones wrote. When he heard an officer some fifty yards to the rear shouting 'withdraw', Jones complied, sending 'men off in driblets, letting them use cover as they liked'. When most were shot down, Jones 'abandoned the attempt' and 'lay listening to the groans and shouts of men lying invisible somewhere behind us, caught by the machine-guns on their way back'.

In retrospect, Jones believed that he and his men should 'have made a dash for it, all at once, every man for himself'. Jones, writing in 1934, pondered his decision, which may have cost lives:

> Almost every man who commanded men in action during the war, if he is not completely self-satisfied, must know of one or more occasions when, had he done something different lives would have been saved. Probably the professional soldier does not allow this to trouble him; he is trained to consider death – his own or that of others – as part of the game; and if one makes a false move at chess and loses a piece or two, what matter? One must accept some such explanation, for otherwise nearly all generals would have committed suicide. But to the civilian in khaki who had held life sacred, the minor commander who knew his men as friends, the problem is not so simple… It may be pleaded in my favour that I had been in a similar position before; at Beersheba I had lain out in front of the line, taking cover with my men from machine-gun fire; and in due time the battalion had come through and saved us; they might well do so again. I must admit, too, that I had failed to learn a lesson of war; that the wounded are of no importance when action is to be considered. For my part, I couldn't face the idea of leaving them; and had promised Murphovitch that if we went back I'd take him in; while Tiny, the huge corporal I had borrowed from 14 platoon, insisted that he too should lend a hand. So we stayed where we were.

Soon Jones's position was outflanked by the Turks, who approached to within twenty yards. Jones drew his rifle to shoot a Turk. A 'sledge-hammer blow hit my left arm above the elbow', he recalled, 'knocking my rifle out of my hand. I had been hit at ten yards range, and as my arm was crossing my body at the time the bullet had missed my heart by about two inches.' Jones, lucky to be alive, suffered combat shock. 'I have read several accounts by modest and truthful men of how they went on fighting when wounded once, twice, even thrice', he noted. 'Either wounds differ or those men are made of different stuff from me; for that tremendous blow knocked all the fight out of me; it seemed to hit me in the brain. I could do nothing but crawl behind the nearest rock; and there I lay.'

Jones was soon joined by three other men, all unwounded. 'They're all dead in front', a noncommissioned officer from 'C' Company announced. 'Whether he meant our men or Turks I did not think to ask; I took it he meant our men, but no Turks came on', Jones remembers. After a time that seemed to last for hours, a private serving as lookout announced in a half-whisper, 'They're only about twenty yards away; they're looting the wounded.' When Jones looked from his hiding place, he saw 'a Turk in a *Khaki* overcoat, the fruit, probably, of an abortive attack by one of our battalions a fortnight before. Beyond him, on the far hill, I saw two or three men scrambling down the hill side, singly.' Jones immediately decided that 'This was no place for a wounded man. To my slow-working brain came an inspiration.' He told the noncommissioned officer from 'C' Company, 'I'm going.' He rose and began to walk the some fifty yards to the next ridge and cover:

> I made no attempt to run; I felt that it would be fatal to do so. Half of my mind was saying 'Hurry, you fool,' while the other half said 'Take it slowly.' Were not some of the Turks wearing *khaki* overcoats? And had I not shed my equipment? So I trudged on, waiting for a shot to hit me in the back. That walk seemed to last hours; but no shot came, till I was within five yards of the top, when one hit the ridge to my left. Then I went up the rocks like a leaping deer, turned half left to follow the line of rocks and shambled back towards our line.[44]

Jones and his platoon had initially exposed themselves to enemy fire when a Turk had pretended to surrender. Lieutenant Chipperfield, 180th Machine Gun Company, who commanded a section of four

Vickers guns that had been attached to the 179th Brigade, had a similar experience. At daybreak, he observed the Turks advancing on his left. He didn't bother with cover. He got his two guns on top of a ridge and began to:

> …blaze away. Suffer two casualties while doing this – Bereton, shot through the stomach, dies later. Almost as soon as we start firing, the enemy put up a white flag. Having seen this happen before, get the third gun up and give them all we've got. Eventually have to stop firing as infantry commander wants to send a party out to capture these would-be prisoners. As soon as our fellows get into a sort of quarry below the enemy, they are bombed to blazes. We spend the rest of the day committing atrocities, shooting everything that moves – wounded, stretcher bearers, Red Crescent parties… Constant barrages and attacks. We are mainly firing short bursts at anything we can see. Fool of a Turk coming up to take his place in the line, stands at full height to fire his rifle from the shoulder. Give him five rounds, knock his head off and see it fall before he drops.[45]

The fierce fighting in the hills north of Jerusalem on December 27–29 brought out the best and worst in the men. Captain Case, a junior engineer officer in the 60th Division, was filled with admiration for the courage and tenacity of Britain's citizen soldiers. 'Can you picture to yourself the terrible stress and individual strain of this trying period; can you imagine the hardships (*on ½ rations*) of those 3 cold and wet days and nights, the fatigue entailed in attacking over such awful country, and most of all can you picture the men who achieved so magnificently this task. As poor physiqued, and pallid faced Londoners in 1915?! On such occasions one can almost believe that war has a few good points.'[46]

On the other hand, the accounts by Jones and Chipperfield reflect the savage, no-holds-barred character of the fighting in this and other battles for the control of the Holy City. Bernard Blaser, a scout in the London Scottish, 179th Brigade, 60th Division, described the killing of prisoners on the eve of Jerusalem's fall. The Turks had kept up a steady fire until the British were upon them. When they tried to surrender, according to Blaser, 'the sight of the recumbent and bleeding forms of our comrades lying around did not tend to promote feelings of mercy, and the tactics of the Turks had so incensed us that bayonets got to work slick and sure. Turks who had been doing their utmost to mow us down were now on their bended knees; angry oaths were uttered, and cries for mercy arose above the din; but no quarter was given; a few bayonet thrusts, a few shots fired point-blank, and they toppled over dead.'[47]

With the British now fighting in a populated region, civilians also became casualties of war. Lieutenant Buxton, now serving with the 20th Brigade, Royal Horse Artillery, confessed that the war was making him callous. 'I have seen a troop of villagers shelled by the Turks, as they fled from their village – my only inward comment has been "Thank God our own troops are not bunched on the sky line like that." I have hurried over the same ground afterwards in the press of business, noticed the dead civilians with "interest," and its been a good few hours before I have realised the cruelty and horror of war, that exposes men, one day quiet in their homes, the next caught in a battle and accidentally killed, in which they were taking no part.'[48] Buxton concluded: 'In our rotten half developed world, we have to submit to one evil that good may come. But I can't help feeling that this war will leave a stigma on all who have participated in it, a slight increase of hardness and bitterness, which will make them less fit for the building afterwards.'[49]

Once desperate Turkish counterattacks against the front of the 60th and 53rd Divisions were checked with heavy loss to the attacker, the XX Corps resumed the offensive all along its front. By the end of December, the Jaffa-Jerusalem line had been secured, but not without hard fighting. Earlier the 52nd Division, XXI Corps, in a brilliant operation, had crossed the River Auju, which flows into the sea about four miles north of Jaffa. This successful operation on the night of December 20–21 resulted in pushing the Turkish line some eight miles from Jaffa.

The Territorial-dominated offensive in Palestine was the one bright spot on Allied battlefields in late 1917. The prolonged British offensive in Flanders had ended with heavy loss and no strategic gain.

Britain's allies had fared even worse. As the year ended, the French army was still recovering from a serious mutiny, the Russians had been knocked out of the war, and the Italians were hanging by a thread after their rout at Caporetto. Turkey had not been driven from the war, but she had been psychologically wounded by the collapse of the Gaza-Beersheba front and the loss of the Holy City. Moreover, Allenby's advance helped secure the British position in Baghdad and Mesopotamia, encouraged the Arab revolt, and inflicted irreplaceable losses on the Turkish army.

But British success in the Middle East had not come cheaply. Allenby had lost approximately 30 per cent of his fighting strength since October 30 (28,000 out of 97,000),[50] and his services of supply had difficulty sustaining even this diminished force on the Jaffa-Jerusalem front. As Allenby admitted to Robertson on January 3, 'I could not deploy more troops, even if I had them, until my railway line is doubled.'[51] Nor had the capture of Jerusalem brought Britain's primary rival, Germany, any closer to defeat. In fact, Britain was confronted with the frightening prospect of Germany winning the war on the Continent before the United States could make its presence felt on European battlefields. Rather than strengthen Britain's position on the western front, Lloyd George's response was to redouble his efforts to give British grand strategy a new direction. He believed that all offensives on the western front – German or Allied – were doomed to failure, and he was determined to give first priority to British forces in Palestine in 1918.[52]

9

Changing Priorities

If Lloyd George had his way, the Middle East would become the focus of Britain's military effort in 1918. His agile mind saw political as well as military advantages in giving priority to Allenby's forces. With Russia faltering and with France in a defensive mood after its army mutinied, Lloyd George believed British gains at the expense of Turkey might serve as an insurance policy in the event of an inconclusive end to the war. 'If Russia collapsed', he once told the War Cabinet, 'it would be beyond our power to beat Germany, as the blockade would become to a great extent ineffective, and the whole of the enemies' forces would become available to oppose the Western Allies. We could not contemplate with equanimity the prospect of entering a Peace Conference with the enemy in possession of a large slice of Allied territory before we had completed the conquest of Mesopotamia and Syria.'[1] Russia's headlong decline during the last half of 1917 especially concerned the imperial-minded members of the government. If unrestrained by Russian pressure, the Turko-German alignment posed a formidable threat to Britain's imperial position in both Africa and Asia.

Robertson, however, kept his eye firmly on the main body of the German army, insisting that the war would be won or lost on the western front. He recognized Lloyd George's 'eastern' (or indirect) as opposed to 'western' approach for what it was: a policy designed primarily to protect and expand the British Empire rather than defeat Germany. However, his support of Haig's controversial offensive in the mud of Flanders (popularly known as the Passchendaele Offensive) seriously undermined his standing in the War Cabinet during the summer and autumn. When Allenby took Jerusalem in December, he lost what was left of his credibility as the War Cabinet's strategic adviser.

Before the rupture of the Gaza-Beersheba front, the general staff (on the War Cabinet's instructions) had asked Allenby about his requirements to capture and defend Jerusalem. This request was accompanied by a 'personal and secret' telegram from Robertson that warned Allenby that he 'should take no chances [in his estimates] because of the many uncertain factors. You should also remember that transport, supply, water, time and space are imperfectly realised here and therefore they may need emphasising'.[2] Allenby subsequently shocked the ministers when he requested an additional thirteen divisions. Yet without these massive reinforcements, he routed the Turks and took Jerusalem two months later. Believing that they had been misled, the ministers demanded answers. Robertson tried to defend Allenby's inflated estimate of potential Turkish strength upon which his extraordinary request for an additional thirteen divisions had been based. 'If we had under-estimated the Turk and failed we should have deserved to be hung', he told an angry and disbelieving prime minister.[3]

Allenby's success made Lloyd George even more determined that Britain's main military effort in 1918 would be in the Middle East. On December 13, the War Cabinet instructed the general staff to consider two policies: the conquest of Palestine which would involve an advance of about 100 miles; or a distant advance to Aleppo to cut Turkish communications with Mesopotamia.

Although the Turks were reeling from their defeat at the hands of the Egyptian Expeditionary Force, the Jaffa-Jerusalem line probably represented the limit that Allenby's half-starved and diminished force could achieve during the rainy season. His Territorials, both foot and mounted, were exhausted from continuous marching and fighting. 'Lord! What would I give for this ruddy war to cease', Buxton wrote home:

Of course, one gets a sort of alive feeling out of a really exciting battle, but its an artificial excitement... The kind of enjoyment I want again is the sort you bask in, and purr, like the end of a days hunting, or dancing with pretty girls, or smelling fish scales... or looking at the top leaf of a tree from a deck chair, with a gentle puff of methylated spirits occasionally wafting from the silver kettle on the tea table... would be infinitely more enjoyable than one minute of this present war.[4]

Private Blunt's thoughts also turned to home as he ushered in the New Year while standing guard. 'What an occurrence to think I should be looking over sleeping Jerusalem this night above all others. Well I hope this time next year to be back in the dear old home at Charlbury. How I thought of mother and all of them.'[5]

The new year began with Allenby's forces paralyzed by a break-down in logistics. On January 13, Adams, a brigade major to the 231st Brigade, 74th (Yeomanry) Division, noted in his diary: 'One's sole interest in life is food and I feel sure we shall be soon cutting each other's throats in the night for a tin of bully. There have lately been a good many cases of men stealing each other's iron rations in the regiment.'[6] Allenby's mobile arm, the Desert Mounted Corps, with the exception of the Yeomanry brigades, had suffered few casualties during the recent fighting. But both the troopers and their horses faced starvation if they stayed at the front. 'At present, I have had to send two divisions of my mounted troops and the Imperial Camel Corps south of Gaza', Allenby informed Robertson. 'As I can't feed them, with certainty; and, even now, a fortnight's heavy rain would bring me near starvation.'[7]

Robertson continued to stress to the War Cabinet the difficulty of supplying Allenby with the men and supplies he needed for a distant advance, whether into northern Palestine or all the way to Aleppo. But his central argument remained the same: Britain could not defeat Germany in Palestine but might lose the war by diverting its military assets to that front. 'I would submit that the War Cabinet should, before deciding to undertake the Palestine campaign, con-sider closely the probability of the enemy attempting to force a decision on the Western front, including Italy, early in 1918, and the possibility of his succeeding in doing so if we do not concentrate our resources there.'[8]

With Robertson's influence now at its nadir, Lloyd George moved to bypass him and implement his Palestine obsession. The Welsh wizard had earlier played a leading role in creating the Supreme War Council with an inter-Allied general staff located at Versailles. His stated rationale was the co-ordination of Allied strategy; his real purpose was to sidetrack Robertson and redirect British strategy. He had found another general more amenable to his ideas – General Sir Henry Wilson, whom he selected as Britain's permanent military representative at Versailles. Through Wilson, he intended to play a deciding role in the formulation of Allied military plans in 1918.

The tall and ungainly Wilson was widely viewed by many senior officers as being a political general. Whatever the justice of this charge, Wilson certainly got along well with the British ministers. In part, this was due to his willingness to treat their views on military matters with respect, whatever he might privately believe. He also had a relaxed demeanour and a quick and self-deprecating sense of humour, once remarking that if a letter were addressed to the ugliest man in the army, he would receive it.

Wilson's tenure at Versailles did little to enhance his reputation. When asked by the politicians to divine German intentions in 1918, he resorted to war gaming. To get inside the mind of the Bosch, he told his staff to wear their hats backwards to imitate German officers. He apparently believed that the western front was 'safe & two or three divisions from Palestine would make no difference',[9] and he lobbied the members of the inter-Allied staff for a major effort to drive Turkey from the war in 1918. His advocacy of a major offensive in the east was based on the view that 'the present condition of Turkey is one of almost complete material and moral exhaustion'.[10]

Lieutenant Colonel A.P. Wavell, who had been acting as the Chief of the Imperial General Staff's liaison officer with Allenby, was sent to Versailles by Robertson because of his intimate knowledge of the Palestine theatre. He attempted to pour cold water on the idea that Turkey was ripe for the picking. According to Wavell, 'No one in Palestine ever doubted that we could beat the Turk, but no responsible person saw how we could advance at the rate the Government wanted.' Wilson, who apparently had 'persuaded himself that if we got to Damascus the Turks would throw out the Germans and make a separate peace', dissented. He told Wavell, 'If I was a German standing on the Pera Bridge at Constantinople, looking at the Golden Horn, I should be saying to myself – Mein Gott, I hope Allenby doesn't attack Damascus.'[11]

To Robertson's dismay, Lloyd George, with Wilson working as his spear carrier, succeeded in getting qualified approval from the Supreme War Council for Joint Note No.12, which called for a 'decisive offensive against Turkey with a view to the annihilation of the Turkish armies and the collapse of Turkish resistance'. The destruction of Turkey, it was claimed, 'would not only have the most far-reaching results upon the general military situation, but might also, if not too long deferred, be in time to enable the Allies to get into direct touch with, and give effective help to, such elements of resistance to German domination as may still exist in Roumania and Southern Russia'.[12]

To ensure the implementation of Joint Note No.12, Lloyd George immediately sent Smuts to confer with Allenby. As Smuts packed his bags for a voyage to Egypt, Robertson composed a cautionary message to Allenby, reminding him once again that his proposed operations might have a detrimental impact on the main theatre in France. As for reinforcements, the EEF could expect very little. 'I see no prospect whatever of sending you more divisions than you now have, except perhaps one from Mesopotamia and even this is doubtful. Similarly as regards drafts.'[13]

Smuts, however, proved far more optimistic about augmenting Allenby's forces for a decisive campaign. An important qualification imposed by the French in supporting Joint Note No.12 was that no British troops in France could be deployed in Allenby's theatre. Smuts therefore proposed that Indian troops be used, both from the Indian Army and from Mesopotamia. Smuts also played the strategist, but the suggestions he offered bore little resemblance to Allenby's later campaign.[14] Soldiers such as Chetwode were distinctly unimpressed with some of the South African general's ideas. The commander of the XX Corps wrote to Wavell after the war: 'With regard to the Smuts/Amery interview. Were you there? If so do you remember the frightful nonsense they talked in the garden of our headquarters in Jerusalem. They suggested that we should cross the Jordan and use the Hedjaz railway to, what they called "turn the Damascus position," quite forgetting that we had no rolling stock on it nor were the Turks likely to leave any; to say nothing of the fact that we were at the extreme end of our supplies in the Jordan valley, let alone Amman.'[15]

On March 6, the War Cabinet unleashed Allenby, giving him the green light to advance 'to the maximum extent possible, consistent with the safety of the force under his orders'.[16] Robertson's restraining hand no longer rested on Allenby's shoulder. He had been forced out as CIGS in mid-February. Wilson, who seemed more concerned about the German threat to the British Empire than to Paris or the Channel ports, took his place in the War Office. If preventive measures were not taken, which included an offensive by Allenby, Wilson warned the ministers, 'we run a grave risk of permitting the Germans to establish themselves in a position which will eventually lead to the downfall of our Eastern Empire'.[17]

As the Germans massed their troops in front of the British defences on the Somme, Allenby focused on his offensive preparations. To enlarge his force, he took the initial steps to create a third corps – the XXII, commanded by Barrow with Wavell as his chief of staff. These officers were busily at work on March 21 establishing the new corps when the EEF attempted its crossing of the Jordan River. Even before the Smuts mission, Allenby had outlined his initial objectives to Robertson, which included an attack across the Jordan River. After consolidating his position and developing his communications, he planned to extend his right to include Jericho. His next move was to cross the Jordan, advance on Amman, and cut the vital Turkish Hejaz railway (the 800-mile line that that ran from Medina to Damascus). 'If I could destroy 10 or 15 miles of rail and some bridges; and get [in] touch with the Arabs under Feisal – even temporarily – the effect would be great',[18] he told Robertson. (Emir Feisal, assisted by T.E. Lawrence, had made headway in mobilizing

Arab tribes against the Turks and was advancing east and south-east of the Dead Sea.)

Allenby chose Shea, the aggressive commander of the 60th Division, to lead this assault across the Jordan and into the mountains of Moab. 'Shea's Force', as it was called, consisted of the 60th Division, ANZAC Mounted Division, Imperial Camel Corps Brigade, one heavy battery, a mountain artillery brigade, and bridging and pontoon units. Normally the Jordan was easy to cross, but this was the rainy season when the river overflowed its banks, doubling its size, with a current running at twelve or more miles an hour. Initially it had been hoped that the existing fords might be used to get heavily equipped men across. A company of the London Scottish, 179th Brigade, 60th Division, was sent to find the ford thought to be located at El Mandesi, some three miles from Ghoraniyeh. In darkness on March 6, the men of the London Scottish found their way to the Jordan with difficulty. 'Men waded in all directions, only to be swept off their feet by the swift current. Casts were made up and down stream, all without result', Lieutenant Colonel J.H. Lindsay of the London Scottish later recalled. The next evening, the men returned with stakes and ropes. But according to Lindsay, the two men who tried to swim the river 'were swept away like corks'.[19]

The British now had no choice. The 2/17th and 2/19th Battalions of the 180th Brigade, 60th Division, were assigned the dangerous task of forcing a crossing at Ghoraniyeh and Hijla. Matters went disastrously for the 2/17th Battalion (Poplar and Stepney) at Ghoraniyeh when on March 21 its men moved into position at midnight. 'Everything was terribly quiet', Sergeant A.V. Young remembered as he carried his raft to the river's bank. 'One man went in to swim across, in fact did cross, on the other side he clutched a root to pull himself up on to the bank, when it gave way. This gave the alarm for challenges rang out & we were soon the object of a sweeping fire from machine guns. Another attempt was made higher up... but two swimmers were *lost* & we had severe casualties.'[20] Brave soldiers drowned when their barges, made of tarpaulins stretched over a wooden framework, were pierced by enemy fire and became waterlogged. Improvised rafts made of wood fared no better. The order had to be given to withdraw.[21]

As the fighting could be heard upstream at Ghoraniyeh, the 2/19th Battalion (St Pancras) went into action at Hilja. From the cover of scrub on the bank of the Jordan, Major Vivian Gilbert observed true grit as men struggled, some being killed or wounded in the process, to bridge the river. Eight strong men had been picked from many volunteers to swim the treacherous river and attach a rope to the other side to make possible the construction of a pontoon bridge. 'The Turkish watch fires rose and fell, at times casting a lurid glare over the valley, at others lighting up the obscurity of the river and causing the naked bodies of the swimmers to stand out pale and golden as they hesitated for a moment to adjust the ropes before plunging into the dark, mud-laden waters that swirled with an eerie sighing towards the Dead Sea', Gilbert remembered.

'I could follow our swimmers on their perilous journey', Gilbert continued, 'for the small white patches their shoulders made in con-trast to the brown coloured river stood out clearly. I knew when a man was hit by a bullet or got into difficulties, because the small patch became a big one as the whole body came to the surface, was buffeted about in the current for a time, and then disappeared out of sight.' It is Gilbert's recollection that all eight men failed to effect a crossing. G.E. Jones, a young lieutenant, eventually succeeded in securing a rope to a tree trunk. A flat-bottomed boat with thirty-two men was then pulled across. All became casualties, according to Gilbert, when the Turks scored a direct hit. More men were wounded or killed before steel chains could be attached to trees and a temporary bridge built.[22] By March 23, most of Shea's Force was across the Jordan, but the operation was now behind schedule, with the Turks rushing forward men to defend Amman and its important railway.

The mountains of Moab proved no less an obstacle than the Jordan when the weather turned nasty on March 25. Heavy rain mixed with sleet continued almost without cease throughout the remainder of the operation. This atrocious weather slowed the advance of troops and forced the British to leave behind their artillery except for a few mountain guns. The infantry, their boots clogged with mud and their packs and clothing soaked through, took the main road that led to Es Salt and then on to Amman, the primary target of the raid.

Weary troops continued their mountain climb as darkness approached. With the disappearance of light, the pack animals rebelled. 'First to go were the Mess donkeys, which one after the other subsided on the track and resolutely refused to try any more. Some of the mules caught the infection and also stopped', an officer in the London Scottish 179th recalled. 'The camels under the Transport Officer had long since dropped hopelessly to the rear. Men began to drop in their tracks, not because they could march no further, but because they were falling asleep. It looked as though the Scottish had at last been set a marching task which was beyond their powers.'[23] The cavalry, followed by the 'Cameliers', advanced by tracks further to the south in the direction of Amman. These narrow paths, according to Bluett, 'would have given a mountain goat the horrors, across wadis and nullahs so steep that the horses had to be let down by ropes and hauled up the other side, while the "Cameliers" had to build their roads as they went along, a camel being rather an inconvenient beast on which to scale the slippery sides of a cliff'.[24]

A.S. Benbow rode with the 9th Company, Imperial Camel Corps Brigade. His adventure had begun when he led his camel across a pontoon bridge over the turbulent Jordan River. 'Pontoons had to be secured very strongly and yet allow for any sudden rise or fall', he noted. 'These conditions made it a hazardous movement for mounted men, any break during the transit causing immersion in the raging water with little or no hope of surviving.'[25] When the mounted forces finally reached Amman, the Turks had collected some 5,000 rifles and fifteen guns for its defence. Hampered by the weather and the rugged terrain, and with almost no artillery support, Shea's Force tried without success to take Amman, with its railway bridges and tunnels, in several days of desperate fighting.

A.S. Benbow was especially apprehensive as he went into battle because his brother Allen was at his side. 'I decided that to go into action with one's own brother was an unnecessary cruelty, an anxiety to be realised only by those who have had that particular experience',[26] he concluded. They were awakened at 3.50a.m. for 'stand-to'. The order to advance, however, was not given until after 2p.m. 'My heart was heavy for Allen as we obeyed our O.C.'s orders to don our equipment', he wrote. Allen moved out in the first wave, and he followed in the second. 'Precisely at 2.14p.m. every rifle and machine gun of the second wave belched forth a covering fire and I breathed an earnest prayer for the safety of dear old Allen.' When it was his turn to advance into the hail of bullets, however, he discovered that:

…it was quite impossible now to wonder how Allen was progressing so I was forced to think only of myself. Men fell on every side and the bullets spat and hissed and make a terrible cracking sound as they hit the stones, just as I was completing the third stage of our advance and was rushing over a demolished stone wall I tripped and losing my balance for a second the fall was ensured by my haversack containing two hundred rounds of ammunition swinging to the front and jamming between my legs; down I went breathless and lay there too exhausted to do anything.

After discovering that his comrades had gone on, he decided to wait for the third wave. But only three men of the third wave made it to him and could advance no further. Exposed, Benbow dug desperately with his fingers 'in the soft ground already covered with young barley three or four inches in height'. But he quickly discovered that he 'could only dig a hole large enough to put my head in' without drawing the attention of enemy fire. 'Feeling truly thankful for my preservation thus far I pushed my head as deeply into the hole as I could and with arms folded along the front of this miniature dugout as an additional protection for my head and neck I lay perfectly still. This was by no means an easy task as bullets were slashing up the ground and glancing off stones all round me and their sickening thud and splash made me wince in a most uncomfortable manner.'

Soon Benbow was more concerned about friendly fire than enemy bullets. 'To my horror our guns now joined in our support for the first time and began to send over small "H.E." [high explosive] shells evidently to ascertain the range for they were falling alarmingly short… one came screaming and hissing from the rear and burst with a terrific explosion on a line with and not more than thirty feet from me sending earth and stones in showers all over the place.' Fortunately the British guns got their range, and soon darkness allowed Benbow, who had been lying out in the open for about four hours, to move forward. 'I glided by several bodies lying in the barley and one or two men called me by name and asked for stretcher bearers; taking note of their position I pushed on and arrived at the wall where the orderlies were attending as best they could to the wounded.'[27] Among the wounded he found Allen, who had been hit by shrapnel in his lower stomach.

The next day, with his brother on his way to the rear and eventual recovery, Benbow engaged in a fierce firefight with Turks and Germans, who attempted to overrun his position as darkness fell. Alerted by a shot from his company's listening post, he grabbed his rifle, attached his bayonet, and took his position in the line. Once the enemy was in range, 'every rifle and machine gun burst out as hard as they could go all along the line supported by dozens of machine guns tucked away on advantageous slopes behind us, and I pitied "Jacko" out in that storm, as I banged away with my trusty old rifle I could see the flashes in the long grass of the Turkish weapons and aimed low accordingly. I fired until my rifle was almost red-hot, I had to drop it after about fifty rounds.'[28]

The enemy was driven back, but before falling asleep, Benbow had the 'melancholy duty' of carrying one of his fallen comrades to a dressing station for burial. When he returned to the line, he learned that an attack by his brigade was scheduled for 3a.m. Several hours later, while the rain continued to pour, 'a stealthy figure came down the line prodding everyone with the butt of his rifle and we awoke conscious of the ordeal before us'. Promptly at 3a.m., he advanced in extended order with his fixed bayonet pointed upward. 'Several shots rang out slightly to our left and then instantaneously the ground in front became alive with flashing rifles and machine guns, and hoarse shouts in guttural German and Turkish Arabic added to the increasing excitement.' After the initial Turkish defences were overrun, 'orders now came to rally, and in a downpour of rain the first and second waves joined up and advanced in the face of a brisk fire from snipers and isolated enemy machine guns across the top of the redoubt. In the distance on all sides could be heard the shouts of the other attacking parties.' In the darkness and rain, Benbow's brigade lost contact with the rest of the attacking force and found itself in a precarious situation.

'Dawn had now shown itself', Benbow wrote in his diary, 'and most of us saw that unless something drastic was done to dominate the surrounding hill tops well held still by the enemy, though the main portions of the position was already in our hands, we should have to retire or face a murderous fire, the accuracy of which would be made more deadly by daylight.' Benbow went to ground behind a stone wall and spent the rest of the day surviving shelling and snipers. 'All at once a shell struck the top of the wall immediately above where I was amongst a bunch of No. 7 men and although the explosion made practically no impression it was obvious if the gun kept steadily on our protection would crumble away in no time and then–! After some dozen shots most of which buried themselves in the wall with a thud the gunners ceased – probably because our Indian Mounted Battery was beginning to find them.'[29] When darkness fell, orders arrived to retreat. Under a full moon, long columns of troops retired, passing through a line of men in extended order (which included Benbow) serving as a rear guard. Benbow concluded his diary entry of March 30 with the words, 'none of us sorry to leave behind forever, we hope, a nightmare of a most terrible nature'.

Many officers in his brigade had been killed, including his company commander, Captain Newsam, who had been shot by a captured German officer who had concealed a weapon. When his men had endangered themselves by carrying him to a dressing station, Newsam exclaimed, 'Kill me boys, and dump me.' Benbow lamented, 'we lost many of the oldest and best hands whose loss, as is always so, was not fully realised until they had gone'.[30]

A dejected British force completed its withdrawal across the Jordan on April 2. The infantry had marched and fought almost continuously in the mud and rain for ten days. The mounted forces had suffered almost as much in both the advance and retreat. In particular it had been a nightmare for wounded being conveyed in their camel cacolets. Camels slipped and fell with their wounded, and the cacolets often banged against the rocks along the narrow paths.

Bluett suggests that 'as a triumph over privation and fatigue, and for extreme gallantry under most trying conditions of battle, the venture is without parallel in British military history, especially in regard to the infantry, who had marched and fought almost continuously for ten days'.[31] But the operation left a bitter taste. For the first time since 2nd Gaza, the British had been defeated. Total British casualties had been 1,348, and the primary objectives of the mission had not been fulfilled. It is now known that both Shea and Chetwode opposed the attack on Amman, believing that both the season and the small size of the force dictated against its success.[32]

This setback was eclipsed by momentous military events on the western front. On March 21, the day that Shea's Force first attempted to bridge the Jordan, the Germans launched a powerful assault on both sides of the Somme. The results were catastrophic. Outnumbered 750,000 to 300,000, the British front collapsed. In a single day, the Germans captured more territory on the Somme than the British had in their prolonged offensive in 1916. On March 23, the War Cabinet learned that the Germans had advanced twelve miles and captured as many as 600 guns. Wilson gloomily reported that 'the British Army was now attacked by a large proportion of the German Army, and was menaced with a possible attack by the whole'.[33] With the loss of 160,000 men and 1,000 guns, Britain had suffered its worst defeat of the war. Robertson's prophecy that the war would be won on the western front never seemed truer.

Panic reigned in London. Each day seemed to bring new demands for the recall of men and guns from Allenby's theatre. On March 23, the War Office instructed Allenby to hold in readiness one of his divisions for dispatch to the western front. As Allenby responded to this order by selecting the veteran 52nd (Lowland) Division for immediate embarkation, he was told to send nine Yeomanry regiments to France to be formed into four and a half machine gun companies. On March 27, he was told to table his offensive plans for 1918. With his forces now on the defensive, the War Office asked for a second division (Allenby chose the 74th) and any heavy artillery that could be spared. As British losses mounted, the War Office continued to draw on the EEF for reinforcements. Between May and August 1918, the 53rd, 60th, and 75th Divisions were completely reconstituted. All but one battalion from each brigade was sent to France, their place being taken by Indian Army battalions. The reforming of the 10th was almost as drastic, with eight of its twelve battalions being replaced by Indian battalions. Only the 54th Division, which at one time was under orders to go to France, was left wholly British.

To stem the German tide in France after March 21, Allenby eventually contributed some 60,000 men: two divisions (the 52nd and 74th), nine Yeomanry regiments, twenty-three British battalions (the equivalent of two more divisions), and five and a half siege batteries and five machine gun companies. His mounted arm, however, was little affected by this massive transfer of Territorials to the western front. Although he had to give up some of his Yeomanry regiments, including the stellar Bucks Hussars, his cavalry was slightly larger when he resumed the offensive in September.

The rapid transfer of troops for embarkation to France served as a testament to the logistical system developed by the British in this so-called side show. The memoirs of signaller R. Loudon, with the 1/4th Royal Scots, 156th Brigade, reflect the rapid transit of the 52nd Division following its relief at the front by the 7th (Indian) Division, which had arrived in Egypt from Mesopotamia in January. 'On 3rd April reveille was at 3.15a.m., and the 4th R[oyal] S[cots] left at 6a.m. for the railway station at Ludd, which we reached at about 7a.m., wearing greatcoats and in marching order. The Bn. entrained at 9a.m., the rest of the Bde. leaving at intervals during the day. We stopped at Gaza and El Arish, and reached Kantara shortly after midnight… I got a new uniform and equipment. We paraded at 6p.m. and entrained in trucks, leaving at 9p.m. On 5th April we reached Alexandria at 6a.m. We went on board U.C.M.S. "Leasome Castle."'[34] According to James Young, the commander of the 1/3rd Lowland Field Ambulance, he and his men knew that 'something important was afoot' but had no comprehension of the precarious position of British forces on the western front. 'Vistas of home leave opened before us', he recalled. Many men had been away for nearly three years, and rumours spread 'that we were going home for a long rest'.[35]

The Lowland Scots, who had led the advance across the Sinai, were the oldest division of this theatre. Unsettled by their rapid transit and uncertain of their destination, some combat-weary Scots became infuriated when no leave was granted and took matters into their own hands. 'Many of the men went ashore without it', Loudon claimed. 'There was considerable rioting and fighting with the military police, with some casualties, before the men could be got aboard again. Many were drunk, and one 4th R[oyal] S[cot] man died from the effects of what he had drunk.' Young, however, presents a more sanitized version of this incident in his published account. 'Some gallant youths, determined to steal another few hours ashore, hit on a happy plan. Regardless of the risks and penalties of detection, with bayonets fixed they formed up on deck. An N.C.O. gave the command, "Attention – form fours – right," and with perfect composure the whole party stepped off across the gangway to the shore, everybody making way for them, in the belief that they were marching to some detailed picquet duty. Later on, after they had had their fling ashore, they marched back in the same soldier-like fashion.'[36]

Those who followed the Royal Scots had no illusions about their destination. On May 23, Calcutt learned that his battalion was among the battalions in the 60th Division ticketed for France when he returned to his unit after collecting water. '"Heard the latest?" "No. What?" "We are going to France!!!" No rumour this time... Not all the Battalions in the Division are going. The 13th are staying in our Brigade, but *we* are unlucky. Cheer up. You will soon be dead now. No camels in France. All thumbs down.' Calcutt and many other soldiers took the news stoically. 'France and its shadow is over all', Calcutt's diary continued. 'We suddenly find that Palestine is not such a bad place. And it is going to be such a soft front we decide... We have done all the dirty work and now [that] it is just sitting tight and holding on we are to go to France.' Calcutt's reaction: 'Ah well. What is to be, is to be, and if you are going to "stop one," it has got your name on it already.'[37]

Yeomanry regiments had an especially difficult time abandoning their horses. 'Out of the blue', noted a member of the Lincolnshire

Yeomanry, 'we were told that our horses were to be handed over to the Indian cavalry and that we were to be sent to France and retrained as machine-gunners.' A ceremony was held at Gaza to mark the occasion. 'Items of saddlery and spurs, etc. were buried and a wooden memorial erected bearing the inscription (much abbreviated): "Stranger pause and shed a tear – A regiment's heart lies buried here."'[38]

The men of the 60th Division, many of whom had already served on two fronts before arriving in Egypt and Palestine, sang the following song when they returned to France for a second time: 'Oh, we're the boys who tour the world, who've been on many a front. We sampled every kind of war and every kind of stunt. We've seen the East, we've seen the West, we want to see no more. But some old blighter's sent us back, to where we were before.'

The men who returned were very different soldiers from the ones who had arrived in the land of the Pharaohs several years earlier. Soldiers in the 74th Division had been in Egypt and Palestine as long as the Lowland Scots, but they had served first in Yeomanry regiments in the Libyan Desert against the Senussi before being dismounted and formed into the first-rate 74th Division. 'It was a "hard-boiled unit" that landed at Marseilles in the summer of 1918. We were all burnt to a mahogany colour by the desert sun; we were practised in gunnery of all possible varieties, gunners and drivers were skilled workmen and knew their jobs and were proud of their skill', wrote A. Douglas Thorburn, who had now become the second in command of the 268th Brigade, RFA, 74th (Yeomanry) Division. He continued, 'No one who had seen us sail away from the same port in November 1916 would have taken us for the same battery. I do not think I exaggerate when I say that as a fighting machine we were ten times the value of the inexperienced organisation that had left the Western Front two-and-a-half years before.'[39]

The 74th, arriving on May 7 at Marseilles, was soon on its way by train to Noyelles. The change of scenery reminded them of home after their long tour of duty in Egypt and Palestine. 'The contrast from the East was indeed marked and delightful, and the long train journey passed quickly in our joy at seeing once more green fields and green trees, villages and farms, long fair hair and fair complex-ions',[40] the history of the division noted. The front lines, however, presented a different picture and were unlike anything that the EEF had witnessed in its drive to take Jerusalem. 'The tragedy of desola-tion and destruction which met our eyes on every side.... a mangled maze of withered woods and torn roads leading to towns that are now nothing but empty, gaping things', James Young, 1/3 Lowland Field Ambulance, 52nd Division, recalled. 'There broken walls stand amid a ruin of debris like shattered gravestones brooding in silent protest over their desecrated dead.'[41]

Many veterans of the trench warfare on the western front were quick to inform these new comers that this was the 'real' war. 'We came to France with our breasts filled with pride at the deeds of our division', Young continued, 'but we found that few knew us and fewer seem to care. If they spared us a thought, it was probably to sympathise with our position and to wonder of what use we could possibly be in France, with nothing but the experiences of wild campaigns to our credit.'[42] This was especially true of senior British officers, who believed that the reinforcements from the East, most of whom were Territorials, had to be retrained to fight on the western front. This attitude infuriated Sergeant John F. Jones of 'D' Company, Civil Service Rifles, who took note of the wide gulf between regular army officers and the ranks on the western front. This was something that he had not experienced fighting with the Territorials in the East. 'The air of cheerful confidence to which we were accustomed, the feeling that everybody was on the same side, from generals to privates, was not found in France.' The attitude of the generals, according to Jones, 'seemed to show that in France the 'troops' had never ceased to be an object of scorn and annoyance to the lordly officers of the peace-time army'.[43]

Jones and other 'irregulars' had had few preconceived notions about the art of war when they had volunteered. Experience rather than any training manual had been their instructor in the Sinai and the Judean Hills. In one training exercise, Jones experienced the ire of the brigadier who was observing his company advancing across open country. 'We took a certain pride in the job', Jones wrote. 'We thought we could show these trench-bound soldiers a thing or two about taking advantage of cover, and about getting over the ground quickly.' When they reach their objective and then formed up in platoons, the brigadier exploded. 'What the hell do you mean lining up like this? Where are your sections? What's the sergeant think he's doing in the rear?' According to Jones, 'we had tried out the "sections" method years before and found it wanting... fighting by sections was an absurdity with platoons varying from fifteen to forty, N.C.O.s varying from one to three or so, and officers numbering two or three to the company. The platoon was our unit, anyway.' Jones and his men marched back to camp with an 'uneasy feeling that the powers that be, although they now wished the troops trained in open-order warfare, had forgotten the elements of it themselves, and were still labouring under the delusion that an ounce of drill-book was worth a ton of experience'.

His new superiors even found wanting the marching of Jones's brigade. Although the 60th Division had marched further and under more difficult circumstances than any British division in France, Jones and the other Palestine veterans were taken to task because they did not march with parade-ground precision. 'We had come to realise that while it was not necessary to be as sloppy as the French', Jones says, 'a certain amount of elasticity was more effective than perfect dressing and 120 thirty-inch paces to the minute.'[44]

Jones was certainly not the only soldier to make unfavourable comparisons between his new superiors and the leadership he had known in Egypt and Palestine. This was especially true of battalions torn from their old divisions and used to reconstitute battered British divisions reduced to cadres. Captain N.E. Drury, from the 6th Royal Dublin Fusiliers, 30th Brigade, 10th (Irish) Division, had his battalion placed in a division which had suffered heavy losses in 1918. 'It is the 66th and it is in the process of reorganising', he grumbled, 'so we don't know yet how we stand. It is an enormous pity that the good old 10th Division could not have come over complete and with our own staffs, whom we know and who knows us.'[45]

Another example of what happened to battalions being shipped from the east to the western front is provided by three battalions that have played a prominent role in this narrative: the London Scottish, the Civil Service Rifles, and the Queen's Westminster Rifles from the 179th Brigade, 60th Division. After arriving in France, they became the 90th Brigade of the 30th Division, which had originally been a New Army formation drawn from Lancashire. The 30th Division had been practically destroyed when Germany's March offensive had broken the Fifth Army's front. Many Territorials in their resuscitated division resented the severe discipline they encountered. For the first time, Calcutt saw men subjected to 'field punishment'. 'Four Royal Scots each tied to trees', he observed in his diary. 'Nothing very terrible physically but most galling and humiliating mentally I should think. I should hate it.'[46]

Sergeant Young was startled that his new front was so different from Palestine. He and other Territorials had 'to master a thousand and one new regulations regarding administration and discipline and all other matters – the accretions which the system in France had gradually gathered round it during years of war'.[47] The spit-and-polish rules seemed petty and unrelated to the fighting efficiency of the unit. Too often, officers came across as uncaring martinets. 'I did not realise the awful abyss of ignorance', Sergeant Jones asserted, 'in which a brass-hat could dwell unknowing until I had the pleasure of a personal encounter with the G.O.C. of the division to which we now belonged; for when, in honour of his approach I called up to attention a party of men who were sitting on the ground, I was greeted with the remark: "Damn your eyes, sergeant! Don't you know that men won't obey you unless you shout at them."'[48]

The warriors from the East were unfamiliar with chemical warfare; the Turks had never used poison gas against them. Hence training in the use of gas masks was welcome. But the training for open warfare they received, according to Thorburn, was useless, 'corresponding to make-believe contests with buttoned foils for a duelist experienced with a sharpened rapier'.[49] Allenby's former soldiers found even less use for bayonet training. No British force had depended on the bayonet as much as the EEF. As a tactical study by the 60th Division's general staff concluded, 'The rifle and bayonet remain the supreme weapons of the infantryman. This has been proven in every fight.'[50]

What was true in Palestine, however, was not necessarily true in France, where artillery and the high explosive shell dominated the battlefield.

Hidebound regular army officers did not alone account for the differences in methods and leadership the men of the EEF experienced when they were shipped to France. The gigantic scale of the war in France made the conflict much more impersonal. 'Our first and dominating impression, and it was one which remained with us throughout in France, was that here we were mere small cogs in a vast machine', Young surmised. 'In a smaller army a division is an important unit.'[51] Commanders in France also seemed especially remote and the purpose of their operations unclear to the rank and file. Signaller Marchant, who served in the 53rd (Welsh) Division, believed that in the east, 'all our actions were at all times clear to us. There was never confusion or acting blindly in the dark; often before an action the general idea of the movement was given to us, and this seemed a guide to direction and made us feel a part of a whole instead of acting in an isolated manner out of touch with the general movement.'[52] In trench warfare, 'you really could not see what you were doing', General Shea remarked. 'Whereas in Palestine the great part of it was that you were in open warfare... You could see what your troops were doing, and you could use your reserves as you wish, when it was necessary.'[53] Thus, in Palestine, where subordinate commanders of all ranks were given more freedom to make decisions on the spot, they were more likely to gain the trust of their men.

Another reason for the rapport between leaders and the led in Palestine and Egypt was that there was often plenty of time for training, and many officers remained with their men during several campaigns. On the western front, as the official British history grimly noted, casualties were so great among platoon commanders and noncommissioned officers that there could be little 'continuity of leadership; the battalions engaged in an attack were unable to profit by the lessons of the last'. But in the east, 'as a rule losses were not so great as to affect seriously the fighting quality of the unit. Good junior officers and non-commissioned officers nearly always remained, becoming craftier fighters and better leaders of men as they gained experience; and the spirit of the rank and file was not blunted by the prospect, on forming up for an attack, of one-third or two-thirds of their numbers being killed or wounded by nightfall'.[54]

10

Jordan Valley

On April 1 1918, Allenby described the impact of the German March 21 offensive to the military correspondent for the *Daily Telegraph*, Captain C.W. Battine: 'Here, I have raided the Hedjaz railway, 40 miles East of Jordan, & have done much damage but my little show dwindles now into a very insufficient affair in comparison with events (?) in Europe.'[1] His theatre had returned overnight from being the government's first priority to a 'sideshow'.

Allenby, however, had difficulty accepting a passive role, despite the altered military landscape. Contrary to his comments to Battine, his assault across the Jordan had left the key bridges and tunnel of Amman intact. Undeterred by this failure, Allenby still planned to seize Amman and other territory east of the Jordan, cut the Hejaz railway, and establish contact with Feisal's forces on his right. This was no simple 'raid', as it is often described, because Allenby planned to maintain a British force in the area to block a Turkish counterattack. His ambitious objectives bordered on the reckless, especially if Arab assistance proved illusory.

The timetable for another Transjordan operation was advanced by some two weeks when envoys from the large Beni Sakhr tribe, encamped about nineteen miles south-east of the Ghoraniyeh bridge-head, offered to add their weight to the Egyptian Expeditionary Force operation if it took place before May 4. After that date, they would have depleted their supplies and would have to withdraw. Some

British officers had already concluded that the irregular Arab warriors were second-rate soldiers and had little chance against the more
disciplined and better-armed Turks in any set battle. Meinertzhaggen,
for example, had earlier lectured Lawrence in December 1917 that
the Arabs 'were just looters and murderers, they would not stand
casualties and were well understood by the Turks who refused to
enlist them in combatant units'.[2] General Headquarters, however,
took this Arab offer to disrupt Turkish communications as being
genuine although in the view of the British official history, the reli-
ability of the desert Bedouins was 'as shifting and unstable as their
own sands'.[3]

On the evening of April 29, a force of infantry and mounted
troops, commanded by Chauvel, assembled on the Jordan. The main
Turkish force of about 5,000 was dug in around Shunet Nimrin.
Another 1,000 or so Turks were positioned to defend Es Salt.
Chauvel, concerned about his transport, had persuaded GHQ to
limit the first stage of the operation to the capture of Es Salt; Amman
might follow in the second stage. Clauvel assigned the 60th Division
the task of pinning down the Turks at Shunet Nimrin while his
cavalry enveloped Es Salt. Once that town fell, a force would be sent
down the road from Es Salt to Shunet Nimrin to block the line of
the Turkish retreat. This relatively simple plan, however, was flawed
by intelligence lapses. The Turks were stronger than anticipated and
had made preparations, including the construction of a pontoon
bridge across the Jordan at Mafid Jozele, for a counterattack against
the vulnerable British left flank in the Jordan Valley.[4]

The British attack soon degenerated into a welter of confusion
because of the alacrity and strength of the Turkish response. Despite
repeated and costly attacks, the 60th Division made little headway
against the main Turkish defences. Meanwhile, Turkish troops west of
the Jordan crossed by their secret bridge at Mafid Jozele and drove
down the centre of the Jordan Valley, breaking through Chauvel's left
flank and threatening to cut off the cavalry's escape route from the
hills. The mounted forces, at first unaware of these ominous develop-
ments, continued their operation. The mountains rather than Turkish
resistance initially represented the greatest obstacle for the troopers. 'It

is well to note that the so called track was made by my Bde and none existed when we first came up to Es Salt', recalled Brigadier General P.J.V. Kelly, the commander of the 5th Mounted Brigade. 'Places were so steep that personally I could only get up by holding on to my horse's tail and most of the way we had to struggle up on foot from the valley, no mean performance for the men carrying their rifles and over a hundred rounds of ammunition in full marching order.' As his brigade approached Es Salt, it was 'strung out over a distance of possibly 2 miles or more, all being in single file'.[5] Darkness fell before the last trooper in the brigade reached the plateau and bivouacked for the night.

When Kelly learned the next morning that Es Salt was in British hands, he sent his troopers through the town to take up a position on the road near the Huweij Bridge leading toward Shunet Nimrin. The going was difficult and Turkish resistance strong. Hence Kelly was alarmed when Major General Hodgson ordered his brigade and the 2nd Light Horse Australian Brigade to capture the bridge and vigorously attack the rear of the Turkish force locked in combat with the 60th Division. After sizing up the situation, Kelly and Brigadier General G. de L. Ryrie, the commander of the 2nd Light Horse, agreed 'that to attack down the Es Salt road was doomed to failure'. At Kelly's request, Ryrie phoned Hodgson and bluntly told him that 'the ground is impossible and the position impregnable'. Hodgson was unmoved and refused to cancel his order.[6]

Reports of a Turkish counterattack on British outposts north-east of Es Salt, however, soon created a new situation. Hodgson withdrew one of Ryrie's regiments to defend Es Salt and suggested to General Chauvel that the offensive down the Es Salt road be broken off. General Chauvel, who believed that the 60th Division might still triumph if assisted by an attack against the Turkish rear, insisted that the attack go forward, no matter what the cost. But he also withdrew the last of Ryrie's regiments to assist in the defence of Es Salt. This meant that Kelly was expected to succeed with three regiments when he had argued that he could not do the job with five. 'This was just as well', Kelly sardonically noted, 'as the greater number of troops employed the greater would have been the loss of life, and no further result could have been attained.'[7]

Kelly later described the 5th Mounted Brigade's predicament as it attempted to capture the Turkish position above the Huweij Bridge:

We were on low ground. The enemy had an Artillery O.P. on the top of the high ground overlooking us and the Huweij Bridge. No movement on our part was possible without heavy shelling from an invisible How. Battery. We had already experienced the accuracy and deadly effect of this fire in various reconnaissance which had taken place. The attack was carried out by elements of 2 regiments [Gloucester and Notts Sherwood Ranger Yeomanry] and a very weak 3rd regiment held in reserve. The only covering fire was that of a mountain pack artillery battery which had accompanied me. M.G.s [machine guns] and Hotchkiss had to be quite early in the advance left behind, as the ground was found to be impassable to any form of pack. The attacking regiments had no opportunity of ever firing a shot, nor did we ever see any of the enemy… The advance, over a distance of about 1 mile from the point of assembly to the hill domineering and commanding the Huweij Bridge, took between 6 & 7 hours – during most of this time the advancing troops were under continuous and heavy How. fire from shrapnel and H.E. I remember that 5 very good officers were literally blown to bits… There was no question of breaking off the attack, it simply spent itself, and elements of the Bde really straggled back, some wounded, others helping wounded.[8]

Kelly incurred Hodgson's wrath for not pushing in his reserves 'to the last man'. But Kelly believed that 'it would have been nothing short of criminal to have pushed in a very weak reserve where twice their numbers had failed. Remember the attack had inflicted no casualties whatsoever on the enemy.'[9] Kelly's most compelling defence was that he was there and his two superior officers were not. Neither Hodgson or Chauvel nor any of their staff had come to inspect the ground over which his men were ordered to advance. Kelly, called 'an outstanding figure' by Captain Cyril Falls, was removed from his command by Allenby the next year because he failed to capture the German commander in chief at Nazareth in September. The charge against him was once again that he was too cautious, weakening his force by clearing two villages on the way to Nazareth.[10]

When Allenby and Chauvel conferred on the afternoon of May 3, the situation looked bleak. The Beni Sakhr had taken no part in the operations and had broken camp, Es Salt was threatened from three sides, the Turkish stronghold at Shunit Nimrin showed no signs of cracking, the troopers in the hills had exhausted their three-day rations, and ammunition was running short. Allenby had no choice but to order a withdrawal of his mounted forces from the hills before they were cut off. Kelly later commented: 'Well do I remember the Australians cheering and throwing their hats in the air when they were withdrawn, as soldiers they knew the attack was hopeless.'[11]

The Londoners of the 60th Division may not have thrown their hats in the air, but they were just as relieved when their futile assaults against strong positions were halted and they were withdrawn the next day to the Jordan. Their losses had been much greater than the mounted forces. Blaser described the removal in wagons of some of the dead for burial:

> Each lifeless body was lifted into the wagons; ten, twenty, thirty and more, the very best of fellows; men with whom we had lived, with whom we had laughed, men with who we had discussed the past and planned the future, now all covered with blood and dust, tattered and disfigured – dead. It was a horrible sight. As each corpse was lifted up, we half expected to hear the old familiar laugh or the same cheerful voice. There had been no last look, no parting words. Not a sound broke the grim silence save the dull thud as each limp form found its place at the bottom of the wagon.[12]

When Chauvel expressed regret to Allenby about the failure of his operation, his commander in chief responded, 'Failure be damned! It has been a great success!'[13] But the facts suggested otherwise. Both the planning and the execution of this battle reflected overconfidence, if not poor judgment. The best-executed operation of the entire battle had been General Hodgson's withdrawal from the hills. In his two Transjordan operations, Allenby had tasted defeat for the first and only time in his campaign. He argued at the time that 'the fact of our having undertaken this enterprise, at a time when all Egypt and Syria know that my troops are being depleted will have a good moral effect all around'.[14] Allenby's losses (1,649) during the second Transjordan operation favoured the British but this offered little solace. For the second time in two months, the Arabs had seen his forces fall back in disarray to the west bank of the Jordan River. Es Salt and Amman remained in Turkish hands. The Turks celebrated by parading nine captured Royal Horse Artillery 13-pounder guns, the only artillery pieces lost to the enemy in the course of Allenby's campaign. If anything, the apparent revival of Turkey's military fortunes made the wavering Beni Sakhr tribe even more inclined toward neutrality.[15]

After suffering a strategic defeat at the hands of the enemy, Allenby's prospects for the near future appeared bleak. 'My own projects have been modified, and the scope of my operations limited, by the requirements of the European battlefield', he wrote to the king of England. 'I have been called upon to supply battalions for France; and have, consequently, been compelled to abandon all ideas of a vigorous offensive.'[16]

On May 29, the new Chief of the Imperial General Staff, Sir Henry Wilson, shared his global vision with Allenby. The war news continued to be ominous, with the Germans on the move both in France and the east. With the War Cabinet contemplating Japanese and American intervention in Siberia to block the German advance eastward,[17] Hindenburg launched his third offensive of the year, this time breaking the French front on the Aisne and creating panic in Paris. Although Wilson expressed confidence that Germany's offensive power would wane by late 1918, he did not expect a decisive Allied victory in the west until 1919 or even 1920. It was during the interim – 'say 12, 18, 24 months' – that British emphasis would return to the outer theatres to contain Berlin's threat to their imperial realms. 'I want to see Aleppo joined to Mosul joined to Baku joined to the Urals joined to the Japanese army; and from that base an advance against the Boches',[18] he wrote to Allenby.

Allenby was pleased that Wilson had big plans for his theatre in the future, but he worried that the continued demands on behalf of the beleaguered western front would cripple the offensive power of his forces. He was encouraged by London's attempts to involve Tokyo more deeply in the war, and he inquired whether he might get three or four Japanese divisions to replace the infantry he was losing to the western front. 'There must be available, I should think, lots of trained Japanese; spiriting for a fight... If I could have the Japanese Divisions, too, I could do big things.'[19] It quickly became obvious, however, that Tokyo had no intention of sending troops to the Middle East – or of fighting Germans in Russia, for that matter.

Allenby's request for Japanese soldiers reflects his growing anxiety about his forces. In mid-June he reacted sharply when he learned that the War Office planned to recall the Australian Mounted Division as drafts for the Australian infantry and his only remaining all-British Division, the 54th. 'I know, well, the importance of concentrating all effort on the Western Front; but the addition of one Division will not save you there; here its absence may lose you the war. The Arabs are behaving well; but they watch us, anxiously. If we fail them, they might join the Turks. Whatever strategical purists may say about side shows, you are committed deeply here; and, if you lose Egypt, you lose the Empire which hinges thereon.'[20] The ministers subsequently overruled Wilson; Allenby retained the Australian Mounted Division as well as the 54th Division. Although he ultimately lost some 60,000 men to the western front after March 21, including most of his British infantry and nine of his Yeomanry regiments, Allenby retained a formidable force: four mounted and seven infantry divisions. All were well-equipped and at full strength. But the composition of his force was now very different from the one previously dominated by Territorials.

In the summer of 1918, Allenby commanded a multinational and multicultural force perhaps without precedent in British military history. Only one of his divisions out of eleven, the 54th, was fully British. His 'rainbow' army was composed of soldiers from many countries and regions, including Armenia, Britain, Burma, Algeria, Australia, New Zealand, India, South Africa, Italy, France, Singapore, Hong Kong, the West Indies and Egypt. In addition, he received three battalions of Jews, the 38th, 39th and 40th Royal Fusiliers. After the

Balfour Declaration of November 1917, which promised a Jewish national home in Palestine, Jews had been recruited in Britain, the United States and the Middle East to fight in the Holy Land. These Jewish soldiers, who sported armbands with a golden Star of David, included a future prime minister of Israel, David Ben Gurion.

Indian troops, forty-four battalions in all, represented the primary source for Allenby's new manpower. Fully half of these Indian battalions had never seen action and included many raw recruits who had not even had musketry training. Specialists such as signallers, Lewis gunners, bombers and transport drivers were also in short supply. The junior British officers in these battalions were green, and most could not speak Hindustani. In one battalion, only one Indian officer spoke English, and only two British officers could communicate with their men. It remained to be seen whether this army was capable of delivering victory. 'Odds and sods, like Jewish battalions and regiments of Hottentots, are useful in a way; but they won't win wars',[21] Allenby had rather crudely informed Wilson in June.

After Allenby's failure to capture Es Salt, the front of the opposing armies stabilized on a line from Arsuf on the Mediterranean, across the Plain of Sharon, into the hill country, and then down to the southern end of the Jordan Valley, where it terminated on the shores of the Dead Sea. Trenches were dug and wired, but the nature of the country made a continuous line of trenches impossible. Although there were gaps and not enough soldiers to strongly defend a front of almost seventy miles, a virtual stalemate existed for the next four months. The Turks were too weak to present a serious threat, and Allenby, with his offensive plans on hold, focused on reorganizing his forces.

The twenty-five-mile section of the front in the Jordan Valley, which was nearly 1,300 feet below sea level, proved to be an inferno for the Desert Mounted Corps stationed there. The army's official handbook for Palestine claimed that 'nothing is known of the climate of the lower Jordan Valley in summer time, since no civilized human being has yet been found to spend a summer there'. The arrival of summer brought soaring temperatures as high as 131 degrees Fahrenheit. Lieutenant Goodsall, who served with the Royal Field

Artillery, recorded the following in a letter home: 'Monday morning, 7a.m., surely a suitable time for letter writing: as a matter of fact the early hours of the day are the only time one has the energy to do anything... During the day we sleep, if it is possible to do so in a temperature of 110 degrees or more... It must be the most enervating spot in the world, and there is a great deal of sickness.'[22] The stifling heat affected the diet of the men because canned meat quickly melted into a concoction of oil and fibre that tasted disgusting and was volatile to the stomach. Veterans of the campaign in the Sinai were of course no strangers to high temperatures, but the excessive humidity of the Jordan Valley created an especially oppressive atmosphere. As Goodsall noted, 'The air is full of moisture due to the proximity of the marshy jungle bordering the river which makes matters worse.'

The troopers in the Jordan Valley had to contend with more than extreme temperatures, high humidity, and blowing clouds of dusts that nearly suffocated them. Waiting to puncture their skin were malaria-bearing mosquitoes, huge black spiders, lice, six-inch-long centipedes, and scorpions. And then there were the flies. Although Goodsall says that flies 'nearly drove us crazy', he found the tiny sand flies an even greater source of discomfort. 'Sand flies are the worst insect pests I have ever encountered or ever hope to', he wrote. 'They are almost too small to see and they find their way into everything, clothes, bedding and through mosquito netting. Wherever they bite they set up the most violent irritation, and as they attack in hundreds all over the body life becomes a mild form of hell. To scratch one's self is useless.'[23] (Sand flies not only extract blood, they also lay eggs in human skin. The resulting parasite may remain in the body for long periods, damaging the organs of the affected. American soldiers in Iraq called these festering sores the 'Baghdad Boil'.)

In normal circumstances the mounted troops would have been held in reserve, but Allenby did not think he had enough infantry divisions to hold his front while simultaneously undergoing a radical reorganization of his army that involved extensive training. Nor did he believe that he could deploy his mounted troops in the hill country. Chauvel was involved in the decision to place his troopers in the Jordan Valley. 'He [Allenby] practically gave me the option of withdrawing from the actual valley if I thought it better but told me that, if I did so, I would have to retake the bridgeheads over the Jordan before the autumn advance.' To Chauvel's way of thinking, he was left with only one choice. As he commented later, 'I considered that I would lose more lives retaking the Valley than I would through sickness in holding it and, furthermore, there was neither room nor water for large bodies of cavalry in the jumble of hills overlooking the Southern end of the Valley and the climate was precious little better.'[24] An additional concern for Allenby was that he would lose touch with the Feisal's Arabs on the Hedjaz railway. The result, he feared, was that 'the Turks would regain their power in the Hedjaz. The Arabs would make terms with them, and our prestige would be gone.'[25]

Without question the mounted troops in the Jordan Valley suffered the most from fatigue and disease during the summer. But long-range Turkish artillery made life uncomfortable for troops elsewhere on the front. This was especially true for recently conscripted soldiers being sent out from Britain. Norman Francis Rothon, a married man with children, had been called up on June 1 1917, his thirty-eighth birthday. Unlike the earlier volunteers, he was a reluctant warrior and loathed the military. He was attached to the 13th Mountain Howitzer Battery, 8th Brigade, RGA, 7th (Indian) Division, as a mule driver and arrived on the front lines near Nabula at the beginning of April to discover 'what it is to hear the shells overhead and the bullets singing'. His baptism of fire terrified him. 'It puts a cold feeling down the spine when you see them bursting overhead, the pieces of the shells go moaning & sighing through the air, quite a number of the animals were hit including my mule, but not seriously, a man standing near me had a piece through his overcoat, one man named Williamson on the H.Q. Staff was killed and a few wounded', he wrote in his diary. 'The steel helmet is my constant companion. In fact I wear it all the time now, and don't mind the weight very much.'[26]

Rothon's diary for the next seven weeks was filled with references to the long-range artillery duel between British and Turkish guns, including the following:

On April 9: Did nothing all afternoon except listen to the shells going over. Like Giants playing tennis.

On April 11: Up about 5 o/c after about the worst night I think I have ever spent in my life. The fighting has been very severe and going on most of the night. Bombs, Machine Guns, Rifles and Artillery quite close to our Lines several times. I thought my last hour must be approaching... How horrible it all seems. God grant that it may soon finish.

On May 17: I have noticed repeatedly just lately that when the guns fire unexpectedly and it startles me, that as well as jarring my ears, I feel it in my *tongue!* A kind of tingling sensation like electricity more than anything else.

On May 26: Had some H.E. Shells over this morning too near to be pleasant, they made the Wadi rattle. It is when I hear these moaning through the air and then bursting that my inside turns over and I wonder whether I shall ever seen home again.

On May 27: Had a brute of a H.E. Shell over this morning which burst up the Wadi side near our mules when on the way to water... How this existence palls on one, feel sometimes as if it will drive me mad.[27]

Static trench warfare led to boredom. 'This is a wretched life at best', Rothon believed. 'Most of the men don't know what to do with themselves during their spare time. Another week gone, how long will it all last?'[28] Some soldiers created their own entertainment. Robert H. Wilson, a lieutenant with the Royal Gloustershire Hussars, 5th Mounted Brigade, recalled a trooper who was especially proud of a fighting scorpion he kept in his cigarette tin. A fight was arranged between his scorpion and a tarantula with an equally impressive record. A cardboard box served as the ring. 'After a bit of preliminary sparring which went in favour of the scorpion – naturally more nimble on his feet than the spider – who obviously felt he had got his opponent weighed up. He sailed in to deliver his blow, which took the form of a rapid swing of his long tail over his back and head. But the spider also knew what to do. He just stood his ground then, with one nip, pinched the scorpion's tail in half and leisurely proceeded to devour his foe.'[29]

The high command did what it could to provide diversions for the men with organized sports and concert parties. Attention was also given to soldiers' stomachs. Although weather and conditions at the front might reduce a soldier's diet to the bare minimum of canned meat and biscuit, rations were much better than they had been during the early days of British occupation of southern Palestine. As railway connections with Kantara improved, so did the diet of the soldiers. Tea was brought in from Ceylon; sheep and goats from the Sudan, Cyprus and later Syria; flour from Australia, India and Canada; and frozen meat from Australia, South Africa and Argentina. The meat supply imported from Australia sometimes included rabbit. From Kantara, this rabbit would be transported by railway to a railhead. It might be several days before it was allotted to a specific unit; the rabbit would then be dispatched by lorries, or by camel if there were no roads. When it reached its destination, it would be unpacked, revealing a layer of ice between the skin and flesh. That members of the EEF occasionally enjoyed rabbit from Australia serves as a striking illustration of how much better British soldiers were supplied than the half-starved Turk he faced on his front.

Despite the EEF's improved infrastructure, soldiers serving in Palestine continued to believe that their counterparts in France were better off in some important respects. 'You ask if sometimes, I'm not very sorry not to be in France – in many ways, yes, but on the whole assuredly, no – I should be near all of you, able to see you often, letters by return of post, everything you want for the asking, comfortable billets whenever you are pulled out of the line, and a knowledge you are right at the heart of things; but on the other hand, this is our war out here, the victories are our victories, the difficulties have been surmounted by us',[30] Buxton reported to his mother in August 1918.

Although home leave remained almost impossible for most members of the EEF, the high command generously granted leave to destinations in Egypt and Palestine. For the first time, many soldiers gained entry within the walls of Jerusalem. Initially, Jerusalem had been strictly off limits. Allenby, knowing the fighting man's propensity for looting, was determined to protect the numerous religious sites. After his triumphal entry into the city, he took a quick tour 'to see if all was in order'. He did not, however, visit any of the holy places. 'I have forbidden this', he wrote to his wife, '& have them all guarded – otherwise they would be pulled to pieces for souvenirs!'[31] With his forces established in the vicinity of the Holy City during the first half of 1918, however, GHQ began to grant permits that included safeguards. Parties were limited to twelve and had to be accompanied by an officer who was held responsible for the conduct of the men under his supervision.

Upon entering the city, many soldiers were repulsed by the filth, noise, and especially the rampant commercialism. Robert H. Wilson, for example, was:

> …very disappointed, you want to be full of imagination to believe half of it. Calvary, the Garden of Gethsemane and the Golden Gate are the only genuine things and of course, they do bring a lump in your throat. The Holy Sepulchre was the most disgraceful display I have ever seen, one mass of gaudyness – dozens of flags with rubbishy designs on them, paper flowers of every colour and the whole thing apparently designed to make it as little sacred and impressive as possible. To put the finishing touch to it they have dotted horrible trashy wax-works of Christ and the Virgin Mary at various places. I felt quite wild to think that a place which could be made to mean more to a Christian than any other should be so hopelessly spoilt by the money-grabbing Greeks, Armenians and any other sect that could creep in.[32]

Simpson-Baikie was even more critical in a letter to his mother-in-law:

> It is really in many ways a most delightful place of interest but I know of few things or places that would so soon choke me off excessive Religion than a detailed visit of inspection to the Religious shrines of the Holy Land – Never mind, if the Religious orders, monks, priests etc are Roman Catholic, Armenian, Syrian, Greek Church, or of any other sect or order; the two mainsprings of their life and conduct appear to be incessant strife with any other Christian domination and a soul-absorbing determination to make every possible penny out of every possible pilgrim or tourist… The attitude of such sects &

denominations towards each other in Jerusalem is the greatest travesty
I have ever seen (or heard of) of the teachings of our saviour.[33]

It appears that Wilson's and Simpson-Baikie's views on Jerusalem were held by a majority of first-time visitors. But some soldiers were able to get beyond their first impressions. 'One's first view of the Holy City, with its Germans and its beggars and its priest craft, and its smells and its eternal sycophancy battering off other people's religions is repellent, but soon all that feeling gets numbed, and the place does grow on you',[34] Buxton reported to his mother after staff duties kept him in the city for three days.

Many members of the EEF also developed an appreciation for Palestine – its rugged peaks and gorgeous ravines, wildflowers, blue skies, and magnificent sunsets. But many were as contemptuous of the Arab inhabitants as they had earlier been of the impoverished Egyptians. Ignoring the scarcity of water which made cleanliness difficult, they found both the local Arabs and their homes dirty and unkempt. Lieutenant H.R.P. Collett, an observer in the 21st Balloon Company, was appalled by the conditions he encountered when he visited a village near Jerusalem. 'The village, like most of its kind, was most disgustingly filthy', he recalled in his memoirs. 'The narrow passages between the stone hovels were littered with refuse, while the flat roofs of the houses were communal manure heaps, the most antique of which assumed a dome-like appearance. This village boasted of an immense flock of goats – hence the domes! What these hovels were like after the soaking winter's rain, I should hate to think, though some attempt to fix gargoyles of tins or broken pots was made in one or two cases.'[35]

Arabs were not only thought dirty and smelly; they were also characterized as being crooked and untrustworthy. John Harding, who commanded the 162nd Brigade Machine Gun Company, 54th Division, responded sharply when asked about his views of the natives of Palestine in an oral interview. 'Not much. We hated the Palestinian Arab, he's a terrible chap.' When asked why, he responded: 'Well they rob the dead, they mutilated the wounded and they made themselves thoroughly objectionable.' He then quoted the doggerel called the 'Australian soldier's farewell to Egypt':

Land of sand and stinking socks,
Syphilis and dripping cocks,
Arabs' heaven and soldiers' hell,
Land of bastards, fare thee well.[36]

Allenby, hoping to enlist Arab support, ordered his men to behave correctly toward the local Arabs. As the Allied military situation in France improved and as the campaign season approached, he also intensified the training of his men just as he had done before 3rd Gaza. Rothon's diary entries reflect the rigorous preparation and strict discipline:

On August 9: Speech of complaint by O/c i/c Lines tonight on the general slackness of everything connected with the Drivers, such as Mules, Harness, discipline in fact everything is awful except the gunnery, privileges which we enjoy ? are to be withdrawn and extra parades piled on if there is not a vast improvement within a week, words fail me to write what I think of such despicable treatment meted out to men who have left their homes to finish off the War, not to be bullied and badgered by men who fancy themselves superior to the ordinary Run [?] because they have a stripe or a pip. One cannot help feeling bitterly when we are very often treated like school children.

On August 17: I think those in charge here are trying to break the mens hearts with their petty orders and punishments etc.

On August 20: One man tied to limber wheel for 1 hour tonight, doing No. 1 Field punishment for 14 days for quite a trivial offence.

On August 21: Defaulter again tied to Limber Wheel, he broke down in hysterics just previous to being tied up and was a very pathetic sight, especially when letters from home were being called out just near him.

On August 23/24: What a battery this is for punishment. Tonight there is one man strung up to the Limber Wheel! B & C Subs on one hour extra grooming!! 4 men doing Pack Drill!!! And one man being tried by little Willie [a new and unpopular officer in charge of the lines]!!!! And then they wonder how it is they cannot get the best out of the chaps.

On August 31: They gave us a rare march last night in the dark and I arrived back in an awful state of perspiration and almost done. We get no consideration whatever here now and are not allowed to leave the Camp to get a wash even, and then we read in the papers about the Troops cheerfully carrying on.

On September 11: 10 men on Pack Drill tonight for various trivial offenses. 'Britons never shall be slaves.'[37]

Allenby's demanding training before his breakthrough on the Gaza-Beersheba front had improved his men's effectiveness and might do so again. But the intense training tested his force's endurance. As the war entered its fifth year with no end in sight, all of the major European armies experienced a crisis of confidence and declining morale. It is not surprising that signs of rot could be discerned in the EEF. 'Everybody concerned is heartily fed up with the whole affair and wants to get back home',[38] Rothon grumbled. When Sergeant John Francis Jones visited Cairo on leave, he heard stories of a desert camp filled with deserters 'who sent men in on pay-day to draw money, and others daily to draw rations; my informant declared that these had once been rounded up by cavalry with aeroplanes co-operating to discover the camp. The tales may of course have been completely untrue', Jones opined, 'but I found on a visit to the base camp that they had been very generally believed.' From his own experience, Jones knew of an officer's batman in his regiment who had 'accompanying his officer to a course of instruction, had disappeared with the latter's best boots and breeches', and was not heard of again until he was admitted to a hospital with a venereal disease.[39]

Whatever the state of morale in Allenby's force – and it was almost certainly much better than the British Expeditionary Force's, which had suffered huge losses since March 21 – the decline of the Turkish forces in Palestine since the Transjordan operations was not in doubt. Ironically, German successes at the beginning of the year, although they had drained Allenby of his best infantry, had improved British prospects on the Palestine front. In the west, the German offensive had sent the Allies reeling. In the east, the Russians had formally exited the war in March by signing the annexationist treaty of Brest-Litovsk, which forced them to withdraw from the Anatolian provinces and to return the Trans-Caucasian territory that they had gained in 1878. The ambitions of the Pan-Turkish elements, fed by German military success in France and an open door to the Caucasus, now knew few limits. Armenia, Georgia, Azerbaijan and even northern Persia seemed within their grasp. Palestine for the moment was forgotten and neglected. The Turkish army in Palestine, starved of both men and supplies and riddled with malaria, was in a disastrous state by September 1918. Despite the presence of lorries with machine guns patrolling roads behind the front, there were 'more deserters than men under arms'.[40] The British official history's description of the forces opposing Allenby is striking: 'Hungry, ragged, verminous, comfortless, hopeless, out-numbered, is it to be wondered that the Turkish soldiers lost heart? It is unlikely that any other troops in the world would have remained without collapse for so long a period of warfare under such condition.'[41]

11

Megiddo

Megiddo is located on the southern end of the Plain of Esdraelon, where it commands the roads connecting Palestine with Syria. This ancient settlement has been the scene of many battles. It is also the site of Armageddon, which, according to the Book of Revelation, is where the final battle between good and evil will be fought. Allenby's naming of his decisive victory over the Turks, Megiddo, may thus have a double meaning.

In the summer of 1918, German fortunes waned on the western front. In July, their fifth attack of the year was quickly repulsed by the French at the Second Battle of the Marne. The initiative passed to the Allies. When General Erich Ludendorff, architect of these German drives, asked Field Marshal von Hindenburg what options Germany now had, he hotly responded: 'Do? Do! Make peace, you idiot!'[1]

Germany's decline coincided with the approach of the campaigning season in the Middle East. Since talking with Smuts in January, Allenby had formulated his own plan. In its simplest form, it represented the reverse of how he had broken the Gaza-Beersheba front. Before 3rd Gaza, he had given the Turks reason to believe that he planned to break through along the coast at Gaza while he secretly massed his forces before Beersheba on the Turkish left flank. Now, however, he planned to make his breakthrough along the coast while giving the Turks the impression that his primary blow would fall on their left flank in the Transjordan region.

Allenby was determined that the Turks would not escape his cavalry this time as they had during 3rd Gaza. He expected his infantry to create a wide breach of some eight miles in the Turkish defences on the Plain of Sharon. After making a rightward move (similar to a swinging door with its hinges on the right), the infantry would drive the demoralized Turks into and through the foothills. Through this doorway, the massed cavalry of the Desert Mounted Corps would pass. Horse soldiers would sweep along the wide coastal Plain of Sharon until they turned north-east through passes in the Samarian Hills, enter the Plain of Esdraelon, and head straight for El Affule and then on to Beisan in the Valley of Jezrell. The seizure of El Affule and Beisan would cut the enemy's lateral railway communications and prevent any retreat in a northern or north-easterly direction.

Concentration, surprise and speed were key elements in the blitz-krieg warfare planned by Allenby. The Egyptian Expeditionary Force in September had at least a two-to-one advantage in manpower along its front. These raw numbers, if anything, understated the EEF's superiority when the firepower, morale and physical condition of the two armies are compared. By massing three cavalry and five infantry divisions along the coast, Allenby was able to achieve a massive superiority at the point of attack. The Turks manned their coastal sector with only about 8,000 troops. Yet Allenby positioned the XXI Corps (3rd, 7th, 54th, and 75th Divisions), reinforced by the 60th Division from the XX Corps, on his left flank. This gave his army at the point of attack a 4.4-to-1 advantage in infantry, or 5.5-to-1 when mounted troops are included. He also had three times the enemy's artillery.[2]

To achieve such overwhelming superiority on his left, it was necessary to assemble this strike force in secrecy. This would have been impossible without control of the skies. The naval and military air forces had been merged on April 1 into the Palestine Brigade, Royal Air Force. It had two wings, a total of seven squadrons, one of which was Australian. The Royal Air Force's dominance was so great by the last half of 1918 that almost no enemy pilot dared venture over Allenby's front. Although the RAF had an advantage in numbers, the greater speed and climbing power of its more advanced flying machines explain its almost total control of the air.

By marching in darkness and hiding in orange groves during daylight, the infantry's movement could be concealed without great difficulty. Lights were forbidden, and field kitchens used solidified alcohol to prevent smoke. The transfer of masses of mounted troops from one end of the front to the other, however, was more difficult to hide. Nightly, brigade after brigade left the Jordan Valley and Judean Hills to trek some fifty miles to the coast. To mask the cavalry's withdrawal, dummy horses and camps were constructed. According to Robert Goodsall, a lieutenant in the RFA, 'Stout stakes were cut from the undergrowth along the banks of the Jordan, to form the legs of the dummy animals, bundles of straw formed the bodies, and a stout stick bound round with straw, and a knob of straw on the end, formed the neck and head. Every horse on the lines had its dummy counterpart erected beside it, while sham men, similarly constructed were dotted about the camp… It was positively uncanny to ride about the valley and come suddenly upon a camp peopled by such natural looking-fakes.'[3] Hundreds of bivouac fires also burned brightly every night in these dummy camps. Clouds of dust to simulate mounted troops going for water were created by mules dragging sleighs across the valley floor.

As the date for Allenby's offensive approached, the red bands and tabs of staff officers became prominent in the streets of Jerusalem. The presence of so many staff officers was part of an elaborate ruse to convince the Turks that Allenby planned to strike inland in the Transjordan region rather than along the coast. The Fast Hotel, which had been managed by the Army and Navy Canteen Board for officers on leave, was closed, it was said, to be used as his general headquarters.

Allenby even took pains to keep his plans secret within his own army. Brigade and regimental commanders, for example, were not given their assignments until Allenby personally briefed the divisional staffs two or three days before 'H' hour (September 19). Many ordinary soldiers, however, knew that something was afoot as training intensified and the front erupted with preparations for an offensive.

'In future "men" are to walk with 2 Mules each to the Dump, this will mean a 14 mile tramp in the heat of the day. This is a Battery for taming Lions! I think they are training us up for a big stunt that will probably be coming off later on',[4] Private Rothon, a mule driver in the artillery, complained in his diary. Elsewhere on the British front, the Royal Engineer Case informed his family, 'A bridging school started on the Auja, the roads were thoroughly repaired and separate highways made for both cars and heavy traffic, detachments of the 60th Div. R.E.s came down to practice bridging, the gas helmets were collected for repairs and so on, and we began to smell a rat... Then orders came round stating that secret orders were to be strictly kept, and that documents marked "Strictly Secret" were to be opened and seen only by Officers, and only then when they were intimately affected by their contents.'[5]

As 'H' hour approached, troops and artillery were concentrated close to the front. 'Artillery was seen in the mornings dotted haphazard over the plains, but they were certainly not there on the previous mornings'. Case continued in his description of the final preparations: 'Then Coy. equipment was made right up to strength, and on one pretty morning (the 17th) we noticed several orange groves, literally *packed* with troops who were not allowed outside during the day, while no natives were allowed to cross the boundary of the River Auja... Dawn of the eighteenth saw the orange groves packed to overflowing with troops, and I got instructions to be ready to move on that evening.'[6]

James Calderwood Jones, a member of the Lowland Brigade RFA, who had not been transferred to France with the 52nd Division, was part of this massive concentration, taking his place in the line at 9p.m. as part of an ammunition column. 'What a mass of horses & transport. Stand-to all night, lie down with our equipment on the horses being hooked-up to the wagons',[7] he wrote in his diary.

No one had greater expectations than the cavalrymen as Allenby's forces prepared for the final push. 'The moment was at hand which had been in the hopes and imagination of every British cavalry soldier west of Suez during the past four years', Major General Barrow, the commander of the 4th Cavalry Division, Desert Mounted Corps, wrote. 'We felt confident that on the morrow those hopes would for us be realised and that we should go through the gap for the first, and what would probably be the last, time in the history of the cavalry.'[8]

Artillery preparations were especially impressive and represented the heaviest concentration yet of guns in the Turkish theatres. The 385 guns, or one for every fifty yards of front, were capable of firing 1,000 shells a minute. Major V.H. Bailey, formerly of the 54th Division, was now attached to the 53rd Brigade RFA, 3rd (Lahore) Division. 'Dressed for war', he anxiously waited in a telephone dugout, some 300 yards from the front, for zero hour, or 4.30a.m. His equipment included a belt, field glasses, revolver and ammunition, water bottle, haversack with maps, orders and notebooks, some food, compass and 'Tin Hat'. 'I lay down to try and get some sleep, but it was no good. I got up at 4.10a.m. and found I was shivering and my teeth simply chattering, so I hoped I was cold',[9] he wrote in his diary.

Allenby could not afford a repeat of his unsuccessful Transjordan operations. This time his preparations had been meticulous and his superiority in men and material truly overwhelming. 'My preparations are as complete as I can make them, and tomorrow they will be tested',[10] he wrote to Wilson. Allenby anticipated a lightning thrust and a quick breakthrough. 'The infantry will advance to the assault under an artillery barrage which will be put down at the hour at which the infantry leave their positions of deployment. This hour will be known as the "XXI Corps Zero Hour." There will be no preliminary bombardment',[11] he emphasized in his Force Order No.68. Following their breakthrough, Allenby expected his infantry to roll up the front, driving the remnants of the Turkish 8th Army eastward into the hills.

Bulfin, the tough Irish commander of the XXI Corps, impressed upon his men that 'time is the enemy, not the Turks'. His operational orders read as follows: 'The whole of the success of these operations depends on the rapidity of movement of the infantry, in order to allow no time for the enemy to meet our onslaught. All commanders must carefully guard against embarking on side issues, and must keep steadily in view the gaining of their objectives well east in the foot-hills, and ensure that their troops are ready to continue the pursuit without pause or delay as long as the enemy are in front of them.'[12]

From his vantage point at the front Bailey described the action as the battle opened. There had been a bright, nearly full moon. When it set around 3.30a.m., the infantry 'crawled out across no man's land close to the enemy's wire'. At precisely 4.30a.m., an artillery barrage of hurricane force to support the infantry's advance began. 'Every gun opened simultaneously.' Trench mortars and machine guns joined in, as well as two destroyers offshore. Outnumbered and dazed by the weight of metal descending upon them, the Turks put up little fight. Mist and dense clouds of smoke and dust slowed the infantry almost as much as Turkish resistance. As Bailey rode into no man's land, one of his signallers' horses fell into a shell hole. 'We had to sit and wait while he pulled it out and got on again. If we had gone on he would never have found us again, the smoke from shells was so thick that sometimes we could not see 50 yards.'[13] By 3p.m. Bailey had his guns in the middle of the Plain of Sharon near Kalkilieh supporting the infantry advancing into the hills as they turned rightward. 'We fired as long as we could, and when they got out of range we had orders to bivouac there',[14] he recorded in his diary.

Shea's division, which had recently been moved to the coast from the Judean Hills, made an impressive advance. Formerly made up of Londoners, the 60th Division had lost nine battalions to the western front after March 21. Some of the Indian replacements, especially the Punjabis, however, were excellent soldiers. After breaching the enemy's front along the coast for the passage of the 5th Cavalry Division, the 60th Division marched on Tul Karm, a distance of about sixteen miles. Private E.C. Powell, formerly of the 60th Division, who had been assigned to the Camel Transport Corps to supply water to the troops, described this advance. 'We marched all day, on and on, scorched by the sun, parched with thirst, nearly dead with fatigue and want of sleep, struggling painfully through heavy sand. Camels rolled over, men were fainting, but still we pushed on. Night came and still we were marching. Kipling's verse, "Boots, boots, boots, rising up and down again" ran through my mind. I thought to myself: "If we who are advancing feel like this, my God, what must the Turks feel who are retreating?"' Powell was encouraged in his trek by the sight on his left of 'long columns of cavalry passing us at a canter'.[15]

As the infantry made war with its legs and lungs, the massed cavalry of the Desert Mounted Corps (less the ANZAC Mounted Division which remained in the Jordan Valley) began its long ride north. 'From 10.00 hours onwards, a hostile aeroplane observer, if one had been available, flying over the Plain of Sharon would have seen a remarkable sight – ninety-four squadrons, disposed in great breadth and in great depth, hurrying forward relentlessly on a decisive mission – a mission of which all cavalry soldiers have dreamed, but in which few have been privileged to partake',[16] Lieutenant Colonel Rex Osborn later exclaimed in *The Cavalry Journal*.

The Turks had no reserves worth mentioning to bring forward to plug the gap. This was partially the fault of General Liman von Sanders who had succeeded Falkenhayn in March. Von Sanders had distinguished himself as a dogged trench fighter at Gallipoli. Believing with some justification that the Turks fought best from trenches, he hoped to avoid a war of movement. Almost all of his available forces were thus established close to the front. On the other hand, given the resources available to Allenby in September, von Sanders faced what many would consider hopeless odds no matter how he deployed his forces.

'Can you imagine the bewildered surprise of the unsuspecting Turk, as we suddenly rushed his lines, and poured thousands and thousands of cavalry and infantry thro' the gaps? Thousands of prisoners were marching back to the cages within 2 hours of zero',[17] Case reported to his family in England.

Panic, exacerbated by the disruption of communications, prevailed on the Turkish side. The Palestine Brigade attacked key communication centres, including the headquarters of the Turkish 8th Army at Tul Karm and the 7th at Nablus. The chief German air base at Jenin was put out of commission, and planes harassed retreating Turkish troops on the roads. Not fully cognizant of the magnitude of his defeat or the rapid advance of the Desert Mounted Corps, von Sanders was almost taken from his bed (his housekeeper says that he fled in his pyjamas) by a detachment of the British cavalry on the morning of the 20th at his general headquarters in Nazareth.

Allenby, in close personal touch with the battle as it developed, began to sense an overwhelming victory. 'We attacked, at 4.30a.m., today', he wrote to his wife. 'Now – 3p.m. – the Turks are breaking everywhere... my cavalry is many miles north of Arsuf; making for the Turks' communications in the valley of Esdraelon. His infantry and artillery are falling back; hunted by my airmen, with machine gun fire and bombs. So far, many guns and 2,500 prisoners have been caught... I am beginning to think that we may have a very great success.'[18]

After an exhausting ride in the blazing sun and later under a bright moon, the Desert Mounted Corps reached the enemy's lateral communications to his rear. The 4th Cavalry marched seventy miles in thirty-four hours. Even the lorries could not keep up. When the sun set on the 20th, Allenby's cavalry formed a picket line from El Affule to Beisan waiting for the retreating and demoralized Turks to emerge from the hills.

Lieutenant Colonel E.F. Lawson, the commander of the Middlesex Yeomanry, had an amazing tale to tell. As his division (the 4th Cavalry under Barrow) moved through the Valley of Jezreel on its way to Beisan, he rode some distance ahead of his regiment to reconnoitre. Surprised by a Turkish detachment retreating from Jenin into the valley, he was taken prisoner. What followed suggested that all fight had gone out of many Turkish units. According to Barrow, Lawson 'explained the situation to the Turkish officers and showed them on his map how hopelessly they were placed with British troops on all sides of them. This strange conference held in indifferent French, ended in the position of captured and captors being reversed; and the officer led back to his regiment 800 armed Turkish officers and men as prisoners of war. This must be nearly a record capture by a man single-handed.'[19] Lawson, one of the first Territorial officers to be promoted to major general, went on to gain recognition as a commander of artillery during the retreat to Dunkirk in 1940.

The 10th and 53rd divisions of Chetwode's XX Corps faced the stiffest resistance. Following the success of the XXI Corps along the coast, Allenby ordered Chetwode to advance through the hills towards Nablus. He began his attack shortly before 8p.m. on September 19, with the 10th and 53rd divisions pressing forward over rugged country, capturing enemy strongholds with the bayonet. Allenby was determined to give the enemy no respite. The 53rd Division advanced to block the Turk's escape route from Nablus along the Wadi Farah to the Jordan River. The 10th Division was entrusted with the occupation of Nablus. Although both divisions were dead tired, Allenby and Chetwode drove them on without regard to the exhaustion of men and animals, Allenby personally showing up to urge on the lead battalions of the 10th Division. 'The moment demanded a great effort', the official history approvingly noted, 'and hearts had to be steeled against suffering.'[20] The 53rd Division's advance was halted on the evening of September 21 when the retreating Turks along Wadi Farah road came under attack by aircraft, as will soon be described. The division took 1,195 prisoners. The 10th Division continued its offensive until Nablus was occupied. In two days of continuous marching and fighting, the 10th captured 1,223 prisoners and, according to the official history, earned 'an honourable place in our military records'.[21]

The Turks, fleeing east from Nablus along the Wadi Farah road in an attempt to cross the Jordan at the Jisr ed Damiye ford, were given a deadly demonstration of air power. One stretch of this road had a deep, menacing gorge on one side and a steep stony bank on the other. This narrow defile became the focus of a devastating attack by the Palestine Brigade on September 21. The lead vehicles and guns were struck first, bringing the convoy to a stop. A little over nine tons of bombs were dropped and 56,000 machine-gun rounds expended on the terrified men and horses of this stalled column, converting the road into a charnel house. Desperate soldiers tried to escape by either descending into the gorge or climbing out of the Wadi. Some prostrated themselves on the ground while others frantically waved their arms trying to surrender. According to the RAF historian H.A. Jones, many pilots were sickened by the slaughter.[22]

Major Lord Hampton, a squadron commander in the Worcestershire Yeomanry, was stunned when he first observed the carnage in the 'Valley of Death'. 'A few hundred feet below us the main road wound down the gorge and, as far as the eye could reach, it was blocked by guns, wagons and motor lorries. Many had fallen over the precipice and lay shattered in the wadi bed. Dead or wounded animals lay thick between the wagons and added to an indescribable tangle',[23] he later recalled. James Calderwood Jones was assigned the grisly task of burying the dead. 'Our salvage party gathered the Turks in wagons & dumped them into holes & buried them in hundreds. This was the biggest rout I have saw',[24] he wrote in his diary.

On the evening of September 21, the Turkish 7th and 8th Armies had been virtually destroyed. 'I was able to motor into Nablus where I was joined by Allenby the same evening also in a motor, both of us being well ahead of our advance guards', Chetwode later wrote. 'The country was a mass of half starving bodies of Turks, some armed and some not, and it was quite ordinary to see an Indian havildar [sergeant] emerging from the mountains followed by 20 or 30 fully armed Turks who had surrendered to him.'[25]

Allenby reported his success to Sir Henry Wilson on September 22: 'The two Turkish armies west of the JORDAN have practically ceased to exist. Captures up to date are estimated at at least 25,000 prisoners and 260 guns, with the whole of the transport of the armies.'[26] When Allenby had conferred with Chetwode in Nablus, he continued to emphasize that there must be no let-up in exploiting the Turkish rout. 'I think very few high commanders have ever been seen before, personally driving on tired men and horses at a time when his personal influence just meant the extra mile or two which closed the last hope of escape to the enemy', Chetwode later commented. But at the time Chetwode was worried that his infantry was 'completely done in with fatigue and scattered over a distance of 10 or 20 miles' and that he only had a handful of cavalrymen available. Allenby, however, reassured him that the number of British troops did not matter for 'one shot from a British rifle' would 'turn the Turks into the Cavalry net'.[27] And he was right.

The infantry phase of the battle was essentially over once the enemy's front was broken. Casualties had been relatively light: 1,617 battle deaths, wounded and missing in September. Approximately one half of these casualties were Indian, a reflection of their importance to

Allenby following the departure of most of his Territorials to France after March 21.[28]

Allenby's breakthrough along the coast had thus far left the Turkish 4th Army in the Jordan Valley and hills of Moab untouched. Ignoring orders to withdraw, the able commander of this Turkish force, Mohammed Djemal the Lesser, had initially held his position as the right flank of the Turkish front collapsed. Confronting the 4th Army was a force commanded by Major General Chaytor. It consisted of the ANZAC Mounted Division, the 20th Indian Infantry Brigade and some other units. When Djemal the Lesser finally retreated, Chaytor ordered a vigorous pursuit. On the afternoon of September 23, Es Salt was taken for the third time in six months. Amman, which had remained out of British hands, fell to Chaytor's Force on September 25. Although some Turks had fled north from Amman on the Hejaz Railway the previous day, the British captured the Turkish rear guard.

With the number of Turkish and German prisoners now approaching 40,000 along the broken and expanding front, British authorities did not have the means to cope, especially given the diseased and starved condition of most of these POWs. Blake O'Sullivan, a subaltern in the 1/Connaught Rangers, 7th Brigade, 3rd (LaHore) Division, found himself in a nightmarish situation when he relieved some Australians who had been guarding a compound of some 300 prisoners. No sanitary arrangements had been made or food and water provided. 'The smell and filth were terrible', O'Sullivan recalled.

No sooner had O'Sullivan's detail begun to police the compound than he learned that some 3,000 additional prisoners were arriving from Beisan. 'First came about 200 Germans. Then a flood of Turks, Armenian, Arabs, Jews and Bedouins. Some wounded, some sick, and all filthy and famishing.' Only the Germans displayed 'a disciplined smartness'; and chaos prevailed as O'Sullivan and his men attempted some organization. 'Sick, crippled and exhausted men kept dragging themselves over to me and moaning "moya, moya" (water, water), making signs to their mouths or raising jittering hands to heaven – till I was nearly frantic. I was in the process of getting a representative water-drawing party formed when the second horde from the station bore down on me, and their bellowings, jostlings, and moanings were added to the pandemonium of the first.'

After O'Sullivan segregated the officers in one tent and arranged a water detail, he attempted to attend to the critically ill. 'The sorting out was no easy job because nearly everyone was sick. Very obvious dysentery wherever one looked; scores with malaria; numerous revolting exhibitions of syphilis; even a case of suspected cholera – and to turn the toughest stomach, teeming vermin swarming over all of them. Some men were so worn out that they lay as if dead, whilst flies in a black mass on their faces, crawled unheeded into their mouths, nostrils, and ears; and settling in myriads on the sores that blotched so many of the bodies.' O'Sullivan was stunned. Could this really be representative of the army which had often fought to the EEF to a standstill despite its inferior numbers and material? 'No men could have sunk to those appalling depths in the few days since the invasion had swept northwards', he surmised before falling asleep that night.

The next day, September 27, he returned to the compound after sponging his body with a 'strong permanganate as a forlorn sop to the surrounding filth'. He was greeted by a 'shocking and unforgettable sight'. With the addition of two additional shipments during the night, the compound now held 3,500 men 'packed in shoulder to shoulder. All sanitary discipline had vanished and dysenteric excrement covered every open space. Two men had died and lay on their backs in a cloud of flies. The rising sun, already hot, was drawing a miasmic fog from the rain soaked ground and a languid morning wind brought waves of a putrescent stench from five-week-old horse corpses which lay nearby.'

O'Sullivan twice circled the enclosure, retching 'violently at least six times before summoning up courage to enter the loathsome place. My retching was simply a compulsion ritual to suit the occasion', he confesses, 'as my stomach was completely empty; the unfortunate sentry who tried to salute me was not so lucky. His salute was erased by sudden uncontrolled vomiting.'

Following his inspection, O'Sullivan's spirits were revived somewhat by the arrival of three lorries with biscuits, bully beef and onions for the POWs. But he was concerned by orders to march the prisoners off to Jenin in three and a half hours. A meal was hastily prepared and O'Sullivan saw to its distribution. He divided the food into seventy equal parts and separated the prisoners into groups of fifty. 'Savage fights and frenzied screaming arose on all sides as each fifty-group proceeded to make its man-to-man distribution. The Turkish N.C.O.s inevitably would claim more for themselves and the fittest as usual survived at the expense of the weak.'

As soon as the last batch of fifty had been fed, the escort to take the POWs to Jenin arrived. Two Egyptian policemen had been included in their number. With drawn swords these Egyptians galloped 'round and round the mob, prodding at stumblers and striking at laggards. For all the world as if two rabid wolves had taken over the marshalling of a sheep flock'. O'Sullivan 'thanked god for not being sent on that ghastly march. Starting at noon they straggled into Jenin about 10.00p.m. that night. Three men died en route, and six more died at Jenin.'[29] Within a week, fully half of the men and officers of the Connaught Rangers compound detail were down with some form of illness and had to be relieved of their guard duties.

Despite the EEF's inability to cope with the thousands of captured Turks, the lucky Turks were the ones who fell into British rather than Arab hands. Allenby's interest in the Arabs on his right flank had increased once his forces were established in southern Palestine, and he had actively sought through the enigmatic Colonel T.E. Lawrence the co-operation of the Hashemite Arabs. The Arabs assisted him by threatening Turkish communications and harassing their garrisons. Although the Beni Sakhr tribe had let him down badly during his last Transjordan operations, he had assigned the Arabs a critical role in his present offensive. 'I am counting on Feisal's continued cooperation with me', he wrote Sir Henry Wilson in August. 'Naturally, I can't push far North unless the Hedjaz railway ceases to be a menace to my right flank. I must either be able to detach a strong flank guard, or my flank must be covered by the Arabs.'[30]

Allenby had anticipated that his cavalry could reach the important rail centres of El Affule and Beisan but not Deraa, the Turk's northwesterly escape route. The Turkish rail link from Damascus ran south to Deraa, where it forked. The Hejaz Railway ran south to Amman and beyond, and another line continued westward to Beisan and El Affule. The destruction of the vital railway junction at Deraa was assigned to the Arabs. Their attack had been timed to begin several days before 'H' hour. The so-called Northern Arab Army under Feisal had met its timetable, destroying four miles of track north of Deraa on September 17. Further demolitions during the next few days were carried out, but Deraa remained in Turkish hands. With the Turks demoralized and in flight everywhere, however, the Arab movement was energized. 'They saw their old enemy reeling to destruction; they saw a vision of freedom, and nearer at hand, a vision of loot', the official history noted. 'Their passion for both flamed up and possessed them.'[31] As remnants of 4th Army tried to escape northward by way of Deraa, other Arab factions joined Feisal's force, with horrific consequences for the broken and fleeing Turks.

On September 28, cavalrymen discovered a Red Crescent train near Amman at Qal'at el Mafraq. The sick and wounded had been killed and the trains looted by the local Arabs. The next day, the 5th Australian Light Horse encountered the Mann garrison fleeing north. When Chaytor arrived on the scene, he observed several thousand Arabs from the Beni Sakhr tribe, most of them on foot, 'all round the Turkish position and they were being incited to rush & kill the Turks'. The Turks wanted to surrender, but according to Chaytor, they 'were not willing to give up their arms until a force sufficient to protect them against the Arabs was available'. When Brigadier General G. de L. Ryrie, the commander of the 2nd ALH, arrived, Chaytor left him in charge with the words, 'The job is yours Ryrie do whatever you think best.'[32] Chaytor then visited with a representative from the Beni Sakhr tribe and told him that he 'would exact severe reprisals for any attack on the Turks who were my prisoners'.[33] Meanwhile, Ryrie, a former heavyweight boxer with a rough-and-ready manner, took a gamble that could have destroyed his career. The Australian commander let the Turks keep their guns for their own protection. The night passed with some bizarre scenes. The Australians camped with their enemy, shared their campfires, and cheered them on when they repulsed attacks by the Arabs. 'Go on,

Jacko!' they shouted. 'Give it to the blighters!'[34] The next morning, as they marched off for Amman, Ryrie allowed the Anatolian Turks among the prisoners to retain their rifles and bandoliers. According to his account, 'General Chaytor nearly had a fit when these fine Troops marched into Amman fully armed.'[35]

Further north, the 4th Cavalry Division's advance on Deraa forced the Turks to evacuate this key railway junction. Turks left behind in this town were not as fortunate as those protected by Chaytor and Ryrie. When General Barrow arrived at the railway station of that town on September 28, he discovered a massacre in progress by the Anaizeh Bedouins. 'A long ambulance train full of sick and wounded Turks was drawn up in the station', he wrote. 'In the cab of the engine was the dead driver and a mortally wounded fireman. The Arab soldiers were going through the train, tearing off the clothing of the groaning and stricken Turks, regardless of gaping wounds and broken limbs, and cutting their victims' throats.' These bloodthirsty acts, it has been suggested, were revenge for earlier Turkish atrocities. But to Barrow 'it was a sight that no average civilised human being could bear unmoved'.[36]

Barrow confronted Colonel Lawrence, whom he had met for the first time a few minutes earlier, telling him to halt the slaughter and remove the Arabs. According to Barrow's account, Lawrence said that he could not stop them, 'as it was their idea of war'. Barrow responded, 'It is not our idea of war, and if you can't remove them, I will.' Lawrence then allegedly said, 'If you attempt to do that I shall take no responsibility as to what happens.'[37] Barrow then took charge. He ordered his men to stop the killing and disperse the Arabs.

Barrow's account, if true – and there is really no reason to doubt his word – puts Colonel Lawrence in a bad light. Earlier, Lawrence, who had developed a hatred of the Turks, had participated directly in another massacre. As Lawrence and his Arab allies pursued a retreating column of Turkish and German soldiers, they had ridden through village Tafas. To their anger and horror, they discovered that some of the villagers had been killed by the retreating enemy. No mercy had been shown to women and children, and some of the dead had been horribly mutilated. Lawrence says that he saw a woman, 'bottom upwards, nailed there by a saw bayonet whose shaft stuck hideously into the air from between her naked legs. She had been pregnant, and about her lay others, perhaps twenty in all, variously killed, but set out in accord with an obscene taste.' A furious Lawrence exclaimed, 'The best of you brings me the most Turkish dead.'[38]

The Arabs apparently needed no urging from Lawrence. They attacked a column of retreating Turks. 'We ordered "no prisoners"', Lawrence wrote, 'and the men obeyed, except that the reserve company took 250 men (including many German A.S.C. [Army Service Corps]) alive.' Later, according to Lawrence, the Arabs discovered one of their 'men with a fractured thigh who had been afterwards pinned to the ground by two mortal thrusts of German bayonets. Then we turned our Hotchkiss on the prisoners and made an end of them.'[39]

The breakup of the entire Turkish front and the disintegration of the Turkish armies facing the EEF raised expectations in London. Allenby had initially planned a limited advance that did not take his forces too far north. But the politicians, encouraged by reports of his offensive, favoured a distant advance as far as Aleppo to knock Turkey out of the war. On September 24, Allenby received a communication from Sir Henry Wilson: 'Your success being so complete, I should like you to consider the possibility of a cavalry raid on ALEPPO, to be supported by infantry or not as the situation developed and as opportunities offered.' Although the War Cabinet was prepared to take full responsibility for any 'risks involved', Allenby hesitated. It was about 300 miles from Nazareth to Aleppo. He told Wilson that such a distant raid did not seem feasible unless supported by large-scale military and naval operations at Alexandretta. He preferred an advance in stages, the first stage being an advance to the Damascus-Beirut line.[40] On October 1, Damascus was occupied by the Australians and Arabs. On October 5, the 5th Cavalry Division left the city and pushed on northward to Rayak, an important railway junction. The Australians covered the thirty miles in a day.

Several days earlier Allenby had sent the 7th (Meerut) Division in three columns along the coast from Haifa to Beirut, Syria's second largest city. Private Rothon, accompanying this Indian Division in its artillery train, arrived at Beirut on the evening of October 9, the day after the city had been occupied. He was half-starved and spent. He had covered 226 miles since September 19, an extraordinary forty miles over the last two days. 'If I was asked how I felt when we arrived I should say like a cripple and fairly doubled up and I hope I shall never experience another march like it the men tramping along with hollow cheeks and staring eyes, nothing to eat but the awful Bouilli & Biscuits and lots of the men go without as their stomachs cannot stand the awful repetition (we have had 3 weeks of it)', he noted in his diary. 'My inside yearns for some *ordinary* food & vegetables.'[41]

During the subsequent advance to Aleppo, spearheaded by a small number of mounted troops and armoured cars, the enemy offered little resistance. Exhaustion, stretched supply lines, and especially disease represented the greatest threat to the EEF. A worldwide flu epidemic combined with malaria in striking down many men. 'Sickness is troubling us', Allenby wrote Sir Henry Wilson. 'I had the mosquitos [*sic*] well in hand; and soon the Jordan Valley had become almost a summer health resort. Now I'm in Turkish territory, and malignant malaria is laying a lot of people by the heels. I've a good acting DMS [Director of Medical Services] now; one Luce, and he is doing all he can, but his beds are all full. I want to send some thousands of sick to Malta; but Salonika appears to have filled up most of the beds there.'[42] Trained medical personnel were also in short supply in the east. Manpower shortages on the western front had led to the recall of all Class A orderlies of the Royal Army Medical Corps, which was responsible for the transport of wounded behind the lines and the running of hospitals. Their place had been taken by untrained Arab boys, most of whom knew little or no English.

Gunner James Calderwood Jones was one of the many soldiers felled by malaria. He was admitted to a makeshift hospital established in a convent in Haifa. Filthy and overcrowded, it might as well have been a charnel house. Barely able to lift his pen, he wrote, 'I think I have been unconscious since last night. I have had two glass of milk since I came in here & haven't saw a Doctor yet. Troops arriving all day, mostly all sickness.' Jones found himself in a nightmarish situation. A wounded German officer lay on the floor near him. While

Jones was in the hospital, he never saw the German treated, or even given a drink of water. Jones fared little better. 'There are about 3,000 patients here, three Medical Officers, six European orderlies', he wrote in his diary, 'the remainder of the staff are all Indians. It is the survival of the fittest, if one is able to be up & about there is a chance of getting something to eat, but if a stretcher case, you get no attention whatever, the staff can't cope with the numbers'[43] After a week, Jones decided to take his chances on the outside. He left to rejoin his unit without asking for a discharge.

Rothon had reached his breaking point on October 18, after a fifteen-mile march to Tripoli over mountain passes and across soft, yielding sand. 'Felt absolutely done up when we got here and at times felt like lying down and giving in as I feel as if my very life blood is being drawn from me in these long marches, an addition to which we are only at half strength which means double work for us all',[44] his diary entry read. Sickness soon followed exhaustion for Rothon. In the last days of the war, he found himself in the American school in Tripoli that had been converted into a hospital. According to Rothon, it was 'packed both inside and also in the grounds and the numbers awaiting admission is colossal'. He estimated that there were almost 1,000 patients, many of whom died during the night. 'When the morning Sun spreads its gorgeous rays over all', he wrote, 'it is pathetic to see the bodies covered with the Union Jacks come solemnly across some distant part of the ground. The *Last Muster,* another poor chap gone to his last Rest, another broken heart.'[45]

The advance to victory thus found Allenby's forces crippled with disease, with inadequate medical care for many. The cavalry's distant trek had been accompanied by remarkably few battle casualties, only 650 in five weeks, but disease was another matter. According to Gullet, 'Every headquarters from corps to squadron was more or less a hospital, where the fortunate lay on stretchers, but most had to be content with a place on the floor, or out in the shade of the trees, while they battled with raging fevers.'[46] Tragically, many who served in the infantry as well as the cavalry died after the armistice with Turkey. The EEF's death toll from disease in October and November was 2,158. By contrast, the EEF had suffered only 453 battle deaths during the last two months of the war.[47]

On October 26, the cavalry entered Aleppo, the last city to fall in the campaign. Five days later, an armistice with Turkey went into effect. Since September 19, Allenby's forces had marched hundreds of miles and netted over 75,000 prisoners. The endurance of the 5th Cavalry Division deserves special mention. In thirty-eight days, this division had covered 550 miles. In a letter to his father, Alan-Williams noted that the 5th Cavalry Division (a newly constituted division that included Yeomanry regiments from the 5th Mounted Brigade, which had previously been in the Australian Mounted Division), 'had been in the van since the commencement of operations five weeks ago & I would not have missed what we have gone through for all the wealth of the Indies'. He had not figured out how many miles he had advanced, but he had done little 'but trek on and on doing anything from 15 to 25 miles per day & stopping for the night near some village… So you see we are living very much on the country, only groceries such as tea, sugar, milk & jam catch us up in lorries very fourth or fifth day.'[48]

On November 11 1918, eleven days after the armistice with Turkey went into effect, the guns also fell silent on the western front. The Great War was over, and none too soon for the men who had been the mainstay of the British military effort in Egypt and Palestine, the Territorials.

We conclude this personal account of British operations in Egypt and Palestine where it began, with A.S. Benbow, who in September 1915 had sailed for Egypt. Four years later, after surviving many campaigns and cerebral malaria, he returned to England in 1919. He made the 'stiff climb' up Wimbledon Hill to the Common, where a demobilization camp had been established. There he was relieved of all his military gear, fed, and, after a bath, given a suit, shirt, shoes and undergarments. He also received a 'pocketful of money' that included a bounty given to all ranks. He had climbed Wimbledon Hill as a veteran Territorial; he now descended the hill to the station to make his way home as a civilian.[49]

Conclusion

It is the rash person indeed who offers sweeping generalizations about the experiences of British soldiers serving in the Great War. Each soldier reacted in his own and different way to the routine of army life, his theatre of operations, and combat. Having said this, it is still possible to make some comparisons between those who served in Palestine and Egypt and those who served on the western front. Bluntly stated, you were more likely to survive the war if you served in the Egyptian Expeditionary Force rather than in the British Expeditionary Force. The western front is associated with huge casualties and stalemated trench warfare, the EEF's theatre with open warfare and distant advances. A war of movement, however, could be just as costly as trench warfare, as the battles in 1918 in France and the EEF's advance on Jerusalem abundantly demonstrate. The smaller casualty rate in Egypt and Palestine is explained by other factors. First, the enemy's artillery, the great killer in this industrialized war, was much less a factor in Egypt and Palestine; and second, and most important, none of the EEF's battles approached the magnitude or duration of the great offensives on the western front. The three battles for Gaza were measured in days rather than weeks or months, the capture and securing of Jerusalem took roughly six weeks, and the final offensive, September 18–October 31, was virtually over in less than a week when the opposing Turkish forces were either captured or sent into headlong retreat.

Most members of the EEF understood that they had a better chance of surviving the war because of the theatre in which they fought. Lieutenant D.F. Heath, who served with the Machine Gun Corps, had this advice in September 1918 for his father, who had just been drafted. 'If you think the war is going to last a long time and you want to be alive at the end of it, apply for the East.'[1] F.S. Harries, a soldier in the 53rd Division, considered himself lucky that his battalion had not been selected to stem the German tide after March 21. 'Some of our old friends who left this country for France have had a bad knock. Numerous officers we knew as well as we know our own fellows have been killed or wounded. We all thank our lucky stars we weren't selected to go. Unheroic and mean? Well, perhaps so, but the zeal to get out that one had in 1914 and 1915 has vanished.'[2]

A lower casualty rate, however, did not make Egypt and Palestine, where physical discomfort overshadowed death, a 'picnic'. Brigadier General H.A. Vernon, the commander of the 158th Brigade, 53rd Division, who served in both France (1914–1917) and Palestine, feared that the official history would not give proper emphasis to the incredible hardships faced by the EEF. 'In Palestine, the shelling, the proximity to the enemy and the trench mud of Flanders and France were lacking', he writes, 'but even when a unit was out of the line, water was always scarce, letters arrived at varying intervals sometimes marked "salved from the sea," sometimes having been dumped for a fortnight before transport was available for their delivery. Parcels usually arrived in a damaged condition months after they had been despatched, newspapers were out of date.'

And this was only part of the story, according to Vernon:

> No one can get a real insight into the campaign, who does not realise the absence of comfort, shelter, water, extras, facilities for washing, drying clothes, replenishing boots and clothing, the changes of temperature day and night when extra clothing cannot be carried – which the troops were subjected to. In France in normal periods one was always liable to intense shelling, to far greater danger and momentary exertions almost beyond human endurance. But after a few days (I mean of course when no operation was actually in progress) one

always got back to a few days comparative comfort where food, drink, hot baths and luxuries were available and where one could with some truth say 'Let us eat drink and be merry for tomorrow we die.' In Palestine one's period of rest was generally one of boredom, monotony and discomfort.[3]

Another feature of service in the east was the protracted exile from loved ones. Home leave, especially for unmarried men, was almost impossible to obtain. 'It was the question of leave that rankled most', recalls Major C.S. Jarvis, 'for, though the troops in Sinai and Palestine got an odd day or so in Egypt at infrequent intervals, it was the home town and their own people that they desired to see and not the lurid lights and rather sordid attractions of Cairo and Alexandria.'[4]

When the war ended, the EEF contained a sizable number of men who had been in Egypt since 1914–1915. When demobilization was delayed because of the imperial requirements to garrison the occupied territories and keep down the nationalist unrest that surfaced in Egypt after the war, Allenby confronted a serious crisis in morale. Peace brought boredom and temptation. In a Special Order of the Day (January 1919), Allenby appealed to his troops to behave during their extended stay abroad. He noted that 'special temptations exist with regard to Wine and Women. Both must be resisted. Our relatives and friends are anxiously awaiting our return home, and they will expect to find all those of us who have escaped wounds in action with our physical and our moral energies unimpaired.'[5] Not surprisingly, this appeal had little effect on soldiers who were bored and anxious to return home. Many soldiers had more on their minds than a reunion with the opposite sex or family members. The fear grew that jobs being kept open for returning soldiers would all be taken before they were demobilized. Unrest in the ranks soon bordered on mutinous.

By May, Allenby believed that he had no choice, whatever the danger to Britain's position in the Middle East, to increase the flow of men home. In a series of letters that stressed the 'danger of mutinous conduct on a large scale', he convinced the War Office to accelerate the demobilization of his men. He pointed out that he had 26,000

1914 men and 30,000 1915 men in addition to 10,000 men in administrative service. Many of his soldiers consequently believed that the War Office was not playing fair with its reluctance to send out drafts and reinforcements to allow them to be demobilized.

Some officers sought to blunt this criticism of the War Office by telling their men that they were lucky to be serving in the Middle East. These officers took the position that most of these veterans of eastern warfare would 'have been dead by now – no doubt – if their service had been in France'.[6] The Tommies, most of whom were Terrritorials, were angered rather than humbled by this line of reasoning. And they had a right to be. They might be alive when some of their comrades who served in France were not. But they had passed with flying colours during a long campaign with a worthy foe a test of endurance and stamina almost unequalled in the service of the crown.

Notes

PREFACE

1   Antony Bluett, *With Our Army in Palestine* (London: Andrew Melrose, 1919), 144–45.

2   Not a single regiment of regular cavalry from home participated in this theatre.

3   *Statistics of the Military Effort of the British Empire During the Great War, 1914–1920* (1922; reprint ed., Dallington, Heathfield, East Sussex: Naval and Military Press, 1999), 238–39.

4   Memoir, IWM, Wintringham MSS 78/9/1.

5   Major C.S. Jarvis, *The Back Garden of Allah,* 4th ed. (London: John Murray, 1941), 88.

6   Memoir ('The Chronicle of a Yeomanry Squadron in Palestine, Jordan and Syria', n.d.), IWM, Hampton MSS DS/Misc/82.

I: EASTWARD BOUND

1   Memoir, IWM, Benbow MSS PP/MCA/146.

2   Memoir, IWM, Chamberlain MSS 89/7/1.

3   For Germany's Middle East strategy, see Hew Strachan, *To Arms,* Vol. 1, *The First World War* (Oxford: Oxford University Press, 2001), 694–712, 729–54.

4   A.J. Smithers, *The Fighting Nation: Lord Kitchener and His Armies* (London: Leo Cooper, 1994), 67. See also Ian F.W. Beckett, 'The Territorial Force', in *A Nation in Arms: A Social Study of the British Army in the First World War,* ed. Ian F.W. Beckett and Keith Simpson (Manchester: Manchester University Press, 1985), 144.

5   Smithers, *Fighting Nation,* 71.

6   Yigal Sheffy, *British Intelligence in the Palestine Campaign, 1914–1918* (London: Frank Cass, 1998), 60.

7   Diary entry of October 18 1918 ('With the Forces in Gallipoli and Palestine:

A Diary by Signaller W. Marchant'), IWM, Marchant MSS Box No 102.

8   Edward J. Erickson, 'Strength Against Weakness: Ottoman Military Effectiveness at Gallipoli, 1915', *Journal of Military History* 65 (October 2001): 982. See also Erickson's *Ordered to Die: A History of the Ottoman Army in the First World War* (Westport, Conn.: Greenwood Press, 2001).

9   Trevor Wilson, *The Myriad Faces of War: Britain and the Great War, 1914–1918* (Cambridge: Polity Press, 1986), 92.

10 Stanley George to Dray April 17 1915, IWM, George MSS 97/26/1.

11 Frederick Thomas Mills, *Great Uncle Fred's War: An Illustrated Diary, 1917–1920* ed. Alan Pryor and Jennifer K. Woods (Whitstable, Kent: Pryor, 1985), 14.

12 Memoir, IWM, Frost MSS 81/1/1.

13 Memoir (January 1962), IWM Hiorns MSS 67/34/1.

14 Mills, *Great Uncle Fred's War*, 16.

15 Diary entry of February 3 1918, IWM, Rothon MSS 82/3/1.

16 Anthony Bluett, *With Our Army in Palestine* (London: Andrew Melrose, 1919), 1.

17 Diary entry of September 11 1917, IWM, Earney MSS 81/23/1.

18 Memoir ('Between Two Great Deserts', 1919), IWM, Boord MSS 66/99/1.

19 Memoir (January 1962), IWM, Hiorns MSS 67/34/1.

20 Oral interview, IWM, Acc. No. 007498/09.

21 Diary entry of July 26 1916, IWM, Macey MSS 74/161/1.

22 C. Ernest Fayle, *Seaborne Trade*, Vol. 2, From the Opening of the Submarine Campaign to the Appointment of the Shipping Controller (London: HMSO, 1923), 358.

23 Diary entry of January 1 1917, and introduction, IWM, Calcutt MSS 78/56/2.

24 Diary entry of January 1 1917, IWM, Calcutt MSS 78/56/2.

25 Memoir, IWM, Fletcher MSS 78/9/1.

26 Diary entry of January 1 1917, IWM, Calcutt MSS 78/56/2.

27 This officer was later rescued. Memoir, IWM, Frost MSS 81/1/1.

28 Lynden-Bell to Maurice, January 4 1917, IWM, Lynden-Bell MSS 90/1/1.

29 Diary, n.d. but written after the war, LHCMA, Walters MSS, Single Collection.

30 Bernard Blaser, *Kilts Across the Jordan: Being Experiences and Impressions with the Second Battalion 'London Scottish' in Palestine* (London: H.F. & G. Witherby, 1926), 14.

31 Ibid., 17.

32 Diary entry of December 31 1915, IWM, Tozer MSS 87/13/1.

33 Diary entry of June 13 1917, IWM, Scott MSS 66/133/1(2).

34 Memoir (1960s), IWM, Surry MSS 82/22/1.

35 Blaser, *Kilts Across the Jordan*, 28.

2: LAND OF THE PHARAOHS

1   Lieutenant General Sir George MacMunn and Captain Cyril Falls, *Military Operations: Egypt and Palestine from the Outbreak of War with Germany to June 1917* (1928; reprint, Nashville, Tenn.: Battery Press, 1996), 50N1.

2   For Turko-German efforts to incite the Senussi, see Hew Strachan, *To Arms,*
    Vol. 1, *The First World War* (Oxford: Oxford University Press, 2001), 743–54.

3   Memoir, IWM, Sharkey MSS 86/57/1.

4   Ibid.

5   'Charge of the Dorset Yeomanry at Agagiya', n.d., NAM, Blaksley MSS, Acc.
    8201-23.

6   MacMunn and Falls, *Military Operations,* 128–29.

7   Frank Fox, *The History of the Royal Gloucestershire Hussars Yeomanry, 1898–1922:
    The Great Cavalry Campaign in Palestine* (London: Philip Allan, 1923), 90.

8   MacMunn and Falls, *Military Operations,* 128n1.

9   Ibid., 85.

10 Ibid., 83–84.

11 William Robertson, *Soldiers and Statesmen, 1914–1918* (London: Cassell, 1926),
    2:150.

12 Murray to editor of the *Times,* February 13 1933, IWM, Murray MSS
    79/48/4.

13 Robertson to Wigram, March 24 1915, RA, Geo V MSS Q. 2522/3/172.

14 Robertson to Callwell, October 26 1915, LHCMA, Robertson MSS 7/2/33.

15 MacMunn and Falls, *Military Operations,* 159.

16 Robertson to Murray, December 31 1915, IWM, Murray MSS 79/48/3.

17 Robertson to Murray, March 15 1916, BL, Murray-Robertson MSS Add
    52461.

18 Kitchener to Murray, December 31 1915, in David R. Woodward, ed., *The
    Military Correspondence of Field Marshall Sir William Robertson, Chief of Imperial
    General Staff, December 1915–February 1918* (London: Bodley Head/Army
    Records Society, 1989), 41–43.

19 Colonel A.P. Wavell, *The Palestine Campaigns* (London: Constable and
    Company, 1928), 40.

20 W.T. Massey, *The Desert Campaigns* (New York: G.P. Putnam's Sons, 1918), 26.

21 Major C.H. Dudley-Ward, *History of the 53rd (Welsh) Division (T.F.), 1914–1918*
    (Cardiff: Western Mail Limited, 1927), 60.

22 'Events commencing from evacuation of Gallipoli Dec 1915.' NAM, Barron
    MSS, Acc. 7408-63.

23 Antony Bluett, *With Our Army in Palestine* (London: Andrew Melrose, 1919),
    30–31.

24 Diary entry of May 16 1917, IWM, McGrigor MSS Vol 1/AMM/2.

25 Letter of July 25 1916, IWM, George MSS 97/26/1.

26 Baker to Lettice, March 24 1916, IWM, Baker MSS 85/39/1.

27 Buxton to Blanche, March 18 1916, IWM, Buxton MSS 66/101/1.

28 Diary entry of October 31 1917, IWM, J. Wilson MSS 84/52/1.

29 Memoir, IWM, Matthews MSS 85/32/1.

30 R.C. Case to mother, July 3 1917, IWM, Case MSS P147.

31 Geoffrey Inchbald, *Imperial Camel Corps* (London: Johnson, 1970), 102.

32 Major Vivian Gilbert, *The Romance of the Last Crusade: With Allenby to Jerusalem*
    (New York: D. Appleton, 1923), 69.

33 Case to 'my dear people', July 5 1917, IWM, Case MSS P147.

34 Inchbald, *Imperial Camel Corps,* 103.

35 Memoir, IWM, Loudon MSS 87/17/1.

36   IWM, Fletcher MSS 78/9/1.

37   For prostitution and the Egyptian Expeditionary Force, see especially
     Lieutenant Colonel P.G. Elgood, *Egypt and the Army* (Oxford: Oxford
     University Press, 1924); and Mark Harrison, 'The British Army and the
     Problem of Venereal Disease in France During the First World War', *Medical
     History* 39 (1995): 133–58.

38   James W. Barrett, *The Australian Army Medical Corps in Egypt* (London: H.K.
     Lewis, 1918), 123.

39   Diary entry of August 17 1918 ('The Last Crusade of a Private Soldier in the
     Palestine Expeditionary Force, 1917–1919'), IWM, Blunt MSS 94/5/1.

40   Memoir ('A Soldier in Egypt 1914–1915, n.d.'), IWM, Thompson MSS 71/7/1.

41   Diary entry of March 21 1917, IWM, Calcutt MSS 78/56/2.

42   Diary entry of September 7 1917, IWM, Blunt MSS 94/5/1.

43   James W. Barrett, 'Management of Venereal Diseases in Egypt During the War',
     British Military Journal (February 1 1919): 127.

44   T.J. Mitchell and G.M. Smith, Medical Services: Casualties and Medical
     Statistics of the Great War (London: HMSO, 1931), 215.

45   David Michael Simpson, 'The Moral Battlefield: Venereal Disease and the
     British Army During the First World War' (PhD diss., University of Iowa, May
     1995), 226–28.

46   Jack to Dorothy ['Dolly'] Williams, November 23 1917, IWM, D. Williams
     MSS 85/4/1.

47   IWM, *Middlesex Yeomanry Magazine*, Souvenir Number, 1914–1919, 47.

48   Letter of May 7 1918, IWM, Young MSS, 76/101/1.

49   Allenby to Robertson, August 8 1917, in Matthew Hughes, ed., *Allenby
     in Palestine: The Middle East Correspondence of Field Marshal Viscount Allenby*
     (London: Sutton Publishing/Army Records Society, 2004), 50.

50   Buxton to Blanche, July 13 1916, IWM, Buxton MSS 66/101/1.

51   Ivy to Beer, August 24 1917, IWM, Beer MSS 86/19/1.

52   Jack to his father, October 12 1917; Ivy to Beer, August 24 1917, IWM, Beer
     MSS 86/19/1.

53   Boord to his mother, September 1 1917, IWM, Boord MSS 66/99/1.

3: CLEARING THE SINAI

1   Dawnay to his wife, December 25 1916, IWM, Dawnay MSS 69/21/2.

2   Lynden-Bell to Sir Frederick Maurice, January 16 1916, IWM, Lynden-Bell
     MSS 90/1/1.

3   Ibid.

4   Benbow to his wife, March 18 1917, IWM, Benbow MSS PP/MCA/146.

5   War letter 103, Vol. 11, IWM, McPherson MSS, 80/25/1.

6   'The Memoirs of an Ordinary Man' (1969), IWM, Cadenhead MSS 85/51/1.

7   Lieutenant Colonel P.G. Elgood, *Egypt and the Army* (Oxford: Oxford
     University Press, 1924), p. 84.

8   Brevet Lieutenant Colonel G.E. Badcock, *A History of the Transport Services of
     the Egyptian Expeditionary Force, 1916–1917–1918* (London: Hugh Rees, 1925), 31.

9   Ibid., 36.

10   War letter 104, Vol. 11, IWM, McPherson MSS 80/25/1.

11   War letter 105, Vol. 11, IWM, McPherson MSS 80/25/1.

12   Major Vivian Gilbert, *The Romance of the Last Crusade: With Allenby to Jerusalem*
       (New York: D. Appleton, 1923), 75.

13   'They Also Served, the story of the Egyptian Labour Corps, in Sinai and
       Palestine', n.d., IWM, Venables MSS P 257.

14   Lieutenant General Sir George MacMunn and Captain Cyril Falls, *Military
       Operations: Egypt and Palestine from the Outbreak of War with Germany to June
       1917* (1928; reprint, Nashville, Tenn.: Battery Press, 1996), 243n1.

15   Robert H. Goodsall, *Palestine Memories, 1917–1918–1925* (Canterbury: Cross and
       Jackman, 1925), 79.

16   Case to 'dear people', September 3 1917, IWM, Case MSS P 147.

17   Venables, 'They Also Served', unpublished, n.d., IWM, Venables MSS P 259.

18   War letter 105, Vol. 11, IWM, McPherson MSS 80/25/1.

19   War letter 107, Vol. 11, IWM, McPherson MSS 80/25/1.

20   W.T. Massey, *Allenby's Final Triumph* (New York: E.P. Dutton, 1920), 175.

21   Diary entry of October 31 1917, IWM, Knott MSS P 305.

22   Memoir ('Between the Two Deserts', 1919), IWM Boord MSS 66/99/1.

23   Allenby to Robertson, December 4 1917, in Hughes, *Allenby in Palestine*, 100.

24   Memoir, n.d., IWM, Matthews MSS 85/32/1.

25   Badcock, *History of the Transport Services*, 42.

26   'With Bicycle and Bayonet', n.d., IWM, A.E. Williams MSS 87/22/1.

27   Martin S. Briggs, *Through Egypt in War-Time* (London: T. Fisher Unwin, 1918),
       204.

28   H.S. Gullett, *The Official History of Australia in the War of 1914–1918*, Vol. 7,
       Sinai and Palestine: The Australian Imperial Force in Sinai and Palestine, 1914–1918
       (Sydney: Angus and Robertson, 1923), 81.

29   Chaytor to Director, Historical Section, Military Branch, October 21 1925,
       PRO, Cab 45/78/C.

30   Murray to Robertson, July 22 1916, copy, IWM, O.C. Williams MSS 69/78/1.

31   Diary entry of July 22 1916, IWM, O.C. Williams MSS 69/78/1.

32   Robertson to Murray July 23 1916, copy, IWM, O.C. Williams MSS 69/78/1.

33   MacMunn and Falls, *Military Operations*, 202n1.

34   In addition to the official history, 175–204, informative accounts can be
       found in Colonel A.P. Wavell, *The Palestine Campaigns* (London: Constable
       and Company), 45–51; Marquess of Anglesey, *A History of the British Cavalry,
       1816–1919*, Vol. 1, *Egypt, Palestine and Syria, 1914–1919* (London: Leo Cooper,
       1994) 59–73; and A.J. Hill, *Chauvel of the Light Horse: A Biography of General Sir
       Harry Chauvel* (Victoria: Melbourne University Press, 1978), 73–83.

35   War letter 105, Vol. 11, IWM, McPherson MSS 80/25/1.

36   Captain O. Teichman, *The Diary of a Yeomanry M.O., Egypt, Gallipoli, Palestine
       and Italy* (London: Fisher Unwin, 1921), 72.

37   'Battle of Romani, August 1916', IWM, Sneath MSS 74/23/1.

38   War letter 105, Vol. 11, IWM, McPherson MSS 80/25/1.

39   MacMunn and Falls, *Military Operations*, 195.

40   'I Remember: The Crossing the Sinai Desert July–December 1916',
       unpublished, n.d., IWM, Thompson MSS 71/7/1.

41   Lynden-Bell to Maurice, August 17 1916, IWM, Lynden-Bell MSS 90/1/1.

42   MacMunn and Falls, *Military Operations,* 201n1.

43   Oral interview, IWM, Acc. No. 4200.

44   Lynden-Bell to Maurice, August 17 1916, IWM, Lynden-Bell Papers, 90/1/11.

45   Diary entries of August 4–5 1916, IWM, Williams MSS 69/78/1.

46   Murray to Lawrence, August 1916, IWM, Murray MSS 79/48/3.

47   Lynden-Bell to Maurice, August 17 1916, IWM, Lynden-Bell MSS 90/1/1.

48   Hill, *Chauvel of the Light Horse,* 82.

49   Buxton to his mother, August 13 1916, IWM, Buxton MSS 66/101/1.

50   Diary entry of November 7 1917, IWM, Knott MSS P 305.

51   Memoir, 1960s, IWM, Surry MSS 82/22/1.

52   'I Remember: The Crossing of the Sinai Desert, July–December 1916', n.d.,
      IWM, Thompson MSS 71/7/1.

53   Murray to Robertson, December 10, 1916, in MacMunn and Falls, *Military
      Operations,* 259.

54   Cyril Falls, *Armageddon: 1918* (London: Weidenfeld & Nicolson, 1964), 45.

55   Lieutenant Colonel C. Guy Powles, *Official History of New Zealand's Effort
      in the Great War,* Vol. 3, *The New Zealanders in Sinai and Palestine* (Auckland:
      Whitcombe & Tombs, 1922), 54–55.

56   Ibid., 68.

57   Hill, *Chauvel of the Light Horse,* 89–93.

58   V.H. Rothwell, *British War Aims and Peace Diplomacy, 1914–1918* (Oxford:
      Oxford University Press, 1971), 126–27.

59   Maurice to Lynden-Bell, December 13 1916, IWM, Lyden-Bell MSS 90/1/1.

60   Robertson to Murray, December 15 1916, in MacMunn and Falls, *Military
      Operations,* 260–61.

4: JOHNNY TURK TRIUMPHANT

1   Townsend to parents, March 26 1917, IWM, Townsend MSS 86/66/1.

2   Diary; IWM, A.V. Benbow MSS No. 48.

3   Richard Holmes, *The Little Field-Marshal: Sir John French* (London: Jonathan
     Cape, 1981), 266.

4   Diary entry of July 22 1916, IWM, O. C. Williams MSS 69/78/1.

5   Letter of April 23 1916, in 'Egypt and Palestine, 1916–1917', IWM, Dawnay
     MSS 69/21/2.

6   See Maurice to Lynden-Bell, January 17 1917, IWM, Lynden-Bell MSS,
     90/1/1; and Lieutenant Colonel C.À. Court Repington, *The First World War,
     1914–1918* (London: Constable and Company, 1920), 1:434, 1:436.

7   Robertson, 'Notes on a Proposal to Undertake a Campaign During the
     Winter with the Object of Capturing Jerusalem, 29 December 1916', PRO,
     WO 106/310.

8   Maurice to Lynden-Bell, January 24 1917, IWM, Lynden-Bell MSS 90/1/1.

9   Repington, *First World War,* 1:493.

10   Ibid.

11   Letter of March 23 1917, in 'Egypt and Palestine, 1916–1917', IWM, Dawnay

MSS 69/21/2; 'Personal Notes on First and Second Gaza by Sir C. Dobell', PRO, Cab 45/78/D.

12 Notes by Dawnay, March 17 1917, IWM, Chetwode MSS P 183.

13 Murray to Repington, April 22 1917, in Repington, *First World War*, 1:564.

14 Chetwode to Dawnay, March 11 1917, IWM, Chetwode MSS, P 183.

15 Chetwode to MacMunn, January 12 1925, PRO, Cab 45/78/C.

16 Letter of March 8 1917, 'Egypt and Palestine, 1916–1917', IWM, Dawnay MSS 69/21/2.

17 Colonel A.P. Wavell, *The Palestine Campaigns* (London: Constable and Company, 1928), 73.

18 Chetwode to MacMunn, January 12 1925, PRO, Cab 45/78/C.

19 Diary entry of March 26 1917, IWM, Marchant MSS Box No, 102.

20 Ion L. Idriess, *The Desert Column* (Sydney: Angus & Robertson, 1932), 191–92.

21 See the comments by the artillery officer Major General S.C.U. Smith: 'I was satisfied that the failure of the 53rd Division to push on faster and with fewer casualties was due to the misuse of the divisional artillery by the GOC of that division.' 'Copy of a letter from Major-General S.C.U. Smith', December 27 1925, PRO, Cab 45/80/S.

22 Wavell, *Palestine Campaigns*, 82.

23 Dawnay to his wife, April 2 1917, in 'Egypt and Palestine, 1916–1917', IWM, Dawnay MSS 69/21/2.

24 Marquess of Anglesey, *A History of the British Cavalry, 1816–1919*, Vol. 5, *Egypt, Palestine and Syria, 1914–1919* (London: Leo Cooper, 1994), 104.

25 Wavell, *Palestine Campaigns*, 81.

26 Chetwode to MacMunn, January 12 1925, PRO, Cab 45/78/C.

27 Lieutenant General Sir George MacMunn and Captain Cyril Falls, *Military Operations: Egypt and Palestine from the Outbreak of War with Germany to June 1917* (1928; reprint, Nashville, Tenn.: Battery Press, 1996), 308–11.

28 C.H. Dudley-Ward, *History of the 53rd (Welsh) Division (T.F.), 1914–1918* (Cardiff: Western Mail Limited, 1927), 97.

29 Bailey kept a diary but the above is taken from an account that he wrote later. IWM, Bailey MSS 85/4/1.

30 Diary entry of March 27, IWM, Marchant MSS Box No. 102.

31 Captain O. Teichman, *Diary of a Yeomanry M.O., Egypt, Gallipoli, Palestine and Italy* (London: Fisher Unwin, 1921), 128.

32 Murray's estimate of the losses was almost 500 less than this number. MacMunn and Falls, *Military Operations*, 313–15n1.

33 Oral interview, IWM, Acc. No. 4052.

34 Shorthand version of Butler's speech taken by Private Abel of 'B' Company, included in diary entry of March 28 1917, IWM, Marchant MSS, Box No. 102.

35 Dobell to Director of Historical Section, December 7 1924, PRO, Cab 45/78/D.

36 Desk diary entries of March 26–27 1917, IWM, Murray MSS 79/48/4.

37 MacMunn and Falls, *Military Operations*, 322n2.

38 'Egypt 1917–1918', IWM, Dawnay MSS 69/21/2.

39 Lynden-Bell to Maurice, March 31 1917, IWM Lynden-Bell MSS 90/1/1.

40 Diary entry of April 2 1917, IWM, O. C. Williams MSS 69/78/1.

41 Ibid.

42 Tim Travers, *The Killing Ground: The British Army, the Western Front and the Emergence of Modern Warfare, 1900–1918* (London: Allen & Unwin, 1987), 24.

43 MacMunn and Falls, *Military Operations*, 223–24n2.

44 Dudley-Ward, *History of the 53rd (Welsh) Division*, 92.

45 Diary entry of April 6 1917, IWM, Williams MSS 69/78/1.

46 Randolf Baker to his mother April 11 1917, IWM, Baker MSS 85/39/1.

47 General Staff, 'A General Review of the Situation in All Theatres of War', March 20 1917, PRO, WO 106/311.

48 Milner to Lloyd George, March 17 1917, HLRO, Lloyd George MSS F/38/2/3.

49 David R. Woodward, ed., *The Military Correspondence of Field Marshall Sir William Robertson, Chief of Imperial General Staff, December 1915–February 1918* (London: Bodley Head/Army Records Society, 1989), 29.

50 PRO, WO 106/1511.

51 Robertson, 'Plan for a Campaign in Syria', February 22 1917, PRO, WO 106/311.

52 Robertson to Edmonds, February 4 1926, PRO, Cab 45/80/R.

53 War Cabinet 109, March 30, 1917, PRO, Cab 23/2.

54 Lynden-Bell to Maurice, April 3 1917, IWM, Lynden-Bell MSS 90/1/1.

55 Lynden-Bell to Maurice April 8 1917, IWM, Lynden-Bell MSS 90/1/1.

56 Maurice to Lynden-Bell, April 5 1917, IWM, Lynden-Bell MSS 90/1/1.

57 MacMunn and Falls, *Military Operations,* 349n1.

58 Dawnay to Director of Historical Section, December 4 1924, PRO, CAB 45/78/D.

59 Ibid.

60 S.F. Mott to Director of Historical Section, February 20 1926, PRO, Cab 45/79/M.

61 Lynden-Bell to Maurice, March 3 1917, PRO, Cab 45/79/M.

62 Buxton to L.E.B., April 7 1917, IWM, Buxton MSS 66/101/1.

63 Diary entry of April 18 1917, IWM, Marchant MSS Box No. 102.

64 War letter 109, Vol. 12, IWM, McPherson MSS 80/25/1.

65 'Copy of a letter from Major-General S.C.U. Smith', November 27 1925, PRO, Cab 45/80/S.

66 Diary entry of April 19 1917, IWM, Marchant MSS Box No. 102.

67 War letter 111, Vol. 12, IWM, McPherson MSS 80/25/1.

68 MacMunn and Falls, *Military Operations,* 343.

69 Bailey kept a diary, but this is taken from an account that he wrote later. IWM, Bailey MSS 85/4/1.

70 Ibid.

71 Dawnay to Director of Historical Section, December 4 1924, PRO, Cab 45/78/D.

72 Ibid.; and 'Personal Notes on First and Second Gaza by Sir C. Dobell', PRO, Cab 45/78/D.

73 Murray to Edmonds, May 1 1925, PRO, Cab 45/79/M.

74 Telegram included with Dobell's account, PRO, Cab 45/78/D.

75 Lynden-Bell to Maurice, April 23 1917, IWM, Lynden-Bell MSS 90/1/1.

76 Murray to Edmonds, May 1 1925, PRO, Cab 45/79/M.

77   MacMunn and Falls, *Military Operations,* 348n1.

78   Diary entry of April 19 1917, IWM, Merchant MSS Box No. 102.

79   War Cabinet 122, April 18 1917, PRO, Cab 23/2.

80   Diary entry of April 30 1917, CC, Hankey MSS 1/3.

81   War Cabinet 115 A, April 5 1917, PRO, Cab 23/13.

82   Robertson to Haig, April 15 1917, Woodward, *Military Correspondence,* 174–75.

83   War Cabinet 124, April 23 1917, PRO Cab 23/2.

84   Amery to Smuts, March 15 1917, CUL, Smuts MSS 680.

85   Smuts to Lloyd George, May 31 1917, HLRO, Lloyd George MSS F/45/9/4.

5: 'BLOODY BULL'S LOOSE'

1   A.B. Acheson to Sir James Edmonds and Edmonds to Acheson, July 18 and 19 1950, PRO, Cab 103/113.

2   Robertson to Haig, April 15 1917, in David R. Woodward, ed., *The Military Correspondence of Field Marshall Sir William Robertson, Chief of Imperial General Staff, December 1915–February 1918* (London: Bodley Head/Army Records Society, 1989), 174–75.

3   Edmonds to Acheson, July 19 1950, PRO, Cab 103/113; memoirs, 271, LHCMA, Edmonds MSS, III/2.

4   General Spencer E. Holland to Wavell, n.d., LHCMA, Allenby MSS 6/7/31.

5   Memoirs, 270, LHCMA, Edmonds MSS III/2.

6   Ibid.

7   General Sir George de S. Barrow, *The Fire of Life* (London: Hutchinson, 1942), 44.

8   Hugh O'Neil to Wavell, June 5 1939, LHCMA, Allenby MSS 6/9/46.

9   Archibald Wavell, *Allenby: A Study in Greatness* (Oxford: Oxford University Press, 1941), 294.

10   Diary entry of June 27 1917, IWM, O. C. Williams MSS 69/78/1.

11   Ibid.

12   Lynden-Bell to Maurice, July 11 1917, IWM, Lynden-Bell MSS 90/1/1.

13   Colonel Richard Meinertzhagen, *Army Diary, 1899–1926* (London: Oliver and Boyd, 1960), 219.

14   Wavell, *Allenby,* 188.

15   Wigan to Director, Historical Branch, CID, December 30 1929, PRO, Cab 45/80/W.

16   Lieutenant Colonel Herbert Lightfoot Eason to Wavell, August 17 1937, LHCMA, Allenby MSS 6/8/43.

17   Geoffrey Inchbald, *Imperial Camel Corps* (London: Johnson, 1970), 82.

18   Ibid.

19   Lawrence James, *Imperial Warrior: The Life and Times of Field-Marshal Viscount Allenby, 1861–1936* (London: Weidenfeld and Nicolson, 1993), 116.

20   Allenby to Lady Allenby, July 28 1917, in Matthew Hughes, ed., *Allenby in Palestine: The Middle East Correspondence of Field Marshal Viscount Allenby* (London: Sutton Publishing/Army Records Society, 2004), 45–46.

21   Colonel Reginald Edmund Maghlin Russell to Wavell, August 6 1937,

LHCMA, Allenby MSS 6/8/74.

22   David Lloyd George, *War Memoirs of David Lloyd George* (London: Odhams Press, 1938), 2:1090.

23   Captain Cyril Falls, *Military Operations: Egypt and Palestine from June 1917 to the End of the War* (1930; reprint, Nashville, Tenn.: Battery Press, 1996), part 1, 631.

24   For an excellent recent account of Allenby's political as well as military role, see Matthew Hughes, *Allenby and British Strategy in the Middle East, 1917–1919* (London: Frank Cass, 1999).

25   Lieutenant General Sir George MacMunn and Captain Cyril Falls, *Military Operations: Egypt and Palestine from the Outbreak of War with Germany to June 1917* (1928; reprint, Nashville, Tenn.: Battery Press, 1996), 12n1.

26   Robertson, 'Palestine', July 19 1917, PRO, WO 106/1513.

27   Edward J. Erickson, *Ordered to Die: A History of the Ottoman Army in the First World War* (Westport, Conn.: Greenwood Press, 2001), 166–72.

28   See David R. Woodward, *Field Marshal Sir William Robertson: Chief of the Imperial General Staff in the Great War* (Westport, Conn.: Praeger, 1998), 158–59.

29   'Notes on Palestine', n.d., IWM, Minshall MSS 86/51/1.

30   Ion L. Idriess, *The Desert Column* (Sydney: Angus & Robertson, 1932), 237–38.

31   Robert H. Goodsall, *Palestine Memories, 1917–1918–1925* (Canterbury: Cross and Jackman, 1925), 34.

32   Captain E. Stanley Goodland, *Engaged in War: The Letters of Stanley Goodland Somerset Light Infantry, 1914–1919,* ed. Anne Noyes (Guildford: Twiga Books, 1999), 88.

33   Diary entry of January 1 1918, IWM, Marchant MSS Box No 102.

34   Diary entries of October 10 and November 30 1917, IWM, Blunt MSS 94/5/1.

35   Case to 'my dear people', June 31 1917, IWM, Case MSS P 147.

36   Bernard Blaser, *Kilts Across the Jordan: Being Experiences and Impressions with the Second Battalion 'London Scottish' in Palestine* (London: H.F. & G. Witherby, 1926), 53.

37   Antony Bluett, *With Our Army in Palestine* (London: Andrew Melrose, 1919), 24–25.

38   Ibid., 163.

39   Diary entry of October 12 1917, IWM, Blunt MSS 94/5/1.

40   Case to 'my dear people', June 31 1917, IWM, Case MSS P 147.

41   Diary entry of July 30 1917, IWM, Pope MSS 78/42/1.

42   Blaser, *Kilts Across the Jordan*, 49.

43   Evans to mother, September 8, 1917, IWM, J. O. Evans MSS 96/7/1.

44   Douglas Thorburn, *Amateur Gunners: The Adventures of an Amateur Soldier in France, Salonica and Palestine in the Royal Field Artillery* (Liverpool: William Potter, 1933), 76.

45   *Middlesex Yeomanry Magazine*, Souvenir Number, 1914–1919, 43.

46   Diary entry of August 23 1917, IWM, Calcutt MSS 78/56/2.

47   Blaser, Kilts *Across the Jordan*, 33–34.

48   Diary entry of October 6 1917, IWM, Calcutt MSS 78/56/2.

49   Diary entry of September 21 1917, IWM, Calcutt MSS 78/56/2.

50   Lynden-Bell to Chetwode, July 19 1917, IWM, Chetwode MSS P 183.

51   Case to 'dear people', July 31 1917, IWM, Case MSS P. 147.

52   Blaser, *Kilts Across the Jordan*, 39.

53   IWM, Blunt MSS 94/5/1.

54   IWM, Calcutt MSS 78/56/2.

55   A. J. Hill, *Chauvel of the Light Horse: A Biography of General Sir Harry Chauvel* (Victoria: Melbourne University Press, 1978), 121–22.

56   'The Chronicle of a Yeomanry Squadron in Palestine, Jordan and Syria', n.d., IWM, Hampton MSS DS/MISC/82.

57   'With Horses to Jerusalem', n.d., IWM, Perkins MSS 87/18/1.

58   Moore to 'Dear Folk', October 14 1917, IWM, Moore MSS Con Shelf.

59   September 26 1917, IWM, Calcutt MSS 78/56/2.

60   Diary entry of October 11 1917, IWM, Calcutt MSS 78/56/2.

61   Diary entry of October 11, IWM, J.C. Jones MSS 67/15/1.

62   'Autobiography. A Humble, Simple & True Account', n.d., part 2, and a separate contemporary account of the Sana Redoubt affair, August 19 1917, IWM, Benbow MSS PP/MCA/146.

63   Memoir, IWM, Hendry MSS, 78/42/1.

64   LHCMA, Clarke MSS 1/1.

65   Beer to his parents, September 22 1917, IWM, Beer MSS 86/19/1.

66   Blaser, *Kilts Across the Jordan*, 43.

67   Diary entry of September 23 1917, IWM, Callcutt MSS 78/56/2.

68   LHCMA, Clarke MSS 1/1; IWM, *Middlesex Yeomanry Magazine* 1, no. 2 (October 1917).

69   Diary entry of September 22 1917, IWM, Calcutt MSS 78/56/2.

70   Bluett, *With Our Army in Palestine*, 230.

71   These numbers are taken from Wavell, *The Palestine Campaigns* (London: Constable and Company, 1928), 112–15.

72   See Hughes, *Allenby and British Strategy*, 46–47.

73   Chetwode wrote the following on his copy of this appreciation: 'The above plan was adopted by Gen. Sir E. Allenby on his arrival in Egypt & was carried out – Commencing with the Capture of Bir Saba on Oct 31st & ending with the fall of Jerusalem on Dec 9th 1917.' 'Notes on the Palestine Operation', June 21 1917, IWM, Chetwode MSS P 183.

74   Meinertzhagen, *Army Diary*, 222.

75   Diary entry of October 8 1917, IWM, Calcutt MSS 78/56/2.

76   Diary entry of October 8 1917, IWM, Blunt MSS 94/5/1.

77   Diary entry of September 5 1917, IWM, A.V. Young MSS 76/101/1.

78   MacMunn and Falls, *Military Operations,* 65n2.

79   Diary entry of October 11 1917, IWM, Bailey MSS 85/4/1.

80   Diary entry of October 27 1917, IWM, Bailey MSS 85/4/1.

81   Captain R.E.C. Adams, *The Modern Crusaders, Palestine, October 1917–May 1918* (London: Routledge, 1920), 30–31.

6: BREAKOUT

1   Diary entry of October 30 1917, IWM, Calcutt MSS 78/56/2.

2   Diary entry of October 30 1917, IWM, Blunt MSS 94/5/1.

3   Diary entry of December 27 1917, IWM, Earney MSS 81/23/1.

4   Diary entry of October 31 1917, IWM, Blunt MSS 94/5/1.

5   Diary entry of October 31 1917, IWM, Calcutt MSS 78/56/2.

6   Diary entry of October 31 1917, IWM, Blunt MSS 94/5/1.

7   Letter of February 8 1918, IWM, Case MSS P 147.

8   Lieutenant General Sir George MacMunn and Captain Cyril Falls, *Military Operations: Egypt and Palestine from the Outbreak of War with Germany to June 1917* (1928; reprint, Nashville, Tenn.: Battery Press, 1996), 57.

9   See, for example, Ian Jones, 'Beersheba: The Light Horse Charge and the Making of Myths', *Journal of the Australian War Memorial* 3 (October 1983): 26–37.

10 H.S. Gullett, *The Official History of Australia in the War of 1914–1918*, Vol. 7, *Sinai and Palestine: The Australian Imperial Force in Sinai and Palestine, 1914–1918* (Sydney: Angus and Robertson, 1923), 393–94.

11 Ibid., 393.

12 MacMunn and Falls, *Military Operations,* 58n1; See also Marquess of Anglesey, *A History of the British Cavalry, 1816–1919*, Vol. 5, *Egypt, Palestine and Syria, 1914–1919* (London: Leo Cooper, 1994), 5:144–150; and A.J. Hill, *Chauvel of the Light Horse: A Biography of General Sir Harry Chauvel* (Victoria: Melbourne University Press, 1978), 127.

13 Hill, *Chauvel*, 125.

14 Hodgson to Bar, February 8 1918, IWM, Hodgson MSS 66/145/1.

15 R.M.P. Preston, *The Desert Mounted Corps: An Account of the Cavalry Operations in Palestine and Syria, 1917–1918* (London: Constable and Company, 1921), 29.

16 Diary entry of November 3 1917, IWM, Calcutt MSS 78/56/2.

17 Diary entry of November 3 1917, IWM, Blunt MSS 94/5/1.

18 Memoir (*c.*1960s), IWM, Powell MSS, PP/MCR/37.

19 Diary entry of November 3 1917, IWM, Calcutt MSS 78/56/2.

20 Diary entry of November 19 1917, NAM, Drury MSS, Acc. 7607-69-3.

21 Memoir (n.d।), IWM, Loudon MSS 87/17/1.

22 Dawnay appreciation, n.d., in 'Palestine 1917–1918, Battle of Philistia', IWM, Dawnay MSS 69/21/2.

23 Major Vivian Gilbert, *The Romance of the Last Crusade: With Allenby to Jerusalem* (New York: D. Appleton, 1923), 90–91.

24 Diary entry of November 4 1917, IWM, Calcutt MSS 78/56/2.

25 'XX Corps Order No. 13', November 5 1917, in Captain Cyril Falls, *Military Operations: Egypt and Palestine from June 1917 to the End of the War* (1930; reprint, Nashville, Tenn.: Battery Press, 1996), part 2, 691.

26 Diary entries of November 5–6 1917, IWM, Calcutt MSS 78/56/2.

27 See Paddy Griffith, *Battle Tactics of the Western Front: The British Army's Art of Attack, 1916–1918* (New Haven, Conn.: Yale University Press, 1994), 96–97.

28 Memoir (*c.*1960s), IWM, Powell MSS PP/MCR/37.

29 Diary entry of November 6, IWM, Calcutt MSS 78/56/2.

30 Memoir (*c.*1960s), IWM, Powell MSS PP/MCR/37.

31 Diary entry of November 6 1917, IWM, Calcutt MSS 78/56/2.

32 Colonel A.P. Wavell, *The Palestine Campaigns* (London: Constable and Company, 1928), 134–37.

33 Diary entry of November 7, IWM, Chipperfield MSS 75/76/1.

34 Impey to his father, November 9 1917, part 2, IWM, Chipperfield MSS
    75/76/1.

35 Diary entry of November 7 1917, IWM, Chipperfield MSS 75/76/1.

36 Impey to his father, November 9 1917, part 2, IWM, Chipperfield MSS
    75/76/1.

37 C.H. Dudley-Ward, *History of the 53rd (Welsh) Division (T.F.), 1914–1918*
    (Cardiff: Western Mail Limited, 1927), 128.

38 Castle account, included in diary entry of November 9 1917, IWM, Marchant
    MSS Box No. 102.

39 Judd to Director, Historical Section, August 19 1928, PRO, Cab 45/79J.

40 'The Chronicle of a Yeomanry Squadron in Palestine, Jordan and Syria', n.d.,
    IWM, Hampton MSS DS/Misc/82

41 Ibid.

42 Diary Entry of November 6 1917, IWM, Evans MSS P232.

43 Dudley-Ward, *History of the 53rd (Welsh) Division*, 135.

44 Diary entry of November 6 1917, IWM, Evans MSS P232.

45 Evans to wife, November 11 1917, IWM, Evans MSS P232.

46 Letter of November 15 1917, IWM, Buxton MSS 66/101/1.

47 Letter of November 15 1917, IWM, Ferguson MSS PP/MCR/111.

7: RELENTLESS PURSUIT

1   Dawnay to Wavell, January 3 1938, LHCMA, Allenby MSS 6/8/37.

2   'Nov 8th 1917 (Huj)', November 27 1917, IWM, Alan-Williams MSS
    84/55/1/A.

3   Diary entry of November 8 1917, IWM, Calcutt MSS 78/56/2.

4   'Nov 8th 1917 (Huj)', November 27 1917, IWM, Alan-Williams MSS
    84/55/1A.

5   Shea to Director, Historical Section, CID, May 3, 1928, PRO, Cab 45/80/S.

6   Account written at request of Brigadier General G.A. Weir, *c.*1920, IWM,
    Alan-Williams MSS 84/55/1A.

7   'Nov 8th 1917 (Huj)', November 27 1917, IWM, Alan-Williams MSS
    84/55/1A.

8   Account written at request of Brigadier General G.A. Weir, *c.*1920, IWM,
    Alan-Williams MSS 84/55/1A.

9   Memoir, 'The Last Cavalry Charge', 48, IWM, R. H. Wilson MSS 82/25/1.

10 Captain Cyril Falls, *Military Operations: Egypt and Palestine from June 1917 to
    the End of the War* (1930; reprint, Nashville, Tenn.: Battery Press, 1996), part 1,
    123n1.

11 Shea to Director, Historical Section, May 3, 1928, CID, PRO, Cab 45/80/S.

12 Falls, *Military Operations,* part 1, 123.

13 Alan-Williams to father, November 14 1917, IWM, Alan-Williams MSS
    84/55/1A.

14 Memoir, 'The Last Cavalry charge', IWM, R.H. Wilson MSS 82/25/1.

15 Chetwode to MacMunn, May 17 1926, PRO, Cab 45/78/C.

16 Robert Henry Wilson, *Palestine, 1917,* ed. Helen D. Millgate (Tunbridge Wells,

Kent: D. J. Costello, 1987), 93–94.

17   Captain R.E.C. Adams, *The Modern Crusaders, Palestine, October 1917–May 1918* (London: Routledge, 1920), 54.

18   S.F. Hatton, *The Yarn of a Yeoman* (London: Hutchinson, n.d.), 169, 173.

19   Case to 'dear people', November 13 1917, IWM, Case MSS P 147.

20   Captain O. Teichman, *The Diary of a Yeomanry M.O., Egypt, Gallipoli, Palestine and Italy* (London: Fisher Unwin, 1921), 187–88.

21   Diary entry of November 9 1917, IWM, Blunt MSS 94/5/1.

22   IWM, Blunt MSS 94/5/1.

23   Ibid.

24   Bernard Blaser, *Kilts Across the Jordan: Being Experiences and Impressions with the Second Battalion 'London Scottish' in Palestine* (London: H.F. & G. Witherby, 1926), 219.

25   Simpson-Baikie to Marion, July 2 and August 3 1917, LHCMA, Simpson-Baikie MSS, single collection.

26   IWM, Blunt MSS 94/5/1.

27   Adams, *Modern Crusaders*, 70.

28   Diary entry of December 27 1917, IWM, Earney MSS 81/23/1.

29   Rowlands Coldicott, *London Men in Palestine and How They Marched to Jerusalem* (London: Edward Arnold, 1919), 99.

30   Ibid., 53–54.

31   Brevet Lieutenant Colonel G.E. Badcock, *A History of the Transport Services of the Egyptian Expeditionary Force, 1916–1917–1918* (London: Hugh Rees, 1925), 92.

32   Dawnay appreciation, n.d., in 'Palestine 1917–1918, Battle of Philistia', IWM, Dawnay MSS 69/21/2

33   'With Horses to Jerusalem', n.d., IWM, Perkins MSS 87/18/1.

34   Perkins's account of the charge differs in some respect from the official history. Lieutenant General Sir George MacMunn and Captain Cyril Falls, *Military Operations: Egypt and Palestine from June 1917 to the end of the War* (1930; reprint, Nashville, Tenn.: Battery Press, 1996), Part 1 168.

35   'With Horses to Jerusalem', n.d., IWM, Perkins MSS 87/18/1.

36   Ibid.

37   MacMunn and Falls, *Military Operations,* Part 1 172n1.

38   Case to family, November 13 1917, IWM, Case MSS P 147.

8: SACRED SOIL

1   Colonel A.P. Wavell, *Allenby: A Study in Greatness* (Oxford: Oxford University Press, 1941), 226.

2   'Some Aspects of Lord Allenby's Palestine Campaign, Staff College Lecture', April 25 1923, LHCMA, Shea MSS 6/2a.

3   Fermperley to Director. Historical Section, CID, January 1929, PRO, Cab 45/79/F.

4   J.P. Wilson, *With the Soldiers in Palestine and Syria* (New York: Macmillan, 1920), viii.

5   Douglas Thorburn, *Amateur Gunners: The Adventures of an Amateur Soldier in France, Salonica and Palestine in the Royal Field Artillery* (Liverpool: William Potter, 1933), 171–72.

6   Ibid., 173.

7   Alan-Williams to father, October 24 1917, IWM, Alan-Williams MSS 84/55/1A.

8   Robertson to Falls, January 30 1929, PRO, Cab 45/80/R.

9   Entry of December 6 1917, IWM, Blunt MSS 94/5/1.

10 Buxton to mother, April 5 1917, IWM, Buxton MSS 94/5/1.

11 Buxton to mother, November 15 1917, IWM, Buxton MSS 94/5/1.

12 Diary entry of December 4 1917, IWM, Calcutt MSS 78/56/2.

13 Case to father, n.d., IWM, Case MSS P 147.

14 Memoirs, IWM, Matthews MSS 85/32/1.

15 Dawnay appreciation, n.d., in 'Palestine 1917–1918', IWM, Dawnay MSS 69/21/2.

16 General Sir George de S. Barrow, *The Fire of Life* (London: Hutchinson, 1942), 169.

17 Ibid., 170.

18 'Desert Mounted Corps, Nov 16th 1917–Nov 26th 1917', PRO, Cab 45/75.

19 S.F. Hatton, *The Yarn of a Yeoman* (London: Hutchinson, n.d.), 197.

20 Barrow, *Fire of Life*, 174.

21 Falls, *Military Operations,* Part 1,194.

22 Memoir ('Between Two Great Deserts', 1919); IWM, Boord MSS 66/99/1.

23 Diary entry of December 28 1917, IWM, Earney MSS 81/23/1.

24 Dawnay to wife, November 24 1917, 'Egypt and Palestine, 1916–1917', IWM, Dawnay MSS 69/21/2.

25 Entries of November 23–24 1917, IWM, Calcutt MSS 78/56/2.

26 Major Vivian Gilbert, *The Romance of the Last Crusade: With Allenby to Jerusalem* (New York: D. Appleton, 1923), 129–30.

27 Lieutenant Colonel R.R. Thompson, *The Fifty-Second (Lowland) Division, 1914–1918* (Glasgow: Maclehose, Jackson, 1923), 471.

28 Entry of December 7 1917, IWM, Blunt MSS 94/5/1.

29 Entry of December 7, IWM, Calcutt MSS 78/56/2.

30 Lieutenant Colonel J.H. Lindsay, *The London Scottish in the Great War* (Eastbourne: Antony Rowe, 1926), 294–95.

31 Entry of December 8, IWM, Blunt MSS 94/5/1.

32 For the surrender of Jerusalem, see diary and letter of December 10 1917, IWM, Bayley MSS 86/9/1; and diary, IWM, Chipperfield MSS 75/76/1.

33 Gilbert, *Romance of the Last Crusade*, 173.

34 Venables to Kenyon, February 13 1918, IWM, Venables MSS P 257.

35 Memoir ('N.C.O.'), LHCMA, Jones MSS, single collection. See also entry of December 9 1917, IWM, Blunt MSS 94/5/1.

36 Venables to Kenyon, February 13 1918, IWM, Venables MSS P 257.

37 Barrow, *Fire of Life*, 176.

38 Venables to Kenyon, February 13 1918, IWM, Venables MSS P 257.

39 Ibid.

40 Diary entries of December 24–25 1917, IWM, Blunt MSS 94/5/1.

41 Diary entry of December 25 1917, IWM, Calcutt MSS 78/56/2.

42   Ibid.

43   Memoir ('N.C.O.'), LHCMA, Jones MSS, Single Collection.

44   Ibid.

45   Diary entry of December 27 1917, IWM, Chipperfield MSS 75/76/1.

46   Letter by Case (no address), February 8 1918, IWM, Case MSS P 147.

47   Bernard Blaser, *Kilts Across the Jordan: Being Experiences and Impressions with the Second Battalion 'London Scottish' in Palestine* (London: H.F. & G. Witherby, 1926), 112.

48   Buxton to mother, November 24 1917, IWM, Buxton MSS 66/101/1.

49   Ibid.

50   Allenby to Robertson January 3 1918, in Hughes, *Allenby in Palestine*, 125.

51   Ibid.

52   See David R. Woodward, *Lloyd George and the Generals* (1983; reprint, London: Frank Cass, 2004), 221–52.

9: CHANGING PRIORITIES

1   David R. Woodward, *Lloyd George and the Generals* (1983; reprint, London: Frank Cass, 2004), 162–63.

2   Robertson to Allenby, October 5 1917, in David R. Woodward, ed., The Military Correspondence of Field Marshall Sir William Robertson, Chief of Imperial General Staff, December 1915–February 1918 (London: Bodley Head/Army Records Society, 1989), 232.

3   David R. Woodward, *Field Marshal Sir William Robertson: Chief of the Imperial General Staff in the Great War* (Westport, Conn.: Praeger, 1998), 163.

4   Buxton to B.E.B., January 1 1918, IWM, Buxton MSS 66/101/1.

5   Entry of December 31 1917, IWM, Blunt MSS 94/5/1.

6   Captain R.E.C. Adams, *The Modern Crusaders, Palestine, October 1917–May 1918* (London: Routledge, 1920), 117.

7   Allenby to Robertson, January 25 1918, in Matthew Hughes, ed., *Allenby in Palestine: The Middle East Correspondence of Field Marshal Viscount Allenby* (London: Sutton Publishing/Army Records Society, 2004), 128.

8   Robertson, 'Future Operations in Palestine', December 26 1917, PRO, WO 106/313.

9   Woodward, *Field Marshal Sir William Robertson*, 165.

10   See 'Joint Note to the Supreme War Council by its Military Representatives (Joint Note No 12). 1918 Campaign', PRO, WO 106/314.

11   Wavell to Falls, September 27 1929, PRO, Cab 45/80/W.

12   Joint Note to Supreme War Council…', PRO, WO 106/314.

13   Robertson to Allenby, February 2 1918, in Woodward, *Military Correspondence*, 281–82.

14   Captain Cyril Falls, *Military Operations: Egypt and Palestine from June 1917 to the End of the War* (1930; reprint, Nashville, Tenn.: Battery Press, 1996), part 1, 299.

15   Chetwode to Wavell, March 28 1939, LHCMA, Allenby MSS 6/IX/18.

16   War Cabinet 360 A, March 6 1918, PRO, Cab 23/13.

17   Woodward, *Lloyd George*, 284.

18 Allenby to Robertson, January 25 1918, in Hughes, *Allenby in Palestine*, 127.
19 Lieutenant Colonel J.H. Lindsay, *The London Scottish in the Great War* (Eastbourne: Antony Row, 1926), 318.
20 Diary entry of March 21 1918, IWM, A.V.Young MSS 84/52/1.
21 Lindsay, *London Scottish*, 321.
22 Maj.Vivian Gilbert, *The Romance of the Last Crusade: With Allenby to Jerusalem* (New York: D. Appleton, 1923), 190–92.
23 Lindsay, *London Scottish*, 324.
24 Antony Bluett, *With Our Army in Palestine* (London: Andrew Melrose, 1919), 240.
25 Autobiography, IWM, A.S. Benbow, MSS PP/MCA/146.
26 Ibid.
27 Diary entry of March 28 1918, IWM, A. S. Benbow, MSS PP/MCA/146.
28 Diary entry of March 29 1918, IWM, A. S. Benbow, MSS PP/MCA/146.
29 Diary entry of March 30 1918, IWM, A. S. Benbow, MSS PP/MCA/146.
30 Diary entry of March 31 1918, IWM, A. S. Benbow, MSS PP/MCA/146.
31 Bluett, *With Our Army in Palestine*, 241.
32 See A.B. Robertson to Falls, January 30 1929, PRO, Cab 45/80/R.
33 Woodward, *Lloyd George*, 287.
34 Memoirs, IWM, Loudon MSS 87/17/1.
35 James Young, *With the 52nd (Lowland) Division in Three Continents* (Edinburgh: W. Green & Sons, 1920), 103.
36 Ibid.; and Memoirs, IWM, Loudon MSS 87/17/1.
37 Diary entry of May 23 1918, IWM, Calcutt MSS 78/56/2.
38 France Seely (letter) to the *Times*, May 1 1990, quoted in Marquess of Anglesey, *A History of the British Cavalry, 1816–1919*, Vol. 5, *Egypt, Palestine and Syria, 1914–1919* (London: Leo Cooper, 1994), 220.
39 Douglas Thorburn, *Amateur Gunners: The Adventures of an Amateur Soldier in France, Salonica and Palestine in the Royal Field Artillery* (Liverpool: William Potter, 1933), 92.
40 C.H. Dudley Ward, *The 74th (Yeomanry) Division in Syria and France* (London: John Murray, 1922), 203.
41 Young, *With the 52nd (Lowland) Division*, 106.
42 Ibid., 105.
43 Memoir ('N.C.O.'), LHCMA, Jones MSS, Single Collection.
44 Ibid.
45 Diary entry of July 20 1918, NAM, Drury MSS Acc. 7607-69-3.
46 Diary entry of August 6 1918, IWM, Calcutt MSS 78/56/2.
47 Young, *With the 52nd (Lowland) Division*, 105.
48 Memoir ('N.C.O.'), LHCMA, Jones MSS, Single Collection.
49 Thorburn, *Amateur Gunners*, 95.
50 'Experience Gained in Recent Fighting', n.d., LHCMA, Shea MSS 4/3.
51 Young, *With the 52 (Lowland) Division*, 104–5.
52 Entry of October 18 1918, IWM, Merchant MSS Box No. 102.
53 Shea oral interview, IWM, Acc. 4227.
54 Falls, *Military Operations,* part 2, 643–44.

10: JORDAN VALLEY

1   Allenby to Captain C.W. Battine, April 1 1918, IWM, Battine MSS 90/37/1.

2   Matthew Hughes, *Allenby and British Strategy in the Middle East, 1917–1919* (London: Frank Cass, 1999), 76.

3   Captain Cyril Falls, *Military Operations: Egypt and Palestine from June 1917 to the End of the War* (1930; reprint, Nashville, Tenn.: Battery Press, 1996), part 1, 391.

4   A.J. Hill, *Chauvel of the Light Horse: A Biography of General Sir Harry Chauvel* (Victoria: Melbourne University Press, 1978), 146.

5   Note by Kelly, October 31 1928, PRO, Cab 45/79K.

6   Ibid.

7   Ibid.

8   Ibid.

9   Ibid.

10 Cyril Falls, *Armageddon: 1918* (London: Weidenfeld & Nicolson, 1964), 78–81.

11 Note by Kelly, October 31 1928, PRO, Cab 45/79K.

12 Bernard Blaser, *Kilts Across the Jordan: Being Experiences and Impressions with the Second Battalion 'London Scottish' in Palestine* (London: H.F. & G. Witherby, 1926), 241.

13 Hill, *Chauvel of the Light Horse*, 151.

14 Allenby to Wigram, May 5 1918, in Matthew Hughes, ed., *Allenby in Palestine: The Middle East Correspondence of Field Marshal Viscount Allenby* (London: Sutton Publishing/Army Records Society, 2004), 152.

15 Hughes, *Allenby and British Strategy*, 87.

16 Allenby to Wigram, May 5 1918, in Hughes, *Allenby in Palestine*, 148.

17 David R. Woodward, 'The British Government and Japanese Intervention in Russia During World War I', *Journal of Modern History* (December 1974): 663–85.

18 Wilson to Allenby, May 29 1918, in Hughes, *Allenby in Palestine*, 158.

19 Allenby to Wilson, June 5 1918, in Hughes, *Allenby in Palestine*, 161.

20 Allenby to Wilson, June 15 1918, in Hughes, *Allenby in Palestine*, 163–64.

21 Allenby to Wilson, June 5 1918, in Hughes, *Allenby in Palestine*, 161.

22 Robert H. Goodsall, *Palestine Memories, 1917–1918–1925* (Canterbury: Cross and Jackman, 1925), 168.

23 Ibid., 170.

24 Hill, *Chauvel of the Light Horse*, 156.

25 Allenby to Wilson, June 15 1918, in Hughes, *Allenby in Palestine*, 163.

26 Diary entries of 4/5 and 6/7, 1918, IWM, Rothon MSS 82/3/1.

27 Diary entries dated in text, IWM, Rothon MSS 82/3/1.

28 Diary entry of May 18 1918, IWM, Rothon MSS 82/3/1.

29 Robert Henry Wilson, *Palestine, 1917*, ed. Helen D. Millgate (Tunbridge Wells, Kent: D.J. Costello, 1987), 109.

30 Buxton to L.E.B., August 31 1918, IWM, Buxton MSS 66/101/1.

31 Allenby to his wife, December 14 1917, LHCMA, Allenby MSS 1/8/33.

32 Wilson, *Palestine, 1917*, 113.

33 Simpson-Baikie to Mrs Miller, May 22 1918, LHCMA, Single Collection.

34 Buxton to Lucy Ethel Buxton, October 7 1918, IWM, Buxton MSS 66/101/1.

35   'A Ballonatic in Palestine', IWM, Collett MSS 01/22/1.

36   Harding oral interview, IWM, Acc. 008736/50.

37   Diary entries dated in text, IWM, Rothon MSS 82/3/1.

38   Diary entry of June 1 1918, IWM, Rothon MSS 82/3/1.

39   Memoir ('N.C.O.'), LHCMA, Jones MSS, Single Collection.

40   Falls, *Military Operations,* part 2, 445.

41   Ibid., 446.

II : MEGIDDO

1   James L. Stokesbury, *A Short History of World War I* (New York: William
     Morrow, 1981), 280.

2   David L. Bullock, *Allenby's War: The Palestine-Arabian Campaigns, 1916–1918*
     (London: Blandford Press, 1988), 127.

3   Robert H. Goodsall, *Palestine Memories, 1917–1918–1925* (Canterbury: Cross and
     Jackman, 1925), 171.

4   Diary entry of August 26 1918, IWM, Rothon MSS 82/3/1.

5   Letter of September 22 1918, IWM, Case MSS P 147.

6   Ibid.

7   Diary entry of September 18 1918, IWM, J.C. Jones MSS 67/15/1.

8   General Sir George de S. Barrow, *The Fire of Life* (London: Hutchinson, 1942),
     194.

9   Diary entry of September 19 1918, IWM, Bailey MSS 85/4/1.

10   Allenby to Wilson, September 18 1918, in Matthew Hughes, ed., *Allenby
     in Palestine: The Middle East Correspondence of Field Marshal Viscount Allenby*
     (London: Sutton Publishing/Army Records Society, 2004), 77.

11   Force Order No. 68, September 9 1918, in Captain Cyril Falls, *Military
     Operations: Egypt and Palestine from June 1917 to the End of the War* (1930; reprint,
     Nashville, Tenn.: Battery Press, 1996), part 2, 713.

12   XXI Corps Order No. 42, September 17 1918, in ibid., 716. See also Cyril
     Falls, *Armageddon: 1918* (London: Weidenfeld & Nicolson, 1964), 44.

13   Diary entry of September 19 1918, IWM, Bailey MSS 85/4/1.

14   Ibid.

15   Memoir (*c.*1960s), IWM, Powell MSS PP/MCR/37.

16   Marquess of Anglesey, *A History of the British Cavalry, 1816–1919,* Vol. 5, *Egypt,
     Palestine and Syria, 1914–1919* (London: Leo Cooper, 1994), 262.

17   Letter of September 22 1918, IWM, Case MSS P 147.

18   Allenby to his wife, September 19 1918, in Hughes, *Allenby in Palestine*, 178.

19   Barrow, *Fire of Life*, 203.

20   Falls, *Military Operations,* part 2, 499.

21   Ibid., 502.

22   H.A. Jones, *Official History of the War in the Air* (Oxford: Clarendon Press,
     1937), 6:224–25.

23   Memoir ('The Chronicle of a Yeomanry Squadron n Palestine, Jordan and
     Syria', n.d.), IWM, Hampton MSS DS/MISC/82.

24   Diary entry of September 24 1918, IWM, J.C. Jones MSS 67/15/1.

25   Chetwode to Falls, August 15 1929, PRO, Cab 45/78C.

26   Allenby to Wilson, September 22 1918, in Hughes, *Allenby in Palestine*, 182.

27   Chetwode to Falls, August 15 1929, PRO, Cab 45/78C.

28   *Statistics of the Military Effort of the British Empire During the Great War, 1914–1920* (1922; reprint, Dallington, Heathfield, East Sussex: Naval and Military Press, 1999), 282.

29   'End of Palestine Campaign. A Ranger Subaltern's Letter of 8 October 1918', IWM, J.F. B. O'Sullivan MSS 77/167/1.

30   Allenby to Wilson, August 14 1918, in Hughes, *Allenby in Palestine*, 174.

31   Falls, *Military Operations,* part 2, 566.

32   Ryrie to Director, Historical Section, October 4 1918, PRO, Cab 45/80R.

33   Chaytor to Director, Historical Section, September 7 1918, PRO, Cab 45/78C.

34   Falls, *Armageddon: 1918,* 98.

35   Ryrie to Director, Historical Section, October 4 1929, PRO, Cab 45/80R.

36   Barrow, *Fire of Life*, 211.

37   Ibid.

38   T.E. Lawrence, *Seven Pillars of Wisdom: A Triumph* (Garden City, N.Y.: Doubleday, Doran, 1936), 631.

39   T.E. Lawrence, *Secret Despatches from Arabia Published by Permission of the Foreign Office*, 168, quoted in Richard Aldington, *Lawrence of Arabia: A Biographical Enquiry* (Chicago: Henry Regnery, 1955), 236–37.

40   Wilson to Allenby, received September 24 1918, and Allenby to Wilson, September 25 1918, in Hughes, *Allenby in Palestine,* 185–86.

41   Diary entry of October 10 1918, IWM, Rothon MSS 82/3/1.

42   Allenby to Wilson, October 22 1918,in Hughes, *Allenby in Palestine*, 210.

43   Diary entries, September 29–30, October 1 1918, IWM, J.C. Jones MSS 67/15/1.

44   Diary entry of October 18 1918, IWM, Rothon MSS 82/3/1.

45   Diary entry of October 30 1918, ibid.

46   H.S. Gullett, *The Official History of Australia in the War of 1914–1918,* Vol. 7, *Sinai and Palestine: The Australian Imperial Force in Sinai and Palestine, 1914–1918* (Sydney: Angus and Robertson, 1923), 773.

47   *Statistics of the Military Effort*, 282–83.

48   Alan-Williams to his father, October 26 1918, IWM, Alan-Williams MSS 84/55/1A.

49   Memoir, IWM, Benbow MSS PP/MCA/146.

CONCLUSION

1   Heath to his father, September 13 1918, IWM, Heath MSS P 279.

2   C.H. Dudley-Ward, *History of the 53rd (Welsh) Division (T.F.), 1914–1918* (Cardiff: Western Mail Limited, 1927), 216.

3   H.A. Vernon to Director, Historical Section, November 26 1928, PRO, Cab 45/80/V.

4   Major C.S. Jarvis, *The Back Garden of Allah,* 4th ed. (London: John Murray, 1941), 89.

5   Special Order of the Day, January [?]1919, in Matthew Hughes, ed., *Allenby in Palestine: The Middle East Correspondence of Field Marshal Viscount Allenby* (London: Sutton Publishing/Army Records Society, 2004), 222–23.

6   Allenby to War Office and Wilson, May 16 and 17 1919, in Hughes, *Allenby in Palestine,* 255–56.

Bibliography

ARCHIVAL COLLECTIONS

— British Library (BL)
  Murray-Robertson
— Cambridge University Library (CUL)
  Smuts, J.C.
— Churchill College, Cambridge (CC)
  Hankey, M.
— House of Lords Record Office (HLRO)
  Lloyd George, D.
— Imperial War Museum (IWM), Department of Documents

Alan-Williams, A.C.
Bailey, V.H.
Baker, Sir Randolf
Barrow, Sir George
Battine. C.W.
Bayley, H.
Beer, J.B.
Benbow, A.S.
Benbow, A.V.
Blunt, F.V.
Boord, O.P.
Buxton, E.N.
Cadenhead, W.G.
Calcutt, D.H.
Case, R.C.
Chamberlain, T.H.
Chetwode, P.
Chipperfield, S.J.G.
Collett, H.R.P.

Dawnay, G.P.
Earney, H.J.
Evans, E.H.
Evans, J.O.
Ferguson, V.M.
Fletcher, A.W.
Frost, R.G.
George, B.
Hampton, Lord
Heath, D.F.
Hendry, W.N.
Hiorns, D.H.
Hodgson, H.
Jones, J.C.
Jones, J.G.
Knott, W.
Loudon R.
Lynden-Bell, A.
McGrigor, A.M.

McPherson, J.W.

Macey, R.W.

Marchant, W.T.

Matthews, L.J.

Minshall, T.B.

Moore, L.G.

Murray, A.

O'Sullivan, J.F.B.

Pedler, R.A.

Perkins, C.H.

Pope, H.T.

Powell, E.C.

Rothon, N.F.

Scott, H.S.

Sharkey, G.V.

Sneath, P.G.

Surry, A.R.

Townsend, E.T.

Tozer, J.R.

Venables, E.K.

Williams, A.E.

Williams, D.

Williams, O.C.

Wilson, J.

Wilson, R.H.

Wintringham, J.W.

Young, A.V.

— Imperial War Museum (IWM), Sound Archive
Carless, R.J.
Harding, J.
Horridge, G.
Pollock, L.

— Liddell Hart Centre for Military Archives (LHCMA)
Allenby, Sir E.H.H.
Clarke, F.S.
Edmonds, J.
Jones, J.F.
Robertson, Sir W.R.
Shea, J.S.M.
Simpson-Baikie, H.A.D.
Walters, J.D.

— National Army Museum (NAM)
Barron, W.
Blaksley, J.H.
Drury, N.E.

— Public Record Office (PRO – now part of the National Archives)
War Office 106 Directorate of Military Intelligence and Operations
Cab 23 War Cabinet Minutes
Cab 44/45 Historical Section CID Official War Histories

— Royal Archives (RA)
George V

PUBLISHED MEMOIRS AND DOCUMENTS

Adams, Capt. R.E.C. *The Modern Crusaders, Palestine, October 1917–May 1918.* London: Routledge, 1920.

Allen, Trevor. *The Tracks They Trod: Salonika and the Balkans, Gallipoli, Egypt and Palestine Revisited.* London: Joseph, 1931.

Badcock, Brevet Lieut. Col. G.E. *A History of the Transport Services of the Egyptian Expeditionary Force, 1916–1917–1918.* London: Hugh Rees, 1925.

Bannerman, Capt. Ronald. *4th the Queen's Royal Regiment: An Unofficial War History with Chapter on the 2/5th Battalion.* Croydon: H.R. Grubb, 1931.

Barrow, Gen. Sir George de S. *The Fire of Life.* London: Hutchinson, 1942.

Blaser, Bernard. *Kilts Across the Jordan: Being Experiences and Impressions with the Second Battalion 'London Scottish' in Palestine.* London: H.F. & G. Witherby, 1926.

Bluett, Antony. *With Our Army in Palestine.* London: Andrew Melrose, 1919.

Briggs, Martin S. *Through Egypt in War-Time.* London: T. Fisher Unwin, 1918.

Brown, Malcolm, ed. *T.E. Lawrence: The Selected Letters.* New York: W.W. Norton, 1989.

Coldicott, Rowlands. *London Men in Palestine and How They Marched to Jerusalem.* London: Edward Arnold, 1919.

Gilbert, Maj. Vivian. *The Romance of the Last Crusade: With Allenby to Jerusalem.* New York: D. Appleton, 1923.

[Goodland, Capt. E. Stanley]. *Engaged in War: The Letters of Stanley Goodland Somerset Light Infantry, 1914–1919.* Edited by Anne Noyes. Guildford: Twiga Books, 1999.

Goodsall, Robert H. *Palestine Memories, 1917–1918–1925.* Canterbury: Cross and Jackman, 1925.

Hatton, S.F. *The Yarn of a Yeoman.* London: Hutchinson, n.d.

Hughes, Matthew, ed. *Allenby in Palestine: The Middle East Correspondence of Field Marshal Viscount Allenby.* London: Sutton Publishing/Army Records Society, 2004.

Idriess, Ion L. *The Desert Column.* Sydney: Angus & Robertson, 1932.

Inchbald, Geoffrey. *Imperial Camel Corps.* London: Johnson, 1970.

Jarvis, Maj. C.S. *The Back Garden of Allah.* 4th ed. London: John Murray, 1941.

Lawrence, T.E. *Revolt in the Desert.* New York: George H. Doran, 1927.

— *Seven Pillars of Wisdom.* Garden City, N.Y.: Doubleday, Doran, 1936.

Lindsay, Lt. Col. J.H. *The London Scottish in the Great War.* Eastbourne: Antony Row, 1926.

Livermore, Bernard, *Long 'Un – A Damn Bad Soldier.* Batley, West Yorkshire: Harry Hayes, 1974.

Lloyd George, David. *War Memoirs of David Lloyd George.* London: Odhams Press, 1938. 2 vols.

Meinertzhagen, Col. Richard. *Army Diary, 1899–1926.* London: Oliver and Boyd, 1960.

Middlesex Yeomanry Magazine. 1914–1919.

[Mills, Frederick Thomas]. *Great Uncle Fred's War: An Illustrated Diary, 1917–1922.* Edited by Alan Pryor and Jennifer K. Woods. Whitestable, Kent: Pryor, 1985.

Repington, Lieut. Col. C.À. Court. *The First World War, 1914–1918.* 2 vols. London: Constable and Company, 1920.

Robertson, Sir William. *Soldiers and Statesmen, 1914–1918*. 2 vols. London: Cassell, 1926.

Silsoe, Brig. Lord. *Sixty Years a Welsh Territorial*. Gwasg Gomer, Llandysul, Dyfed: Gomer Press, 1976.

Teichman, Capt. O. *The Diary of a Yeomanry M.O., Egypt, Gallipoli, Palestine and Italy*. London: Fisher Unwin, 1921.

Thorburn, Douglas. *Amateur Gunners: The Adventures of an Amateur Soldier in France, Salonica and Palestine in the Royal Field Artillery*. Liverpool: William Potter, 1933.

Tyndale-Biscoe, Julian. *Gunner Subaltern: Letters Written by a Young Man to His Father During the Great War*. London: Leo Cooper, 1971.

Wilson, J.P. *With the Soldiers in Palestine and Syria*. New York: Macmillan, 1920.

Wilson, Robert Henry. *Palestine, 1917*. Edited by Helen D. Millgate. Tunbridge Wells, Kent: D. J. Costello, 1987.

Woodward, David R., ed. *The Military Correspondence of Field Marshall Sir William Robertson, Chief of Imperial General Staff, December 1915–February 1918*. London: Bodley Head/Army Records Society, 1989.

Young, James. *With the 52nd (Lowland) Division in Three Continents*. Edinburgh: W. Green & Sons, 1920.

SELECTED BIBLIOGRAPHY OF OTHER SOURCES

Aldington, Richard. *Lawrence of Arabia: A Biographical Enquiry*. Chicago: Henry Regnery, 1955.

Anglesey, Marquess of. *A History of the British Cavalry, 1816–1919*, Vol. 5, *Egypt, Palestine and Syria, 1914–1919*. London: Leo Cooper, 1994.

Barrett, James W. *The Australian Army Medical Corps in Egypt*. London: H.K. Lewis, 1918.

— 'Management of Venereal Diseases in Egypt During the War.' *British Military Journal* (February 1 1919): 125–27.

Beckett, Ian F.W. *The Great War, 1914–1918*. London: Longman, 2001.

Beckett, Ian F.W., and Keith Simpson, eds. *A Nation in Arms: A Social Study of the British Army in the First World War*. Manchester: Manchester University Press, 1985.

Brown, Malcolm. *T.E. Lawrence*. New York: New York University Press, 2003.

Bruce, Anthony. *The Last Crusade: The Palestine Campaign in the First World War*. London: John Murray, 2002.

Bullock, David L. *Allenby's War: The Palestine-Arabian Campaigns, 1916–1918*. London: Blandford Press, 1988.

Dalbiac, P.H. *History of the 60th Division*. London: George Allen, 1927.

Dudley-Ward, C.H. *History of the 53rd (Welsh) Division (T.F.), 1914–1918*. Cardiff: Western Mail Limited, 1927.

— *The 74th (Yeomanry) Division in Syria and France*. London: John Murray, 1922.

Elgood, Lieut. Col. P.G. *Egypt and the Army*. Oxford: Oxford University Press, 1924.

Erickson, Edward J. *Ordered to Die: A History of the Ottoman Army in the First World War.* Westport, Conn.: Greenwood Press, 2001.

— 'Strength Against Weakness: Ottoman Military Effectiveness at Gallipoli, 1915.' *Journal of Military History* 65 (October 2001): 981–1011.

Falls, Cyril. *Armageddon: 1918.* London: Weidenfeld & Nicolson, 1964.

Falls, Capt. Cyril. *Military Operations: Egypt and Palestine from June 1917 to the End of the War.* 2 parts. 1930. Reprint, Nashville, Tenn.: Battery Press, 1996.

Fayle, C. Ernest. *Seaborne Trade,* Vol. 2, *From the Opening of the Submarine Campaign to the Appointment of the Shipping Controller.* London: HMSO, 1923.

Fox, Frank. *The History of the Royal Gloucestershire Hussars Yeomanry, 1898–1922: The Great Cavalry Campaign in Palestine.* London: Philip Allan, 1923.

French, David. *The Strategy of the Lloyd George Coalition, 1916–1918.* Oxford: Clarendon University Press, 1995.

Fromkin, David. *A Peace to End All Peace: Creating the Middle East, 1914–1922.* New York: Henry Holt, 1989.

Gardner, Brian. *Allenby.* London: Cassell, 1965.

Griffith Paddy. *Battle Tactics of the Western Front: The British Army's Art of Attack, 1916–1918.* New Haven, Conn.: Yale University Press, 1994.

Gullett, H.S. *The Official History of Australia in the War of 1914–1918,* Vol. 7, *Sinai and Palestine: The Australian Imperial Force in Sinai and Palestine, 1914–1918.* Sydney: Angus and Robertson, 1923.

Harrison, Mark. 'The British Army and the Problem of Venereal Disease in France During the First World War.' *Medical History* 39 (1995): 133–58.

Hay, Ian. *One Hundred Years of Army Nursing: The Story of the British Army Nursing Services from the Time of Florence Nightingale to the Present Day.* London: Cassell, 1953.

Hill, A.J. *Chauvel of the Light Horse: A Biography of General Sir Harry Chauvel.* Victoria: Melbourne University Press, 1978.

Holmes, Richard. *The Little Field-Marshal: Sir John French.* London: Jonathan Cape, 1981.

Hughes, Matthew. *Allenby and British Strategy in the Middle East, 1917–1919.* London: Frank Cass, 1999.

James, Lawrence. *Imperial Warrior: The Life and Times of Field-Marshal Viscount Allenby, 1861–1936.* London: Weidenfeld and Nicolson, 1993.

Jones, H.A. *Official History of the War in the Air.* Vol. 6. Oxford: Clarendon Press, 1937.

Jones, Ian. 'Beersheba: The Light Horse Charge and the Making of Myths.' *Journal of the Australian War Memorial* 3 (October 1983): 26–37.

Liddle, Peter H. *The Soldiers War, 1914–1918.* London: Blandford Press, 1988.

Massey, W.T. *Allenby's Final Triumph.* New York: E.P. Dutton, 1920.

— *The Desert Campaigns.* New York: G.P. Putnam's Sons, 1918.

— *How Jerusalem Was Won: Being the Record of Allenby's Campaign in Palestine.* London: Constable and Company, 1919.

MacMunn, Lieut. Gen. Sir George, and Capt. Cyril Falls. *Military Operations: Egypt and Palestine from the Outbreak of War with Germany to June 1917.* 1928.

Reprint, Nashville, Tenn.: Battery Press, 1996.

Mitchell, J.J., and G.M. Smith. *Medical Services: Casualties and Medical Statistics of the Great War*. London: HMSO, 1931.

Powles, C. Guy. *Official History of New Zealand's Effort in the Great War*, Vol. 3, *The New Zealanders in Sinai and Palestine*. Auckland: Whitcombe & Tombs, 1922.

Preston, R.M.P. *The Desert Mounted Corps: An Account of the Cavalry Operation in Palestine and Syria, 1917–1918*. London: Constable and Company, 1921.

Rothwell, V.H. *British War Aims and Peace Diplomacy, 1914–1918*. Oxford: Oxford University Press, 1971.

Sheffy, Yigal. *British Intelligence in the Palestine Campaign, 1914–1918*. London: Frank Cass, 1998.

Simpson, David Michael. 'The Moral Battlefield: Venereal Disease and the British Army During the First World War.' PhD diss. University of Iowa, May 1995.

Smithers, A.J. *The Fighting Nation: Lord Kitchener and His Armies*. London: Leo Cooper, 1994.

Statistics of the Military Effort of the British Empire During the Great War, 1914–1920. 1922. Reprint, Dallington, Heathfield, East Sussex: Naval and Military Press, 1999.

Stokesbury, James L. *A Short History of World War I*. New York: William Morrow, 1981.

Strachan, Hew. *The First World War*, Vol. 1, *To Arms*. Oxford: Oxford University Press, 2001.

Thompson, Lieut. Col. R.R. *The Fifty-Second (Lowland) Division, 1914–1918*. Glasgow: Maclehose, Jackson, 1923.

Travers, Tim. *The Killing Ground: The British Army, the Western Front and the Emergence of Modern Warfare, 1900–1918*. London: Allen & Unwin, 1987.

Wavell, Col. A.P. *Allenby: A Study in Greatness*. Oxford: Oxford University Press, 1941.

—— *The Palestine Campaigns*. London: Constable and Company, 1928.

Wilson, Jeremy. *Lawrence of Arabia: The Authorised Biography*. London: Minerva, 1990.

Wilson, Trevor. *The Myriad Faces of War: Britain and the Great War, 1914–1918*. Cambridge: Polity Press, 1986.

Woodward, David R. 'The British Government and Japanese Intervention in Russia During World War I.' *Journal of Modern History* (December 1974): 663–85.

—— *Field Marshal Sir William Robertson: Chief of the Imperial General Staff in the Great War*. Westport, Conn.: Praeger, 1998.

—— *Lloyd George and the Generals*. 1983. Reprint, London: Frank Cass, 2004.

List of Illustrations and Maps

All illustrations courtesy of the Imperial War Museum unless otherwise stated

Index

TEMPUS – REVEALING HISTORY

Private 12768 Memoir of a Tommy
JOHN JACKSON

'Unique... a beautifully written, strikingly honest account of a young man's experience of combat' **Saul David**

'At last we have John Jackson's intensely personal and heartfelt little book to remind us there was a view of the Great War other than Wilfred Owen's' **The Daily Mail**

£9.99   0 7524 3531 0

The German Offensives of 1918
MARTIN KITCHEN

'A lucid, powerfully driven narrative' **Malcolm Brown**
'Comprehensive and authoritative... first class' **Holger H. Herwig**

£13.99   0 7524 3527 2

Verdun 1916
MALCOLM BROWN

'A haunting book which gets closer than any other to that wasteland marked by death' **Richard Holmes**

£9.99   0 7524 2599 4

The Forgotten Front
The East African Campaign 1914–1918
ROSS ANDERSON

'Excellent... fills a yawning gap in the historical record' **The Times Literary Supplement**

'Compelling and authoritative' **Hew Strachan**

£25   0 7524 2344 4

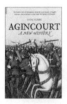

Agincourt
A New History
ANNE CURRY

'A highly distinguished and convincing account' **Christopher Hibbert**
'A *tour de force*' **Alison Weir**
'*The* book on the battle' **Richard Holmes**
A **BBC History Magazine** Book of the Year 2005
£25   0 7524 2828 4

The Welsh Wars of Independence
DAVID MOORE

'Beautifully written, subtle and remarkably perceptive' **John Davies**

£25   0 7524 3321 0

Bosworth 1485
Psychology of a Battle
MICHAEL K. JONES

'Most exciting... a remarkable tale' **The Guardian**
'Insightful and rich study of the Battle of Bosworth... no longer need Richard play the villain' **The Times Literary Supplement**
£12.99   0 7524 2594 3

The Battle of Hastings 1066
M.K. LAWSON

'Blows away many fundamental assumptions about the battle of Hastings... an exciting and indispensable read' **David Bates**
A **BBC History Magazine** Book of the Year 2003
£25   0 7524 2689 3

TEMPUS – REVEALING HISTORY

The Wars of the Roses
The Soldiers' Experience
ANTHONY GOODMAN
'Sheds light on the lot of the common soldier as never before' *Alison Weir*
'A meticulous work'
The Times Literary Supplement

£12.99   0 7524 3731 3

D-Day
The First 72 Hours
WILLIAM F. BUCKINGHAM
'A compelling narrative' *The Observer*
A *BBC History Magazine* Book of the Year 2004

£9.99   0 7524 2842 2

English Battlefields
500 Battlefields that Shaped English History
MICHAEL RAYNER
'A painstaking survey of English battlefields... a first-rate book' *Richard Holmes*
'A fascinating and, for all its factual tone, an atmospheric volume' *The Sunday Telegraph*

£25   0 7524 2978 7

Trafalgar Captain Durham of the Defiance: The
Man who refused to Miss Trafalgar
HILARY RUBINSTEIN
'A sparkling biography of Nelson's luckiest captain' *Andrew Lambert*

£17.99   0 7524 3435 7

   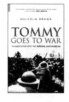

Battle of the Atlantic
MARC MILNER
'The most comprehensive short survey of the U-boat battles' *Sir John Keegan*
'Some events are fortunate in their historian, none more so than the Battle of the Atlantic. Marc Milner is *the* historian of the Atlantic Campaign... a compelling narrative'
Andrew Lambert

£12.99   0 7524 3332 6

Okinawa 1945 The Stalingrad of the Pacific
GEORGE FEIFER
'A great book... Feifer's account of the three sides and their experiences far surpasses most books about war' *Stephen Ambrose*

£17.99   0 7524 3324 5

Gallipoli 1915
TIM TRAVERS
'The most important new history of Gallipoli for forty years... groundbreaking' *Hew Strachan*
'A book of the highest importance to all who would seek to understand the tragedy of the Gallipoli campaign' *The Journal of Military History*

£13.99   0 7524 2972 8

Tommy Goes To War
MALCOLM BROWN
'A remarkably vivid and frank account of the British soldier in the trenches' *Max Arthur*
'The fury, fear, mud, blood, boredom and bravery that made up life on the Western Front are vividly presented and illustrated' *The Sunday Telegraph*

£12.99   0 7524 2980 9

TEMPUS – REVEALING HISTORY

R.J.Mitchell
Schooldays to Spitfire
GORDON MITCHELL
'[A] readable and poignant story'
The Sunday Telegraph

£12.99   0 7524 3727 5

Forgotten Soldiers of the First World War
Lost Voices from the Middle Eastern Front
DAVID WOODWARD
'A brilliant new book of hitherto unheard voices
from a haunting theatre of the First World War'
Malcolm Brown

£20   0 7524 3854 9

1690 Battle of the Boyne
PÁDRAIG LENIHAN
'An almost impeccably impartial account of the
most controversial military engagement in British
history' *The Daily Mail*

£12.99   0 7524 3304 0

Hell at the Front
Combat Voices from the First World War
TOM DONOVAN
'Fifty powerful personal accounts, each vividly
portraying the brutalising reality of the Great
War... a remarkable book' *Max Arthur*

£12.99   0 7524 3940 5

Amiens 1918
JAMES MCWILLIAMS & R. JAMES STEEL
'A masterly portrayal of this pivotal battle' *Soldier:
The Magazine of the British Army*

£25   0 7524 2860 8

Before Stalingrad
Hitler's Invasion of Russia 1941
DAVID GLANTZ
'Another fine addition to Hew Strachan's
excellent *Battles and Campaigns* series'
BBC History Magazine

£9.99   0 7524 2692 3

The SS
A History 1919-45
ROBERT LEWIS KOEHL
'Reveals the role of the SS in the mass murder
of the Jews, homosexuals and gypsies and its
organisation of death squads throughout occupied
Europe' *The Sunday Telegraph*

£9.99   0 7524 2559 5

Arnhem 1944
WILLIAM BUCKINGHAM
'Reveals the real reason why the daring attack
failed' *The Daily Express*

£10.99   0 7524 3187 0

TEMPUS – REVEALING HISTORY

The Defence and Fall of Singapore
1940-42
BRIAN FARRELL
'A multi-pronged attack on those who made the defence of Malaya and Singapore their duty... [an] exhaustive account of the clash between Japanese and British Empire forces' *BBC History Magazine*
'An original and provocative new history of the battle' *Hew Strachan*

£13.99   0 7524 3768 2

Zulu!
The Battle for Rorke's Drift 1879
EDMUND YORKE
'A clear, detailed exposition... a very good read' *Journal of the Royal United Service Institute for Defence Studies*

£12.99   0 7524 3502 7

Paras
The Birth of British Airborne Forces from Churchill's Raiders to 1st Parachute Brigade
WILLIAM F. BUCKINGHAM
£17.99   0 7524 3530 2

Voices from the Trenches
Life & Death on the Western Front
ANDY SIMPSON AND TOM DONOVAN
'A vivid picture of life on the Western Front... compelling reading' *The Daily Telegraph*
'Offers the reader a wealth of fine writing by soldiers of the Great War whose slim volumes were published so long ago or under such obscure imprints that they have all but disappeared from sight like paintings lost under the grime of ages' *Malcolm Brown*

£12.99   0 7524 3905 7

Loos 1915
NICK LLOYD
'A revealing new account based on meticulous documentary research... I warmly commend this book to all who are interested in history and the Great War' *Corelli Barnett*
'Should finally consign Alan Clarke's farrago, *The Donkeys*, to the waste paper basket' *Hew Strachan*

£25   0 7524 3937 5

The Last Nazis
SS Werewolf Guerilla Resistance in Europe 1944-47
PERRY BIDDISCOMBE
'Detailed, meticulously researched and highly readable... a must for all interested in the end of the Second World War' *Military Illustrated*

£12.99   0 7524 2342 8

Omaha Beach A Flawed Victory
ADRIAN LEWIS
'A damning book' *BBC History Magazine*
£12.99   0 7524 2975 2

The English Civil War
A Historical Companion
MARTYN BENNETT
'Martyn Bennett knows more about the nuts and bolts of the English Civil War than anybody else alive' *Ronald Hutton*
'A most useful and entertaining book – giving us all precise detail about the events, the places, the people and the things that we half-know about the civil war and many more things that we did not know at all' *John Morrill*

£25   0 7524 3186 2

If you are interested in purchasing other books published by Tempus, or in case you have difficulty finding any Tempus books in your local bookshop, you can also place orders directly through our website

www.tempus-publishing.com

TEMPUS – REVEALING HISTORY

Quacks Fakers and Charlatans in Medicine
ROY PORTER

'A delightful book' *The Daily Telegraph*
'Hugely entertaining' *BBC History Magazine*

£12.99   0 7524 2590 0

The Tudors
RICHARD REX

'Up-to-date, readable and reliable. The best introduction to England's most important dynasty' *David Starkey*

'Vivid, entertaining... quite simply the best short introduction' *Eamon Duffy*

'Told with enviable narrative skill... a delight for any reader' *THES*

£9.99   0 7524 3333 4

The Kings & Queens of England
MARK ORMROD

'Of the numerous books on the kings and queens of England, this is the best'
Alison Weir

£9.99   0 7524 2598 6

The Covent Garden Ladies
Pimp General Jack & the Extraordinary Story of Harris's List
HALLIE RUBENHOLD

'Sex toys, porn... forget Ann Summers, Miss Love was at it 250 years ago' *The Times*
'Compelling' *The Independent on Sunday*
'Marvellous' *Leonie Frieda*
'Filthy' *The Guardian*

£9.99   0 7524 3739 9

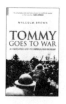

Okinawa 1945
GEORGE FEIFER

'A great book... Feifer's account of the three sides and their experiences far surpasses most books about war'
Stephen Ambrose

£17.99   0 7524 3324 5

Tommy Goes To War
MALCOLM BROWN

'A remarkably vivid and frank account of the British soldier in the trenches'
Max Arthur

'The fury, fear, mud, blood, boredom and bravery that made up life on the Western Front are vividly presented and illustrated'
The Sunday Telegraph

£12.99   0 7524 2980 4

Ace of Spies The True Story of Sidney Reilly
ANDREW COOK

'The most definitive biography of the spying ace yet written... both a compelling narrative and a myth-shattering *tour de force*'
Simon Sebag Montefiore

'The absolute last word on the subject' *Nigel West*
'Makes poor 007 look like a bit of a wuss'
The Mail on Sunday

£12.99   0 7524 2959 0

Sex Crimes
From Renaissance to Enlightenment
W.M. NAPHY

'Wonderfully scandalous'
Diarmaid MacCulloch

£10.99   0 7524 2977 9

If you are interested in purchasing other books published by Tempus, or in case you have difficulty finding any Tempus books in your local bookshop, you can also place orders directly through our website

www.tempus-publishing.com

TEMPUS – REVEALING HISTORY

D-Day The First 72 Hours
WILLIAM F. BUCKINGHAM

'A compelling narrative' *The Observer*
A *BBC History Magazine* Book of the Year 2004

£9.99   0 7524 2842 X

The London Monster
Terror on the Streets in 1790
JAN BONDESON

'Gripping' *The Guardian*
'Excellent... monster-mania brought a reign of terror to the ill-lit streets of the capital'
The Independent

£9.99   0 7524 3327 X

London
A Historical Companion
KENNETH PANTON

'A readable and reliable work of reference that deserves a place on every Londoner's bookshelf'
Stephen Inwood

£20   0 7524 3434 9

M: MI5's First Spymaster
ANDREW COOK

'Serious spook history' *Andrew Roberts*
'Groundbreaking' *The Sunday Telegraph*
'Brilliantly researched' *Dame Stella Rimington*

£20   0 7524 2896 9

Agincourt A New History
ANNE CURRY

'A highly distinguished and convincing account'
Christopher Hibbert
'A *tour de force*' *Alison Weir*
'*The* book on the battle' *Richard Holmes*
A *BBC History Magazine* Book of the Year 2005

£25   0 7524 2828 4

Battle of the Atlantic
MARC MILNER

'The most comprehensive short survey of the U-boat battles' *Sir John Keegan*
'Some events are fortunate in their historian, none more so than the Battle of the Atlantic. Marc Milner is *the* historian of the Atlantic campaign... a compelling narrative' *Andrew Lambert*

£12.99   0 7524 3332 6

The English Resistance
The Underground War Against the Normans
PETER REX

'An invaluable rehabilitation of an ignored resistance movement' *The Sunday Times*
'Peter Rex's scholarship is remarkable'
The Sunday Express

£12.99   0 7524 3733 X

Elizabeth Wydeville: The Slandered Queen
ARLENE OKERLUND

'A penetrating, thorough and wholly convincing vindication of this unlucky queen'
Sarah Gristwood
'A gripping tale of lust, loss and tragedy'
Alison Weir
A *BBC History Magazine* Book of the Year 2005

£18.99   0 7524 3384 9

If you are interested in purchasing other books published by Tempus, or in case you have difficulty finding any Tempus books in your local bookshop, you can also place orders directly through our website

www.tempus-publishing.com

TEMPUS – REVEALING HISTORY

Britannia's Empire
A Short History of the British Empire
BILL NASSON

'Crisp, economical and witty' *TLS*
'An excellent introduction the subject' *THES*

£12.99   0 7524 3808 5

Madmen
A Social History of Madhouses,
Mad-Doctors & Lunatics
ROY PORTER

'Fascinating'
The Observer

£12.99   0 7524 3730 5

Born to be Gay
A History of Homosexuality
WILLIAM NAPHY

'Fascinating' *The Financial Times*
'Excellent' *Gay Times*

£9.99   0 7524 3694 5

William II
Rufus, the Red King
EMMA MASON
'A thoroughly new reappraisal of a much
maligned king. The dramatic story of his life is
told with great pace and insight'
John Gillingham

£25   0 7524 3528 0

To Kill Rasputin
The Life and Death of Grigori Rasputin
ANDREW COOK

'Andrew Cook is a brilliant investigative historian'
Andrew Roberts
'Astonishing' *The Daily Mail*

£9.99   0 7524 3906 5

The Unwritten Order
Hitler's Role in the Final Solution
PETER LONGERICH

'Compelling' *Richard Evans*
'The finest account to date of the many twists
and turns in Adolf Hitler's anti-semitic obsession'
Richard Overy

£12.99   0 7524 3328 8

Private 12768
Memoir of a Tommy
JOHN JACKSON
FOREWORD BY HEW STRACHAN

'A refreshing new perspective' *The Sunday Times*
'At last we have John Jackson's intensely
personal and heartfelt little book to remind us
there was a view of the Great War other than
Wilfred Owen's' *The Daily Mail*

£9.99   0 7524 3531 0

The Vikings
MAGNUS MAGNUSSON

'Serious, engaging history'
BBC History Magazine

£9.99   0 7524 2699 0

If you are interested in purchasing other books published by Tempus, or in case you have difficulty finding any
Tempus books in your local bookshop, you can also place orders directly through our website

www.tempus-publishing.com

TEMPUS – REVEALING HISTORY

Freaks

JAN BONDESON

'Reveals how these tragic individuals triumphed over their terrible adversity' *The Daily Mail*
'Well written and superbly illustrated'
The Financial Times

£9.99   0 7524 3662 7

Bollywood

MIHIR BOSE

'Pure entertainment' *The Observer*
'Insightful and often hilarious'
The Sunday Times
'Gripping' *The Daily Telegraph*

£9.99   978 07524 4382 9

King Arthur

CHRISTOPHER HIBBERT

'A pearl of biographers' *New Statesman*
£12.99   978 07524 3933 4

Arnhem

William Buckingham

'Reveals the reason why the daring attack failed'
The Daily Express

£10.99   0 7524 3187 0

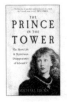

Cleopatra

PATRICIA SOUTHERN

'In the absence of Cleopatra's memoirs Patricia Southern's commendably balanced biography will do very well'
The Sunday Telegraph

£9.99   978 07524 4336 2

The Prince In The Tower

MICHAEL HICKS

'The first time in ages that a publisher has sent me a book I actually want to read' *David Starkey*

£9.99   978 07524 4386 7

The Battle of Hastings 1066

M. K. LAWSON

'A *BBC History Magazine* book of the year 2003
'The definitive book on this famous battle'
The Journal of Military History

£12.99   978 07524 4177 1

Loos 1915

NICK LLOYD

'A revealing new account based on meticulous documentary research' *Corelli Barnett*
'Should fiinally consign Alan Clark's Farrago, *The Donkeys*, to the waste paperbasket'
Hew Strachan
'Plugs a yawning gap in the existing literature... this book will set the agenda for debate of the battle for years to come' *Gary Sheffield*

£25   0 7524 3937 5

If you are interested in purchasing other books published by Tempus, or in case you have difficulty finding any Tempus books in your local bookshop, you can also place orders directly through our website

www.tempus-publishing.com